REAL CHANGE

REAL CHANGE

The Fight for America's Future

■ ■ ■

NEWT GINGRICH

with VINCE HALEY
and RICK TYLER

Since 1947
REGNERY
PUBLISHING, INC.
An Eagle Publishing Company • Washington, DC

Library of Congress Cataloging-in-Publication Data

ISBN 1-59698-589-5 / 978-1-59698-589-6

Published in the United States by
Regnery Publishing, Inc.
One Massachusetts Avenue, NW
Washington, D.C. 20001
www.regnery.com

Manufactured in the United States of America

10 9 8 7 6 5 4 3 2 1

Books are available in quantity for promotional or premium use. Write to Director of Special Sales, Regnery Publishing, Inc., One Massachusetts Avenue NW, Washington, DC 20001, for information on discounts and terms or call (202) 216-0600.

Distributed to the trade by:
Perseus Distribution
387 Park Avenue South
New York, NY 10016

*This book is dedicated to Maggie and Robert and
to the American people, who are the key to their future.*

Contents

Moving the "M"

WHEN I FIRST WROTE *Real Change* I believed deeply that America was on the wrong track and that we needed real change. That analysis is even truer and more important today.

I have to confess that the growing number of challenges facing America since 2004 are larger and more dangerous than I expected.

I date these challenges from 2004 because that was when I wrote *Winning the Future*. At that time I expected things to get worse, but I had no idea the economy would become so mismanaged.

By the time I wrote *Real Change* in October 2007, I was convinced the Republican Party was off track and the Democratic left had learned nothing about reality. That said, I didn't anticipate the collapse of conservative fiscal policies and the explosion of government intervention and unrestrained spending, which began with the $180 billion "stimulus" package in spring 2008. Today, the projected $9 trillion of new debt under President Obama's current budget plan, on top of the huge surge in spending under President Bush, presents a far bigger economic and political threat than I would have thought possible back in 2004.

As our fiscal discipline collapsed, our national security situation also deteriorated, notwithstanding the success of the surge in Iraq. The State Department regained dominance over the Bush White House in early 2008, and the result has been a steady erosion of American interests:

* The North Koreans continue to build nuclear weapons and long-range missiles.
* The Iranians are coming ever closer to achieving their goal of developing nuclear weapons and, ultimately, annihilating Israel.
* Somali pirates have grown richer and more audacious in their attacks.
* Sudan continues to follow vicious policies in Darfur, but now does so with Chinese oil money.
* Robert Mugabe continues to destroy Zimbabwe.
* South Africa is decaying into corruption.
* Pakistan is ceding authority to Islamist extremists and the Taliban in Northwest Pakistan.
* Our southern border remains uncontrolled, and America's own drug abuse problem has financed an explosion of drug cartels in Mexico, leading to a massive increase in violence there.

From electromagnetic pulse attacks to cyber assaults to nuclear proliferation, the threats have grown in recent years far faster than our national security system's capacity to deal with them.

Finally, the liberal judicial class is becoming even more arrogant, showing a greater determination to impose alien values on American citizens. With their attempts to destroy traditional marriage and their usurping the commander in chief's responsibility for national security, the courts are becoming increasingly enthralled by alien elite views that represent fundamental breaks in the American tradition.

The Obama Administration: Radical Spenders, Weak Defenders

All these trends have culminated in the most radical election result in American history. The 2008 campaign began as a repudiation of Republicans for big spending, corruption, and their failure to manage competently challenges like Hurricane Katrina, border security, and the war in Iraq. It ended with the election of the most radical president in American history.

The Obama-Pelosi-Reid team is the most radical group ever to hold the reigns of American power. Its vision of a high-tax, bureaucratic, Washington-centered system dominated by politicians and leading to a secular-socialist future will fundamentally challenge America's role as a beacon of hope, opportunity, and freedom.

The Pelosi-Reid machine had already come to dominate the Bush administration in its last year. The $180 billion stimulus package of spring 2008 was a disgraceful failure and waste of taxpayer money. The astonishing $345 billion housing bailout in July 2008 was of little benefit to most Americans, but served as a huge payoff to ACORN and other leftwing groups. And the $700 billion Wall Street bailout of

September 2008 (more than matched by a $2 trillion Federal Reserve guarantee program) marked the complete collapse of the Bush administration's economic discipline.

With the groundwork already laid, Obama took office and presided over "Bush Plus"—but with an aggressiveness, speed, and scale that shocked most Americans.

The $787 billion Obama stimulus bill was written with such startling speed that no member of Congress had even read the entire proposal before it was approved. The subsequent $404 billion, 2009 omnibus budget bill was passed with over 8,000 earmarks and cheerfully signed by President Obama, even as he reiterated his supposed opposition to earmarks.

And the president's 2010 budget outline forecasts a $9 trillion increase in the national debt. This unprecedented level of deficit spending raises the very real danger of massive inflation in the future. It is troublingly reminiscent of President Carter's legacy of 13 percent inflation and 22 percent interest rates. And incredibly, all the while, the president is proclaiming that he is cutting the deficit.

Under this administration, businessmen and women who make business decisions to earn profits are being usurped by politicians who make political decisions to win votes. The president forced General Motors to fire its CEO—even while claiming he didn't do it. Democratic senators and House members have become dictators of salaries, bonuses, and "appropriate" venues for conferences. Government micromanagement of the economy has now reached a level not seen in over seventy years.

Furthermore, this administration has shown an unprecedented hostility to Christianity. It has nominated a judge, David Hamilton, to the federal bench who once ruled that invoking Jesus Christ in a public prayer is "sectarian" and thus unconstitutional, but praying to Allah is just fine. Before Obama gave a speech at Georgetown University, a Catholic institution, the White House asked that a Christian symbol behind the podium be covered up so it would not appear in pictures with the president.

In foreign policy, the Obama administration has reverted to the weakness and apologetic critique of America that characterized the Carter administration from 1977 to 1980. President Obama bows to the King of Saudi Arabia, cheerfully meets Venezuelan dictator Hugo Chavez, and naively accepts Chavez's backhanded "gift" of a viciously anti-American book.

The administration is determined to shut down domestic oil production and block oil exploration off American shores, but it's enthusiastic about placating dictators who sell us oil. It is a dangerous policy.

The North Koreans test the new administration by firing a long-range missile after repeated warnings not to do so. They even time the missile launch to occur the morning President Obama is giving a major speech in Europe on the need for nuclear disarmament. The irony would be rich in a novel but seems lost on the Left. The president grandly announces that North Korea will be sanctioned and then turns to the United Nations, which of course does nothing.

Also seeking to test Obama, the Iranians announce they have opened their 7,300th centrifuge for making nuclear material. The administration responds by promising to communicate respectfully with the ayatollahs.

An Israeli investigation reveals that the Hamas leadership operated out of a hospital during the terror group's recent armed conflict with Israel, and that Hamas fighters disguised themselves as medical workers and moved around in ambulances. This is ignored by the United

Nations' Durban II "anti-racism" conference, where participants focused on condemning Israel and demanded that the world outlaw criticism of Islam.

Pakistan concedes authority to Sharia (Islamic fundamentalist law— a medieval system of male-dominated tyranny) and to Islamists in Northwest Pakistan. The Islamists respond by demanding Sharia be extended to all of Pakistan. The danger is growing that Pakistan will disintegrate, isolating the NATO forces in Afghanistan and creating an Islamist dictatorship possessing nuclear weapons.

President Obama apologizes for America's supposed arrogance, and the Europeans respond by giving him zero additional combat troops for Afghanistan.

The Obama administration promises to be nice to the Russians, and they promptly block our efforts to sanction North Korea in the UN Security Council. Meanwhile, the Russians continue building up their forces around the nation of Georgia in violation of their cease-fire agreement.

President Obama relaxes restrictions on travel and remittances to Cuba and gets no concession in return—not a single prisoner is released. When Raul Castro simply expresses a willingness to talk to the U.S., his brother Fidel clarifies that nothing will change on the imprisoned island.

We witnessed a brief show of American resolve when Navy SEALs killed several Somali pirates and rescued an American hostage. Yet the following day pirates brazenly captured two more ships. A moment of heroism could not hide the total absence of strategic resolve to protect the freedom of the high seas—something America had done consistently for 200 years, since President Thomas Jefferson sent the navy and the Marines "to the shores of Tripoli," as the Marine Corps hymn reminds us.

Indisputably, the first months of the Obama administration have been characterized by astonishing weakness. If the Carter administration is an indicator, such weakness enhances the dangers that confront America.

There are criminal governments, predators, and aggressors all around the planet. When law-abiding democracies are strong and confident, these forces of predation and disorder tend to lay low. When democracies lose their will, however, these forces can emerge with frightening speed and do extraordinary damage.

What Would Reagan Do? Change the Game

Only time will tell if the Obama administration's foreign policy of apology, self-deception, and appeasement will endanger America. But here at home it is already clear what we are facing and what the consequences will be.

The steady drive toward bigger government, more powerful politicians, and a more secular, anti-religious, and anti-American ideology is not new.

The steady rise of big government, big bureaucracy, and politician-centered decision making was described by then California governor Ronald Reagan in his first nationally televised speech in October 1964. Reagan warned against the dangers of big government again in his speech to the 1976 Republican National Convention. This was also one of the major themes of his 1980 presidential campaign.

In February 2009, my wife Callista and I released *Ronald Reagan: Rendezvous with Destiny*. We made this film with David Bossie and his team at Citizens United. Kevin Knoblock did a great job directing it.

That film reminded me of the unchanging truths of the Reagan movement. I had first met Reagan in 1974, when he was still governor. I campaigned with him in the late 1970s and worked with him as a member of Congress for the eight years of his presidency.

In 1994 I helped design the Contract with America to continue implementing Reagan's values, which were really just core American values: lower taxes, control of spending, a balanced budget, welfare reform, litigation reform, stronger defense, and better intelligence.

As Speaker of the House from 1995 to 1999, I sought to implement the values and principles of Reaganism. We reformed welfare— 65 percent of welfare recipients went to work or to school. We balanced the federal budget for four consecutive years and paid down part of the federal debt for the first time since the 1920s—to the tune of $405 billion.

During my four years as Speaker, federal spending grew by an average of 2.9 percent a year—the lowest growth rate since 1930. Given the dramatic and indeed alarming growth of government under both presidents Bush and Obama, let me repeat that fact. All federal spending, including entitlements, grew by 2.9 percent a year while I was Speaker. (It grew substantially more under Clinton the two years before I became Speaker and the two years after I left the Speakership.)

Yet while I admired and studied Reagan's leadership, there were aspects of his effectiveness I had not fully appreciated.

I strongly recommend Tom Evans's *The Education of Ronald Reagan* as a remarkable study of the impact eight years at General Electric had on Ronald Reagan. While working with Lemuel Boulware, GE's vice president and labor strategist, Reagan delivered 375 speeches to GE employees in an eight-year period. This was part of the most elaborate employee education program about free enterprise, markets, and productivity in that generation.

Boulware enthusiastically gave Reagan books by great free-market thinkers like Hayek, Friedman, and Haslett. Reagan spent hours reading them on the train, which is how he travelled in those days, and this prepared him to talk to blue collar workers about science, technology, free enterprise, and the American system of freedom.

The greatest impact on Reagan was exerted by a model Boulware developed for fundamentally changing the terms of the debate. Boulware called it "moving the M."

Boulware believed every issue had an "M"—the point where the majority opinion on that topic was found. For Boulware, if you could "move the M," you moved the entire framework of the debate. And since politicians stick close to the voting majority, "moving the M" was key to changing the law.

As I read Evans's book, I began to rethink the structure of some of Reagan's greatest speeches. We were at the twenty-fifth anniversary of two of his most consequential speeches—the Evil Empire speech and the Strategic Defense Initiative speech.*

At an event hosted by the American Enterprise Institute, I used Boulware's model to analyze these speeches from this new perspective. I had realized that Reagan was not merely a great communicator in those two speeches, but he was a tremendous educator, affecting the country's basic understanding of the Soviet Union, the Cold War, and the requirements of American national security.

---

* To hear and read these speeches, go to www.newt.org/reagan-twospeeches.

Reagan did not argue within the framework of the leftwing elites. He "moved the M," changing the fundamental framework of the debate and requiring people to think about issues in a completely new way. He armed people with new facts and new explanations of timeless principles so they could understand and support new policies.

The world today requires a similar fundamental reframing of the entire political context. Any effort to argue within the framework of the elite Left's interpretations of reality and the elite Left's policies will lose.

What our elites are now doing is so destructive and so dangerous that if you operate within their framework you will always lose the debate. You will end up endorsing "less destructive, less expensive, slower decay" versions of a lot of really bad ideas.

We are once again in a time when we need "bold colors, not pale pastels," as Reagan argued back in 1975. Indeed, the problems are so fundamental we need a new argument about the very nature of political reality and the very nature of danger in the world.

This kind of argument is more cultural than political.

We are now engaged in a struggle between two cultures rather than two political systems. On the Left is an elite culture that sees the world as safe and America as dangerous. It supports drug legalization over anti-drug enforcement. It believes big government is superior to free enterprise, bureaucrats are more important than entrepreneurs, and government redistribution is better and fairer than individual success.

Our struggle with them is a struggle about the very nature of reality.

Because they know the American people fundamentally disagree with them, they rely on judges to impose radical change on an unwilling America.

Because they know they will lose honest, factual arguments, they routinely engage in dishonest, inaccurate communications.

Conservatives try to be reasonable and to debate within the framework established by the Left. It is a hopeless task. What is needed is a new, bold, and direct approach to reality and to the principles that work and the principles that fail.

This will require a debate and a citizen movement unlike anything we have seen in at least a century.

The tea parties that have recently swept the country may be a first step in that direction. But there will have to be a lot more action to stop and then replace the leftwing machine that now dominates America.

This action is already taking place. At the Center for Health Transformation (www.healthtransformation.net), we work every day to develop a new generation of healthcare solutions that will enable longer lives, greater independence, better health, and lower costs.

At American Solutions for Winning the Future (www.AmericanSolutions.com), we work every day to develop the new solutions and make the fundamental arguments that will create a new dialogue with all Americans and lead to a much better future for everyone.

At Renewing American Leadership (ReAL) (RenewingAmericanLeadership.com), we work every day with people of faith to restore America's core values and principles, our unique history, and our Godly heritage. ReAL is committed to advancing and defending American civilization.

Hopefully, this new edition of *Real Change* will be a further step on the road to restoring our fiscal discipline at home, expanding freedom abroad, and renewing faith in a better future for our children and grandchildren.

PART ONE

A Time for Change

CHAPTER ONE

The Myth of Red America versus Blue America

AMERICANS BELIEVE OVERWHELMINGLY that we need a change in course. Americans are surprisingly united in this belief, and in the conviction that real change will never come from Washington. On this, like so many things, Americans are absolutely right.

The media tell us America is a nation divided between conservative red states and liberal blue states. They tell us that red and blue are equally divided—which is why elections are so close, why Congress seems gridlocked, and why nothing ever seems to get done in Washington.

But that's simply not true. The reality is the American people are united on almost every important issue facing our country. The real division is between red-white-and-blue America (about 85 percent of the county) and a fringe on the left (about 15 percent of the country). Not only have the media perpetuated the myth that the country is equally divided, but the elites on the left fringe have also insisted that their positions hold moral superiority. Neither is true.

Meanwhile, the Republicans have been so lacking in backbone and conviction that they have accepted these myths—but tell themselves that they can manage big government better than the Democrats (which really means managing decline and managing failure).

If you want to know why the American people are frustrated, it is because we Americans are experiencing government that is not responsive to the needs of the nation. We understand what we face and what needs to be done—we just can't convince anyone in Washington to listen. And Americans are getting fed up.

Big Problems, Obvious Solutions

The stakes, I believe, have never been higher. America today is at an extraordinary crossroads. We're standing on the edge of a potential golden age for America. Advances in technology, science, engineering, and medicine hold the promise of benefits our parents couldn't even have dreamed of. If we make the right choices now, America will enjoy a level of prosperity, safety, and freedom unknown to previous generations. But if we make the wrong choices, we will suffer very serious consequences from a set of challenges we choose to ignore. Our country could be devastated by terrorist attacks, our prosperity diminished by the rising commercial giants of China and India, and our children and grandchildren unable to pay for the needs of their families and for the health, pension, and Social Security burdens of their parents.

America's Natural Majority

Hope lies, as it always has, in the American people. America has a natural, overwhelming, center-right majority—and it's a majority that has a better grasp of the challenges facing us than the Washington bureaucrats, politicians, and lobbyists who don't think of finding solutions to problems but of managing "the system."

On issues across the board—from permitting a moment of silence for prayer in our public schools to the issues of war and peace—the American people speak with one voice. I know, because we've asked and we've listened.

Ask the American people if they want a moment of silence for children to pray if they desire in public school, and 94 percent say yes.

Ask the American people if they support making English the official language of the United States, and 87 percent say yes.

Ask the American people if al Qaeda poses a serious threat to our country, and 93 percent say yes.

Ask the American people if they believe it is possible to negotiate with terrorist groups like al Qaeda, and 79 percent say no.

Ask the American people if the Social Security system is broken, and 80 percent say yes.

Ask the American people if it is important for the president and Congress to address the Social Security mess within the next few years, and 96 percent say yes.

Ask the American people if they support the option of a single income tax rate of 17 percent for everyone, with standard exemptions for each adult, married couple, and child dependent, and 71 percent say yes.

Ask the American people if they support drilling for oil off America's coasts to reduce our dependence on foreign oil, and 73 percent say yes.

Ask the American people if they support building more nuclear power plants to cut carbon emissions and reduce our dependency on foreign oil, and 65 percent say yes.

Ask the American people if they support laws that criminalize advocating terrorism or advocating violence against American citizens, and 83 percent say yes.

If the American people agree on so much, why is it that our politicians agree on so little? And why can't we get the policies America wants?

A System of Politics and Government That Doesn't Work

While Americans are overwhelmingly united, the two major political parties foster deep divide and rancorous debate. And neither has truly engaged in trying to find creative solutions to the serious problems we face as a nation.

Democrats can't talk creatively about replacing government failure with a model that works because their power base is largely the very unionized bureaucracies that need to change, and their ideological base is the big-government, highly regulatory, high-tax model that is failing. Republicans can't talk creatively about replacing government failure with a model that will work because the Republicans' proper focus on limiting government, an enormous task, often leaves little energy for serious thought on improving government that has been properly limited. Another challenge for Republicans is that they have written off large segments of the country as unwinnable, as "blue-state America," and therefore not of concern to them.

Both parties are failing America. While Republicans are closer to core American values in their doctrines of lower taxes, limited government, more entrepreneurship, more private sector job creation, and strength in national security, they refuse to think deeply enough about the performance failures of the recent eight years of Republican attempts at governing, and they refuse to invest the energy that is needed to understand the problems plaguing the inner city. Thus, they have failed to create a credible dialogue with people who have been badly served by Democrats but are deeply distrustful of Republicans.

A Republican Party that addressed the issues, that spoke to all Americans as the natural party of commonsense solutions, of entrepreneurship, of a strong national defense, of revitalizing America's core values and principles, would find that it represents the majority of the people by an overwhelming margin. But Republicans are stuck in their historic minority mindset. As a party that labored in the minority for forty long years, Republicans don't know how to provide the kind of sustained leadership necessary to create a long-term majority party. Worse, Republicans have allowed political consultants to do their thinking for them. The most destructive example of this is consultants who convince Republicans that in order to win, they need to run divisive campaigns rather than solution-oriented campaigns.

The Democrats are no alternative. If Republicans are ruled by timidity at their minority mindset, Democrats wrongly assume that their left-wing base—trial lawyers, the Hollywood elite, labor unions, government bureaucrats—represents the values of the American people, when in fact it represents the values of a fringe opposed by 70 to 90 percent of the American people. When Democrats are elected as a majority, it's because of Republican failure.

That was exactly the case in the 2006 and 2008 elections. But really, the problem began much earlier. It started in the 2000 election, and became obvious by the 2004 election.

The Lost Opportunity in 2004

Consider this fact: in 2004, when Democrat John Kerry ran against George W. Bush, Kerry didn't represent half of an evenly divided red-state/blue-state America: he represented the 15 percent fringe.

In recent American history, we have seen two other ideological mismatches similar to the Bush-Kerry matchup. In 1972, liberal Democratic senator George McGovern ran against incumbent Republican president Richard Nixon. McGovern lost the election by 520 electoral votes to 17. He lost every state—including his home state of South Dakota—except for Massachusetts and the District of Columbia. Then, in 1984, liberal former vice president Walter Mondale ran against President Ronald Reagan and lost by 525 electoral votes to 13. Mondale carried only his home state of Minnesota and the District of Columbia.

Senator John Kerry of Massachusetts was as liberal as McGovern or Mondale, and as far removed from red-white-and-blue America.

Consider these polling results from a paper I wrote in July 2004 about the Bush-Kerry matchup: 87 percent of Americans told pollsters they believed in a work requirement for welfare; 72 percent said they believed in government support of faith-based initiatives to help the poor; 73 percent said they believed that American interests were more important than international organizations; 84 percent said they believed that a person who attacks a pregnant woman and kills her unborn baby should be prosecuted for killing the baby; 78 percent said they believed children should be allowed to pray at school.

On these big questions, an average of 79 percent of the people were on President George W. Bush's side and an average of only 16 percent were on John Kerry's side. Senator Kerry was rated by *National Journal* as the most liberal senator in 2003. His vice presidential nominee, Senator John Edwards, came in fourth. The Kerry-Edwards ticket was the most left-wing since George McGovern's 1972 campaign. Kerry's lifetime ADA (Americans for Democratic Action) voting record was more liberal than Walter Mondale's (92 to 90). John Edwards had a lifetime ADA voting record rated more liberal than that of Mondale's vice presidential nominee, Geraldine Ferraro (81 to 79).

The point is this: the 2004 presidential election should have been a Bush landslide. But the Republicans did not run a positive, values-oriented, big-choice campaign. They focused instead on merely turning out their base. The result was a marginal victory—the closest reelection for any winning incumbent president in modern times, with zero political capital to govern effectively. All it proved was that the anti-Kerry vote was slightly bigger than the anti-Bush vote. With no political capital to spend, President Bush had little chance of policy success, and the stage was set for Republican defeats in 2006 and 2008, all because the campaign did nothing to prove to the American people that the Republican Party stood with the 70 percent–plus majority of the American people.

For the Republicans, the 2004 campaign was a tragedy because it deepened the sense of a partisan divide in America. In that setting and with relatively narrow margins in the House and Senate, the premium was on sticking with the Republican team even when it was doing truly stupid things. The result was a blank check for greedy and short-sighted committee chairmen to exploit party loyalty among their members to write pork-laden legislation guaranteed to infuriate the taxpayers and fiscal conservatives. In effect, the very narrowness of the 2004 election sowed the seeds of the bad behavior that led to the collapse of 2006–2008.

For the Democrats, the 2004 campaign was a long-term tragedy, because it allowed them to ignore how out of touch with America the left wing of their party was. The Democrats now consider the fringe left their base. And with the Democrats' victory in the 2008 elections, Americans are gearing up to bear the costs of higher taxes, bigger government, and more regulations and litigation. Americans voted for change in 2008, but there are already signs that this is not the change they were looking for.

Real Change Requires Real Change

Clearly, both parties are out of step with the citizens they should be representing. The answer, however, is not to form a third party—no third party has worked since the Republicans were launched in 1854. The answer is to empower the 70 to 90 percent of Americans who agree on all the major issues that confront the country. The answer is for Americans to force our elected representatives to get serious about real solutions to our problems and real change in our approach to governance—or change who we elect.

Americans have clearly communicated the policies and solutions we must pursue. But to get there, we need transformational change of our current, failed bureaucratic system of government. This change can't come from a president or a Congress alone. It will require transforming every level of government—federal, state, and local—by insisting that federal, state, and local elected officials be truly accountable to "we the people" who elect them. It means demanding from our government the high level of performance that private sector entrepreneurs and workers achieve every day. It means acting on the fact that the main difference between the private sector and the government sector is that the private sector is largely "the world that works," and the government sector is largely "the world that fails." We can no longer afford that failure.

In the world that works, you can track millions of packages (via FedEx or UPS) in real time as they move across the country. But in the world that fails, the federal government can't keep track of the estimated ten to twenty million people living in this country illegally, even if they live in the same community for months or even years.

In the world that works, you can go to an ATM almost anywhere in the world, twenty-four hours a day, seven days a week, insert a plastic card, punch in a four-digit number—and what happens? The information travels instantly to your bank, which verifies who you are and that you have money in your account to cover the amount you want to withdraw. The ATM translates that amount into the foreign currency you need and gives you the money—all in about eleven seconds. In the world that fails, you have situations like what recently happened in California, where a hotel owner was barred by court order from firing an employee who had presented illegal documents when first hired. That worker was the forty-second person to have used the same fraudulent Social Security number. Why is it that your bank can recognize your information instantly, yet the Social Security bureaucracy can't recognize the fraudulent use of a Social Security number the first time, the second time, the third time, or even the fortieth time?

In the world that works, innovators come up with and employ commonsense solutions every day. They do not think challenges can't be met. Accepting failure means losing business. In the world that works, improving services is critical to gaining and keeping customers.

In the world that fails none of this applies, and yet our government is entrusted with the awesome responsibilities of defending our country, preventing terrorism, winning in the global economy, responding to natural disasters, ensuring Social Security benefits, educating our children, and protecting our environment.

In the world that works, if 70 to 90 percent of customers want something, they get it. In the world that fails, if 70 to 90 percent of the people want something, the bureaucracy continues to do what's best for itself, not for the majority of the American people.

Our current system of government is on a course of decay, decline, and disaster. This system won't deliver the change we need. But we the people can force real change, and can secure the kind of future America and our children and our grandchildren deserve. This book is a practical blueprint for real change, addressing problems that our current system of politics and government ignores, and providing solutions that can work. What you hold in your hands is not merely an exhortation for a better America but also a how-to guide that we the people can employ.

But we had better do it soon. Terrorists who want to kill Americans and destroy our way of life, along with economic competitors who are determined to surpass us in every measure of entrepreneurship and innovation, are gathering at the gates. They won't be held off for long. We must embrace real change. Our very survival depends on it.

We are confronted with historic challenges. But both the current teams, Right and Left, have failed to meet the challenges and come up with the solutions America needs. As a conservative and a Republican, let me begin with the failure of my own party to govern effectively and provide real solutions.

CHAPTER TWO

An Unreformed Right: Why Republicans Failed to Govern Successfully

THIS WAS THE MOST DIFFICULT CHAPTER for me to write. I have been an active Republican since 1960, when I volunteered as a high school junior for the Nixon-Lodge campaign. For forty-eight years I have been working to develop a Republican majority in Georgia and in America.

After 1994, it seemed possible to build on the majority President Reagan had created in 1984. The 1994 election broke forty years of Democratic control of the U.S. House of Representatives. This was followed by the election of 1996, which was the first successful Republican House reelection since 1928. But after the 2000 election it became obvious that something was profoundly wrong with Republican political strategies. The patterns used by Republican consultants were beginning to be self-destructive. From 2004, I began to offer an alternative system of strategy and thought.

The GOP Culture of Defeat and Minority Status

To understand how Republicans got into their current mess and how badly the Republican system has failed, it is essential to remember some history. The House Republicans last held a stable majority prior to the election of 1930. From 1930 to 1994 there were only two elections in which House Republicans had a majority (1946 and 1958).

Consider the impact on a party of sixty-plus years in which there were fifteen years of Democratic House control for every year of Republican control. For Republicans, the impact was devastating. Those who could not stand being in a minority in the House ran for the Senate, or for governorships, or took jobs in the executive branch, or left politics.

Those who remained comfortably in the minority learned to accept their minority status, to expect to lose elections and votes in the House, and to work with the majority Democrats in a permissive environment where "good" Republicans would not fight too hard and would get rewarded by Democrats for cooperating. In Speaker Sam Rayburn's phrase, "to get along, go along." That was the culture of the House Republicans when I was elected in 1978, and despite twenty years of work as a member, it remains the culture of too many House Republicans today.

After leaving the speakership, I realized (after five years of painful reevaluation) why the Republican Party had failed to gain not just a majority in Congress but a majority capable enough to govern effectively for a generation or more. It became clear that over the last fifteen years, there had been three significant opportunities for conservative parties to adapt and change by heeding the lessons of history. Yet in each case, the party of the Right failed to learn.

First, in Great Britain, Prime Minister Margaret Thatcher failed to change the culture of the Conservative Party, which reverted to an unthinking, non-reform, tax-increase style as soon as she left office. At about the same time in the United States, President Reagan failed to change the culture of presidential Republicans; the first Bush administration got rid of virtually all the Reaganites as soon as it could, and within two years was cutting deals with the Democrats to raise taxes, despite having campaigned on "read my lips, no new taxes."

The last item in this trifecta of failure happened when those of us who believed in a reform-oriented, majority Republican Party could not change the minority mindset of the House Republicans. Those who want Republicans to become a natural governing majority have to come to grips with how deep and serious the problem is: Republicans must be capable of seizing the moment of change and making it permanent by implementing real change.

When House Republicans won control in 1994, only three of the new Republican committee chairmen had any understanding of what we were trying to do with the Contract with America. Congressman John Kasich became chair of the Budget Committee, Bob Livingston became chair of Appropriations, and Bob Walker became chair of the Science Committee. Virtually every other Republican who later became a chairman would have bet against our becoming a majority as late as Election Day. Ironically, our very success propelled people into positions of power who had spent their entire lives in the minority and were comfortable being in the minority. To them, gaining the majority in 1994 was seen as the end. It should have been considered by them and by all Republicans as merely the first step to creating a governing majority. The minority thinkers had no idea what it had taken to win the majority in 1994, and they had no interest in learning. They already had accidental power by virtue of their seniority in a system that suddenly gave them authority. They were not particularly interested in being exhausted by continuing efforts to develop the new solutions necessary to create and sustain a long-term governing majority.

The problem in the Senate was even worse. Few senators really understood what we were doing. The minority mindset in the Senate went back to the 1980 election. The Reagan tide had shocked everyone by creating a Senate majority when six underdog candidates won by a combined total of 75,000 votes. The problem for the long-term development of the Republican Party was that these victories pushed into chairmanships and other positions of real power older senators who not only predated Reagan, but also despised him.

Senate Republicans remain to this day a tactical collection of individually elected members in a loose alliance. The Senate Republicans' failure to understand why voters had initially elected them has prevented them from creating any coherent governing philosophy to build upon.

With House Republicans mired in a culture of minority status—and the Senate Republicans a collection of minority-minded personal fiefdoms—there was no long-term impetus to develop a governing majority. In this vacuum of leadership, the center of gravity in developing the Republican Party has moved to the consulting community, which is focused only on the short term. That reliance has directly led to the current collapse of the GOP back into its familiar place in the minority.

The Republican Trap: Rule by Consultants

There is an enormous difference in the way Republicans and Democrats have developed as political parties.

Democratic Party candidates are a collection of ambitious people immersed in politics and in policy. They are fascinated by the process of accumulating power in a free society and then using it for their own ideological purposes and to strengthen their allies and their institutional supporters.

Republican Party candidates tend to come from the business and professional world, which operates rationally in a business school–like manner. They often have little interest in or knowledge of politics as a method of accumulating power among a free people. They frequently have strong biases and opinions but remarkably little understanding of how government works or how a particular policy issue is developed over time.

This difference between the two parties was not evident from 1856 to 1930. The great era of Republican domination was also an era of Republican professional politicians and a time when Republican businessmen spent real time and effort in politics. (Note Mark Hanna's career in Cleveland or Elihu Root or Henry Stimson in New York.)

Shortly after he changed parties, then congressman (and later Texas senator and one-time presidential candidate) Phil Gramm told me he was astounded at how much easier it was to be in the minority. The majority has to think through an issue, translate it into legislation, make the compromises necessary to build a majority for the bill, and then manage the committee, the House floor, and the conference with the Senate. In other words, they actually have to govern. The minority simply has to vote no.

Six decades of a minority mindset created a Republican Party in which an amazing number of candidates and elected leaders turned to their political consultants and pollsters for advice about how to win and what to do. The status of permanent minority had depleted the energy level, diligence, and aggressiveness of the Republican members.

As they felt sure they would never be the majority party no matter what they did, it was easy to relax and enjoy their minority status. As the minority they could delegate political and campaign responsibilities to people who had no interest in governing and could focus on the tactics and mechanics of individual elections.

The consultants and pollsters were quite happy to do the job. First, they were getting paid to do it, and the more they did it, the more they could charge. Consider how the presidential campaigns spent millions in the first half of 2007 on high-priced consultants when not a single delegate would be selected before January 2008. Second, as they specialized in the mechanics of politics and in analyzing polling data, the consultants in fact knew a lot more about tactical politics than the incumbents they were advising, and this was seen by the candidates and elected officials as quite useful.

But this evolution into a consultant-defined party has been a huge mistake. Long-term leadership has to be focused on history, not the next campaign cycle. It has to be strategic rather than tactical. It has to involve governing rather than merely campaigning. Furthermore, the person whose name is on the ballot and who ultimately will have to take responsibility for his time in office is inherently more likely to take big risks than the consultants.

No consultant would have advised Abraham Lincoln to give a two-hour long speech at Cooper Union in New York in February 1860 (the only speech he gave that year), which arguably made him president, or to give an extraordinarily short speech at Gettysburg in 1863. Yet Lincoln understood that each speech was exactly right for its time and place. That is why he was Lincoln and they were not.

In his 2007 book *Testimony*, French president Nicolas Sarkozy recounts that when he decided to make a decisive speech announcing that France needed a "clean break" with the policies of President Jacques Chirac, in whose cabinet he was serving, all his major advisors were opposed. Yet it was the decisive move in creating a genuine pro-change candidacy on the right and the key to his election.

When President Ronald Reagan first wrote the words, "Mr. Gorbachev, tear down this wall!" for a speech in Berlin in 1987, the State Department editors took it out twice. Only when Reagan wrote it in a third time and called Secretary of State George Shultz to insist on it did the bureaucracy back down. Two years later the Berlin Wall fell.

Real leadership inherently requires leaders who listen to their advisors but then obey their own instincts, who take risks when the situation requires it. A consultant-dominated system can never compete with a leader-dominated system over time—governing is much harder than campaigning and leading is much harder than consulting.

Governing Is Much Harder Than Campaigning

Even if you assume that consultants are much better at the details of campaigning, it does not mean they are the right people to be at the center of decision-making for a governing party. Campaigning is challenging. Governing is much harder. Once you acquire power, people will measure you by how well you govern, not by how well you campaigned.

Over the past several years, Republicans have begun to discover that their consultants do not know enough to create effective long-term strategies for governing. In retrospect, it seems clear that the two greatest habits of modern Republican consultants were bound to get the GOP in a lot of trouble. The first is emphasizing the partisan divide, and the second is emphasizing the negative. Together they can be summed up as the red-versus-blue fixation. This flawed political focus has had a devastating effect on the party.

Why Red-versus-Blue Fails: The American People Want Red-White-and-Blue Solutions

Red versus blue as a core strategy is an invitation to disaster over time. It can work for one or two election cycles, but eventually it sets up three destructive dynamics.

* First, a red-versus-blue strategy continually narrows the playing field. Candidates give up on persuading anyone on the other side to join their cause and focus instead on narrow, partisan appeals.
* Second, the requirement to maximize turnout with partisan appeals leads to a shrillness that eventually drives away the independent and moderate voter.
* Third, the most effective turnout mechanism is to increase the negativity or scare or anger your side into voting, which in the long run leads to a numbness that convinces all but the hardest partisans that your messages are phony and misleading. The six Republican Senate incumbents who lost in 2006 have to wonder whether their appeal was too narrow and too negative.

Consider the consequences of these destructive dynamics in more depth. Although people will tolerate a very intense, narrow focus in a single campaign for a single election, there is a huge difference between an individual campaign and the growth, effective management, and leadership of a governing system. People expect a party in which they've given their trust to govern the nation to represent the concerns of all Americans. There is a remarkably deep sense of collective identity among the American people about the need to keep the American community together. There is a very deep emotional sense that all Americans are worthy of respect. Any political party that begins each day by writing off a large number of fellow citizens is effectively delegitimizing itself as a choice for long-term governing.

Americans deeply dislike the idea of abandoning their fellow Americans. We don't like it in war, when we demand that our leaders do everything we can to save wounded young Americans. We don't like it in a disaster, when we demand that our leaders rescue people from floods, fires, hurricanes, or earthquakes. We don't like it when faced with deadly disease, when we demand that our leaders do something to help the ill.

Given everything we know about the compassion Americans feel for the American family, how could any party think it could turn its back on Americans of any ethnic group, geographic region, or economic status and still be considered worthy of governing?

President Bush's failure to address the NAACP early in his presidency was a clear signal to the African American community that Republicans did not see them as worthy of engagement in dialogue. The country would have been better off if he had gone there and challenged them to uproot failing school systems, to lower taxes in failing cities, to attract jobs, and to tackle the problem of violence and murder in cities like Philadelphia. It would have shown he was prepared to take seriously the plight of the poorer elements of the African American community, even if the NAACP was too indebted to its bureaucratic and union allies to join him. The only downside was the risk of being booed; the upside was igniting a dialogue to save Americans in the inner cities from decay.

The failure of the major Republican candidates to participate fully in Latino or African American debates in all of 2007 is the kind of red-versus-blue thinking that made sense to their consultants individually, but is collectively a devastating signal for the Republican Party to send to all Americans, especially to minority Americans. If Republicans intend to reverse their recent minority status, they had better decide to drop red versus blue and go back to thinking red-white-and-blue, which was the key to our 1994 victory with the Contract with America.

In order to maximize turnout among the base, Republicans allow their campaigns to be dominated more and more by pandering to small, specific segments of the activist wing of the party. The elite news media are deeply anti-Republican, and they are delighted to stir up as much competition and conflict among the "base" elements of the Republican Party as possible. The media delight in the undisciplined and increasingly shrill appeals by candidates to win over small voter groups at the expense of isolating themselves from the vast majority of Americans. Even when their positions are correct and defensible, their tone and intensity repel most voters not familiar with or committed to that particular issue.

In one election, in the right political environment, intensity is fine. But over a long period of time intensity drives away all but the most intense and limits a party to a small minority base, making appeals to a majority of voters all but impossible. What's more, over time, shrill and hostile messages gradually lose their effectiveness. People simply cease to believe them or cease to attribute to them much importance even if they do believe them.

The steady decay of Republican support in the Northeast from Baltimore to northern Maine and up and down the Pacific Coast is a result of this shrillness as much as anything. Even if people agree on the issue, the intensity makes them very uncomfortable. This decay caused by base mobilization strategy is a significant part of what happened by 2006 and why the Republicans lost every close Senate race involving a Republican incumbent. When you are zero for six there are some pretty big lessons to be learned.

The base mobilization strategy requires a scorched-earth negativity that gradually turns people off because it simply exhausts them. Most voters cannot sustain being angry for very long. We faced this phenomenon in 1994. We knew that the base Republican vote would not be big enough to win the majority by itself, but we also knew that key coalitions of voters were totally turned off by negative campaigns. We could pick up some seats just by the natural attrition of the Democrats having made so many people angry. But we had to offer a proposal so positive and so compelling that it would attract the Perot voters who were both anti-politics and anti-negativity.

The Contract with America campaign was relentlessly positive precisely because of this sense that we had to bring people together in order to get the non-voters to decide to vote again. Our single biggest ad was placed in *TV Guide*. The message was entirely positive. It did not attack President Clinton or the Democrats. It listed ten things Americans wanted, and explained our contract to vote on them in the first one hundred days in office if we won the majority.

So many pollsters, analysts, and reporters have been confused about the 1994 election that I simply want to set the record straight. Joe Gaylord, Frank Luntz, Haley Barbour (then RNC chairman, now governor of Mississippi), and I had a pretty good idea throughout the year that we were making a historic gamble on big issues and big, positive ideas.

In 1994, we achieved the largest one-party vote increase in an off-year election in American history. Nine million more people voted for

Republicans (and one million fewer people voted for Democrats) between the 1990 and the 1994 elections. We elected the first Republican majority in forty years and then managed the House through a confrontation with a liberal president, a government shutdown, and a balanced budget effort that included reforming Medicare. Then we won reelection for the first time since 1928.

What was most misunderstood about our victory by the media and even many in the Republican Party was that even though voters were angry about their government in 1994, they were not anti-government. The Republican Party cannot win over time as the permanently angry, anti-government party because neither appeals to most voters. It can win as the pro-good government and pro-limited government party.

While there were many factors that contributed to the Republican victory in 1994, including voter anger with an out-of-touch and arrogant Democratic Party and a weak president, winning was no accident. Winning was the result of carefully considered, systematic strategies. Yet the strategies of running on big issues with massive bipartisan support that were used to develop the Contract with America were so outside the pattern of the minority-minded, tactically oriented Republican consultants that there was a determined effort not to study them and not to learn from them. The consultant-driven agenda was to use the power granted to the Republicans by the American people to stay in power for power's sake.

For a number of years I kept quiet, but the recent devastation to my party is now so great that I am compelled to speak out explicitly and decisively. A red-versus-blue, base-focused, negative-advertising model is a terrible model for a political party, no matter how good it may be for an individual candidate. If Republicans do not replace this minority-mindset model with a much more powerful, majoritarian, solution-oriented, governing model, they should expect to remain in the minority for another forty years.

As discussed in Chapter One, the failure of the Republicans to run a majoritarian, solutions-oriented governing campaign in 2004 against John Kerry was a tremendous lost opportunity. Had the Republicans run a campaign focused on the extraordinary divide in values and philosophy between the two candidates, it is very possible they would have won a victory comparable to 1972 and 1984. Had that happened, the scale of the defeat would have given the Republicans the strength to govern effectively. It would also have given the Democrats a profound reason to rethink their philosophy.

As for the 2008 campaign, President Bush's unpopularity and the sudden crisis in our financial system made a victory for Senator McCain very difficult. However, it is worth noting that it was the victor, Senator Obama, and not Senator McCain, whose core message was the rejection of red-versus-blue politics.

Senator Obama ran a positive presidential campaign that reached out to many sectors of the population beyond the Democrats' traditional base. The result was not just winning a narrow victory by maximizing turnout in traditionally Democratic areas among people who were angry with President Bush. Obama had reached out to all Americans and was rewarded with victories in North Carolina, Colorado, and other traditionally red states. In fact, it is likely that Senator Obama's victory would have been even more overwhelming if the ideology of the Left were not so fundamentally out of sync with that of the vast majority of Americans. This divergence is addressed in the next chapter.

CHAPTER THREE

An Unreformed Left: Why Democrats Can't Deliver Real Change

THE DEMOCRATS' NEAR-VICTORY in the 2004 presidential election and runaway victory in 2008 are a long-term tragedy for the Democratic Party. They have allowed the leaders to ignore how out of touch with America the left wing of their party is. The combination of left-wing financier George Soros's money with the energy of the liberal lifestyle groups, the labor unions, the trial lawyers, the Hollywood Left, and the antiwar Left enabled the Democrats to generate a sense of momentum. This same sense of media excitement and Internet intensity was also experienced by former presidential candidate and current Democratic National Committee chairman Howard Dean, right up to his collapse within a three-week period in Iowa in January 2004.

While the Republicans failed to learn the lessons of leadership and risk-taking from the 1994 victory, the Democrats are showing no signs of learning the lessons from two of their own failures: the failure of their unionized bureaucracies to help provide growth and progress to every sector of our economy (both public and private) and the failure of their left-wing values to resonate with the American people.

Failures of the Unionized Bureaucracies

There is one very simple way to understand why the Democrats will be unable to deliver real change despite winning the White House in 2008. It's provided in your daily newspaper. When Democratic politicians run for office, they invariably promise new government programs—programs that cost the taxpayers, inflate the bureaucracy, and put more power in the hands of a government that too often doesn't share the people's values. The news media report with a straight face that each of the new government programs will actually deliver the promised results. But buried in the very same newspapers are story after story of government incompetence, inefficiency, waste, fraud, and illegality.

No one since President Reagan and the Grace Commission has seriously tried to bring big incompetence, big inefficiency, big fraud, and big waste of your tax money into the spotlight.

Before the public lets the Left explain its newest idea for paying off its unionized bureaucratic allies and its various special interest groups with your tax money, they should force Democratic politicians to explain why new government programs won't be riddled with the same kinds of waste and fraud that currently plague government programs. Consider the following examples:

* The U.S. Department of Agriculture has paid more than a billion dollars to deceased farmers over the last seven years.

Officials approved payment without any review 40 percent of
the time.

* Between 1996 and 2001, NASA and Lockheed Martin spent
  more than $1 billion on a space plane to succeed the current
  space shuttle. Due to technical problems, the project was can-
  celed before a prototype was even completed.

* According to a report by the Government Accountability Office,
  our country has 55,322 criminal illegal aliens who have been
  arrested at least a total of 459,614 times, averaging about eight
  arrests per illegal alien. Twenty-six percent (about 15,000) have
  had eleven or more arrests. Imagine a government bureaucracy
  so incompetent it can't even remove people from the United
  States when they have been arrested eleven or more times.

It's Not Just the Federal Government

Wasting money and establishing sweetheart deals for government
employees is not simply an issue for the federal government. It is an
issue at every level of government. And at every level of government,
the Democrats are on the wrong side of reform. Consider the California state pension system's scandalous encouragement of dishonest
disability claims:

* A California Department of Corrections (DOC) employee,
  Greg Nelson, claimed that he hurt his back and neck in a workplace fall in 2002. The DOC workers' compensation fraud unit
  caught Nelson on videotape working fourteen-hour days operating heavy machinery at forest fires in Oregon. Despite this, the
  state retirement system awarded him a medical pension of

$22,000 per year, agreeing that his injuries prevented him from working as a corrections officer.

* It is not a crime in California for a public employee to lie while trying to get a disability pension.

* The California Public Employees' Retirement System (CalPERS) cannot request medical examinations for disability pensioners.

* CalPERS investigators do not have the right to obtain employment information about people claiming debilitating injuries. Legislation to correct this, and make it easier to crack down on fraud in disability pensions, was passed unanimously by both houses in 2004 but then quietly shelved.

* Democrats do not want to take action on the anti-fraud bills because the unionized bureaucracy—state employee unions—is one of their biggest allies, and they are worried the governor will replace pensions for state workers with a 401(k) system. The public employee unions oppose this plan, so the Democrats oppose it too.

Then there is the scale of fraud and waste in New York Medicaid. A July 2005 series of articles in the *New York Times* reported that the retired chief state investigator of Medicaid fraud and abuse in New York City said he and his colleagues believed that at least 10 percent of state Medicaid dollars were spent on fraudulent claims. At least 20 or 30 percent more were siphoned off by what they termed abuse, meaning unnecessary spending that might not be criminal. "So we're talking about 40 percent of all claims are questionable," he said, "an amount that would approach $18 billion a year." Eighteen billion dollars a year in questionable claims is simply astonishing.

One year later, a study of New York's Medicaid program by Washington-based consultant Don Muse found jaw-dropping amounts of "unexplainable" spending. State health officials who attended the presentation of the final report in June 2006 were stunned into silence. To this day, that full study remains buried in New York's Medicaid bureaucracy under strict confidentiality agreements. This is extremely unfortunate, because the overwhelming number of providers who treat Medicaid patients are honest. But the amount they are paid by Medicaid keeps declining, partly because federal and state authorities are unable or unwilling to deal with fraudulent activity in a serious way.

The public employee unions have also blocked pension reform, an area in which they have created sweetheart deals for themselves over the years. The local politicians like the arrangement because they can win affection from the union for the next election while giving away money that won't come due for decades. They are burdening their successors with huge debts, but that is not their immediate problem. It is an irresponsible strategy and one that the public employee unions are happy to exploit.

Chris Edwards and Jagadeesh Gokhale, economists at the libertarian Cato Institute, have warned that there is a $2 trillion "fiscal hole" in unfunded retirement benefits and retirement health benefits for state and local workers. They warn that "the prospect of funding $2 trillion of obligations with higher taxes is frightening, especially when you consider that state politicians would be imposing them on the same income base as federal politicians trying to finance massive shortfalls in Social Security and Medicare."

One issue is fairness: not only are we being unfair to our children and grandchildren, but we're also being unfair to today's taxpayers and retirees. As the two economists note, "Federal data shows that state and local governments spend an average of $3.91 per hour worked on employee health benefits, compared to $1.72 in the private sector." So as a taxpayer, you are paying taxes to give bureaucrats 125 percent more benefits than you are getting.

Edwards and Gokhale say the obvious: "The only good options are to cut benefits and move state and local retirement plans to a pre-funded basis with personal savings plans"—exactly what the Left opposes. They conclude, with unwarranted optimism, "Hopefully, most state policy makers appreciate that hiking taxes in today's highly competitive global economy is a losing proposition."

The unreformed Left doesn't understand this at all. It does not understand that hiking taxes in today's highly competitive global economy is a losing proposition. And that's just one reason we can't expect real change from a Democratic Party dominated by an unreformed Left.

An Unreformed Left Dominated by Unreformed Unions: A Codependency of the World That Fails

Historically, unions have played very important roles here in America and abroad. The American union movement, especially the AFL-CIO, played a major role in helping the Solidarity movement liberate Poland from a Communist dictatorship. Today, the bus drivers' union in Iran is a major opponent of the dictatorship there. Conservatives cannot cheer unions overseas and then be blindly anti-union here at home. There are legitimate historic reasons for workers to organize together, and there is a strong need for a healthy, competitive union movement that helps improve the lives of its members and the competitiveness of our country.

Andy Stern, the head of the Service Employees International Union, is the union leader who probably best understands the challenge of the world market and the need to make American union members productive in the face of world competition. Sadly, he is in a distinct minority among union leaders.

A strong, healthy, competitive union movement focused on improving productivity and increasing incomes by increasing competitive capabilities would be a tremendous movement with a worldwide appeal. The failure of most union leaders to rethink their role and to develop a new and more effective union movement weakens America.

The Union Leaders and the World That Fails

Unions are so powerful in California and New York that even popular governors do not effectively control the state government. The real power lies in the unions, which have invested more and more in politics as their popularity among workers has declined. They have replaced worker representation at the local level with political power in state capitals, and now they are trying to apply the same model to Washington.

Governor Arnold Schwarzenegger, the most charismatic California governor since Ronald Reagan, does not run California government. He presides over lifetime bureaucracies defined and dominated by unions and interest groups. When the former movie star staked his political capital on passing a series of initiatives to tame California's public employee unions, he lost and they won. In Sacramento, the head of the prison guards' union is more powerful than the governor.

In Albany, the real governor of New York is Dennis Rivera of the Service Employees International Union, and the elected governor is simply a supplicant begging for change but powerless to get it done without permission.

As the unions have become less and less competitive in seeking members, and as unionized companies have become less and less able to flourish in a free market, their leaders have turned to an overtly political strategy of seeking and holding on to power in the narrowest sense. For union membership, those they can't persuade to join, they intend to coerce. For industries that supply union jobs but that can't deliver goods and services competitively, they seek to make monopolies without competition. What they can't earn in the marketplace they intend to win through political power and government control.

These special interest union leaders are not inherently bad people. They are hardworking, enthusiastic advocates of causes they believe in. They have a deep vested interest in influencing the people who determine their incomes, their pensions, and their work rules, especially for work forces either employed directly by government or drawing their income from government-funded programs (health care and education are two).

Similarly, trial lawyers have a vested interest in ensuring that legislatures rig the game in favor of litigation and in favor of trial lawyer enrichment. Thus they have a huge investment in ensuring that government regulations favor their filing class-action suits and winning large awards so they will have opportunities to increase their personal income.

As a result, union leaders and trial lawyers focus very intensely on raising campaign funds, organizing "volunteer" workers from their union membership, and ensuring that they can maximize their power in the state legislature.

The average citizen and the average small business do not have this direct interest in politics. Their taxes may go up while their services may decay due to bad work rules. They might even be irritated by the arrogance of the special interest groups. But none of these irritations leads them to focus on politics as a life-and-death matter.

For the government employee, the government-financed unions, and the trial lawyers, however, political power leading to legislative power is a matter of life and death. Thus over the last three decades there has been a steady growth of union and trial lawyer investment in politics and politicians. Ironically, the number of Americans who voluntarily join a union has been shrinking as union political power has been growing.

As unions cannot win many secret-ballot elections to organize workers, they have come up with a new solution. It's not to make the union more desirable. It's simply to take away the American worker's right to have a secret-ballot election. This would repeal reforms to protect workers from intimidation and extortion that go back to 1935. It's not an idle left-wing fantasy: it actually passed the House of Representatives in early 2007 with almost no public notice. Under the Orwellian name of the "Freedom of Choice Act," this legislation is backed by President Obama, who has vowed to sign the measure if passed by Congress, where it enjoys wide Democratic support. Thus the Democratic Congress and president are fighting to eliminate a fundamental American right just to make it easier for their union allies to acquire more members, more dues, and more power. And yet 89 percent of the American people don't want workers to lose their secret-ballot rights.

If you want to know the depth of the Left's commitment to its union allies, all you have to do is look at how the Democrats in

Congress singled out the Office of Labor Management Standards, the lone federal agency responsible for finding and prosecuting union corruption. It was the only major office in the Department of Labor to receive less money in 2007 than in the previous year.

Rigging the Game Against the Average American

Beyond union issues, the Left knows it has a hard time winning among normal Americans, and so it does everything it can to rig the game against the interests of average middle-class taxpayers.

As one of their first acts in the majority, Democrats in Congress passed a resolution to give certain voting rights in the House to delegates from D.C., Puerto Rico, Guam, the Virgin Islands, and American Samoa. But consider this: American Samoa has fewer than 60,000 residents, while the average congressional district represents 600,000 residents. Imagine how average Americans would react if they knew their representative had voted to allow someone representing one-tenth as many people to offset their votes. Furthermore, President Obama enthusiastically supports granting a congressional seat to heavily-Democratic Washington, D.C., despite the fact that such a move would blatantly violate the Constitution, which reserves the right to vote for Congress to residents "of the several States." Washington, D.C. is not a state, of course, and this was noted in a legal opinion drafted by the Department of Justice's Office of Legal Counsel, which found Congress's current proposal for D.C. voting rights to be unconstitutional. In a sign of the importance of D.C. statehood to the Obama administration, Attorney General Eric Holder rejected the opinion and ordered a new one from other Justice lawyers, who conveniently found that D.C. statehood is perfectly legit.

The Left's desire to rig votes and win unfairly is perfectly captured in its attitude toward holding clean, honest elections. For some reason people on the left believe accurate election rolls and honest elections are to their disadvantage. Consider the example of the voting dog.

Jane Balogh of Seattle registered her dog, Duncan, to vote, and submitted ballots in three elections signed with the dog's paw print. Even after this story received national media attention, Duncan remained on the voter rolls because it's "an arduous process" (according to election officials) to remove a name. Election officials said taking someone off the rolls entails a formal challenge and a public hearing. Duncan was registered to vote in April 2006. In November, Duncan sent in a ballot marked VOID. An election official called shortly thereafter and the ruse was revealed, but Duncan still continued to receive absentee ballots for elections in February and May 2007.

As she was sending in Duncan's ballots, Balogh was writing letters to legislators describing her trick and pleading for them to fix the system. The ballots, elections officials said, could have counted had she not blown the whistle on herself.

In 2004, Democrat Christine Gregoire became governor of Washington State by a margin of 129 votes out of 2.8 million cast. In one county alone, officials found 1,800 more votes than people who had signed in to vote at polling stations. After state officials examined the voting rolls, they announced in 2006 that they had deleted 55,000 registrations, including 19,579 names of people who were dead and 35,445 otherwise illegal registrations.

The combination of bureaucracy, waste, union work rules, public employee union special pay, pensions, and benefits all rigging the game against the average American makes it extremely difficult for the Left to offer the kind of real change that America needs. The Left can't possibly hope to reform government until it reforms itself and until it puts the interests of America's red-white-and-blue majority ahead of the interests of bureaucrats, union bosses, and trial lawyers. But the greater difficulty for the Left in trying to establish a governing majority is the enormous gap between its values and those of the majority of Americans.

The Left's Ideological Unacceptability

It is hard for our elites to understand how distant their values are from those of the average American. In the university faculty lounges, the Hollywood cocktail parties, the left-wing activist groups, and the newsrooms and editorial boards of most of the elite media, there is such a unanimity of belief that it is impossible for them to realize that they collectively form a left-wing enclave in a hugely center-right nation. As Obama's victory showed, the only way they can get elected to national office is to obscure their real beliefs and intentions.

In early 2007, I created a nonpartisan organization called American Solutions in order to break partisan gridlock and create commonsense solutions. At American Solutions, we decided to listen carefully to the American people about their values and their understanding of what would work and what they favored. In the summer of 2007, we ana-lyzed a series of six national surveys.*

To understand the gap between the Left and the American people, consider the following:

* 85 percent believe it is very important for a group or organiza-tion in this country to pursue the goal of helping defend Amer-ica and its allies.

---

* The full results are available at www.americansolutions.com.

* 75 percent believe it is very important for a group or organization in this country to pursue the goal of defeating America's enemies.
* 93 percent believe al Qaeda poses a serious threat.
* 85 percent believe Iran poses a serious threat.
* 79 percent would support the death penalty for someone caught and convicted of carrying out a terrorist attack in the United States.
* 83 percent support the establishment of clear laws making it a crime to advocate acts of terrorism or violent conduct or the killing of innocent people in the United States.
* 77 percent support the closing down of terrorist Web sites at home and abroad using the techniques of computer warfare.
* 65 percent favor abolishing the death tax.
* 48 percent favor abolishing the capital gains tax (41 percent oppose; this is included because no one on the left could imagine that without any argument being made and any campaign being waged there are already enough investors in the United States to have a plurality favoring abolishing the capital gains tax).
* 70 percent favor a tax incentive for companies headquartered in the United States.
* 61 percent favor the option of a single income tax rate of 17 percent.
* 74 percent favor the single rate of 17 percent for corporations.
* 68 percent see a direct link to making American corporations more competitive in the United States so they will not move jobs overseas.

* 54 percent believe the wealthiest should pay the same proportion of their income as everyone else, while only 43 percent believe they should pay more. This undermines one of the Left's happiest battle cries of "tax the rich."

The Left is distant from the average American on national security and economics, but the gap becomes cataclysmic when the topic turns to culture and religion.

* 89 percent believe religion and morality are important to them and their families.
* 79 percent believe religion and morality are important to the country.
* 87 percent approve of the reference to "the Creator" in the Declaration of Independence; 6 percent strongly disapprove.
* 88 percent approve of the reference to "one nation under God" in the Pledge of Allegiance; 7 percent strongly disapprove.
* 78 percent approve of the Ten Commandments appearing in courthouses across America; 12 percent strongly disapprove.
* 81 percent oppose removing crosses and other such monuments from public parks and other public property; 8 percent strongly approve.
* 94 percent approve of a moment of silence allowing children to pray to themselves if they want to in public schools; 3 percent strongly disapprove.
* 90 percent approve of a Christmas tree or menorah being placed on public property during the holiday season; 5 percent strongly disapprove.

This is not just a matter of cultural values. The average American absolutely believes that these values make a difference in defining who we are and the freedoms we enjoy.

* 84 percent agree that references to God in the Pledge of Allegiance and the Declaration of Independence are important because they make clear that certain rights can't be taken away by the government; only 9 percent strongly disagree.
* 93 percent believe that it is still important to acknowledge that our rights come from our Creator today; only 3 percent disagree.

When given a choice between two hypothetical candidates, one who believes that most of the problems our country faces are because America is no longer as religious and moral as it once was, and a second candidate who believes that religion and morality have little to do with America's problems and that our problems are a result of changes in the economy, war, public education, and other issues, the American people choose the candidate of religion and morality by 65 percent to 30 percent. This choice is rooted in a deeper understanding of how relevant our Founding Fathers and their values are to twenty-first-century America.

To reinforce the primacy of traditional American beliefs, values, and history, consider the results of a choice between a candidate who believes that statements regarding religion and morality made by the Founding Fathers don't have much to do with America today, and a candidate who believes that statements regarding religion and morality made by the Founding Fathers are just as important today as they were two hundred years ago. The American people favor a candidate who respects the lessons of the Founding Fathers by 86 percent to 12 percent over the secular candidate.

Given a choice between a candidate who believes the best way to protect religious freedom is to protect all religious references and symbols, including those on public buildings, lands, and documents, and a candidate who believes the best way to ensure religious freedom is to remove all religious references and symbols, Americans by 81 percent to 14 percent pick the candidate who would protect religious symbols.

I strongly agree with those who believe America's roots are to be found in the endowment of our Creator. I wrote *Rediscovering God in America* (also now available as a DVD walking tour of Washington that my wife, Callista, and I co-host) to prove that from the Declaration of Independence ("we are endowed by our Creator with certain unalienable rights") to the Constitution (signed in "the Year of our Lord") to the great leaders of America, most Americans are right and those who insist on anti-religious bigotry are simply wrong.

Yet if a massive majority (averaging between 80 and 90 percent support on question after question) recognizes the important role of religion and morality in our public life, then why does this majority keep losing to an anti-religious Left with a hardcore following of only 3 to 9 percent? The answer is to be found in the deliberate strategy of the Left in using the law and the courts to impose on America what they could never win in elections, which I address in more detail in Chapter Thirteen.

CHAPTER FOUR

Katrina, Michigan, and Beyond: How the Old Order Is Failing America

THE RESULTS OF HAVING TWO UNREFORMED and dysfunctional political parties can be seen in an increasingly out-of-date government failing at its core missions of effective governance. It is hard to overestimate the human cost that failed government has on the prosperity and well-being of the American people. Unionized bureaucracies and underperforming government institutions fight hardest to avoid change precisely where change is most needed because they recognize change as a threat to their power. They prefer failure with power to success without power. We have seen this cost of bad government most recently in the aftermath of Hurricane Katrina and most starkly in the state of Michigan and its once great city of Detroit.

Hurricane Katrina

New Orleans and the Gulf Coast are still trying to recover from the damage of Hurricane Katrina. Hurricanes can't be prevented, but the catastrophe in New Orleans that this hurricane caused was completely avoidable. What is hard to explain is how the senior leadership of our government could have been so distant and uninformed as to let it happen.

New Orleans has a special attraction for me. I spent three wonderful years as a graduate student at Tulane University. My youngest daughter was born in New Orleans. My oldest daughter went to Head Start in New Orleans. We made many friends and enjoyed Mardi Gras, the Audubon Park Zoo (today a much better and more attractive zoo under Ron Forman's inspired entrepreneurial leadership), and spent delightful afternoons in the French Quarter and on the St. Charles Avenue trolley.

So for me, as for so many Americans, the disaster of Katrina was personal. And the deepest outrage should be that there is no outrage. Where is the demand for fundamental reform of the government that failed us? Where is the insistence on new and better approaches to responding to natural disasters at every level of government?

As much as any one thing, it was the government's failure to respond to the catastrophe of Katrina that made me determined to launch American Solutions and to insist on a bipartisan national movement to get America back on track.

Here are the unspoken—and apparently unspeakable—facts about the disaster in New Orleans:

The collapse of New Orleans was avoidable.

The collapse of the relief effort among the very poor was avoidable.

The lack of national, state, and local leadership and decisive intervention was avoidable.

The Army Corps of Engineers failed to do its job and ensure that the levees would work when put to the test by a large-scale hurricane, which was a clearly foreseeable situation. The Corps has suffered no consequences for its failure and it has not been reformed. Moreover, before Hurricane Katrina, the one Bush appointee who said the Army Corps of Engineers needed more funding or disasters would result (former Mississippi congressman Mike Parker, who served briefly as assistant secretary of the army for civil works) was fired.

The politicians in Washington clearly had other things they wanted to spend money on and preferred to run the risk of a city-crippling catastrophe. None have paid any costs for their misjudgment, including some key members of the Louisiana delegation who could have fought for levee repair and did not. On the state level, the voters of Louisiana have demanded change by electing as their governor a conservative Republican, Bobby Jindal, who has taken tremendous steps toward transforming Louisiana's state governance.

A Model for Failure

If government is the world that fails, the branches of government that should have responded to Hurricane Katrina failed catastrophically. From the ground up:

The local levee board was incompetent and parochial, and to this day is a hindrance to sound engineering and efficient implementation of change and improvement.

The New Orleans city government is notoriously corrupt and remains so.

The Democratic governor of Louisiana was too timid, too slow, and too ineffective—and worried more about shifting blame to President Bush than about saving New Orleans.

The Louisiana Office of Homeland Security and Emergency Preparedness was under federal indictment for losing more than $50 million in federal funds before Katrina and was incapable of operating effectively.

The Charity system for health care in Louisiana is a state patronage system that delivers inadequate care at absurd costs. It is one factor in Louisiana's ranking as the second most expensive state for Medicare and the state with the worst outcome for senior citizens. Yet the Charity system is a political sacred cow sponsoring so many jobs that it will be very hard to dismantle or substantially change it, no matter how ineffective it is in terms of patient health and cost to the taxpayer. It is a case study of a self-protecting bureaucracy using its political power to avoid competition and change even at the cost of human lives.

The Federal Emergency Management Agency (FEMA) had been allowed to decay and was incapable of operating effectively. Its bureaucratic attitude and arrogance became a stunning indictment of the federal government in the weeks after Katrina. According to the Select Bipartisan Committee to Investigate the Preparation for the Response to Hurricane Katrina, the federal response to Katrina was a "national failure." The report found a dramatic contrast between the government bureaucracy that failed, and which caused "death, injury, and suffering," and the world that works, consisting of individuals "whose exceptional initiative saved time, money, and lives." It is no surprise then that while FedEx resumed service to New Orleans within two weeks, the United States Postal System maintained an embargo on magazines, newspapers, periodicals, and advertising mail going to New Orleans for six months.

The federal government's record of wastefulness and incompetence in helping New Orleans rebuild is well documented. The federal government has spent $7.5 billion for the Road Home program to help homeowners rebuild, but of the 104,000 who have applied for help, only 500 have received grants. The federal government spent $878.8 million on nearly 25,000 manufactured homes; 11,000 went unused because FEMA's own regulations prohibit placing the homes in flood plains, such as New Orleans. Many of the 120,000 trailers and mobile homes provided to people along the Gulf Coast are contaminated with unhealthy levels of formaldehyde, a known carcinogen. In July 2007, House lawmakers released documents indicating that FEMA lawyers tried to block investigation of the contamination for fear of lawsuits.

FEMA spent $67 million on 224.3 million pounds of ice in 2005 for Katrina victims. It was never delivered. Instead, it was sent to storage in twenty-two facilities around the country. After two years, FEMA concluded that the ice was past its shelf life, and spent another $3.4 million to melt it.

The Department of Homeland Security (DHS) was also simply not up to the job of responding effectively to Hurricane Katrina—let alone the three nuclear attacks in one day it is supposed to be able to handle. DHS and the Bush administration did not even learn the lessons of 1992's Hurricane Andrew, when the Army moved in a corps headquarters with all its communications, command and control, and transportation assets. Though Hurricane Katrina was even more devastating than Andrew, the Bush administration did not send an Army corps headquarters to New Orleans. The president clearly was not functioning as a commander in chief. How could he have been so uninformed, or misinformed, as to say, "Brownie [referring to FEMA director Mike Brown], you are doing a heck of a job" four days into the mess? Anyone who had been watching the news channels or had gone to the various Web sites and blogs would have known that Brownie was in over his head, drowning along with New Orleans.

Hurricane Katrina exposed the fact that no one in politics today is letting the facts lead them and inform their decisions. Rather than seek the best solutions for the American people, politicians are too busy looking for the best attack for their partisan advantage. Because the politicians are too busy playing the blame game, no one thinks about transforming government so that we have a twenty-first-century system to meet twenty-first-century problems. Disasters like Hurricane Katrina are an example of settling for failure. With more natural disasters surely to follow, settling for failure cannot be an option.

Michigan and Detroit as a Case Study in the Impact of Bad Policies

No state is a better case study for the impact of the cost of bad government than Michigan, led by a left-wing governor and a cadre of state employee interest groups that insist on avoiding reform even if it cripples the state. The impact of this bad economic policy has been devastating. From 2000 to 2006, Michigan lost 336,000 jobs and is predicted to lose an additional 33,000 by the end of 2008. Its unemployment rate in June 2007 was 7.2 percent, the highest in the nation.

Michigan had a AAA bond rating (the best you can get) and was borrowing money at the lowest rate when Governor John Engler left office in 2003. Within a year it lost that rating and the cost of its debt service began to rise. Under Governor Engler's policies of welfare reform, tax cuts, education reform, and modernizing state government, Michigan reached the lowest unemployment rate in its history, 3.3 percent. Today this rate has more than doubled and is the highest unemployment rate in America. This economic collapse has had human consequences.

* In the fall of 2006, Michigan was the only state to see housing prices fall, decreasing 0.4 percent in one year.
* A 2007 poll found that more than half of the graduates of Michigan's three largest universities planned on leaving the state. About half of the students polled at Michigan State University, the University of Michigan, and Wayne State University stated that they were planning to leave the state to find jobs. Only about 25 percent of students polled answered that they were planning to stay in Michigan. A similar 2004 poll found that 40 percent of college students planned to leave Michigan after they graduated.
* A 2003 Census report found that between 1995 and 2000, Michigan lost more young people than it attracted. The net outflow of young, college-educated, single people from Michigan during that period was 16,018.
* United Van Lines, a moving company, reported that 66 percent of all moves involving Michigan were outbound moves of people leaving the state, tied for highest in the nation. A December 2006 Census report found that Michigan was one of only four states to suffer a loss of total population.

Faced with these losses, the liberal governor of Michigan fought to raise taxes. This policy made no economic sense but a lot of political sense. Economically, the tax increase would drive even more businesses, jobs, and people out of Michigan. Politically, however, it would appease the governor's public employee union allies and protect the government at the expense of the rest of the state. This is a suicidal policy that will ultimately lead to the further decline of Michigan. Nowhere is the example of failure in Michigan more dramatic than in the state's largest city.

Detroit as a Special Example of Bad Outcomes from Bad Policies

Detroit is an amazing case study in the economic and human costs of bad government and bad policies. In 1950, Detroit had 1,800,000 people and ranked first in median income of all major cities in America. Today Detroit has shrunk to 871,000 people and ranks sixty-sixth out of sixty-eight major American cities in median household income.

The Mackinac Center for Public Policy reports that

* Since 1950, Detroit has lost 46 percent of its population, but the number of city employees has shrunk by only 30 percent.
* The city government is the second-largest employer in Detroit, behind only the Detroit public school system.
* Of the city's twenty-five biggest employers, 40 percent of jobs are provided by state, county, and city governments.
* The city of Detroit has a ratio of residents per city employee of 50. Compare this with 68 for Chicago, 78 for Houston, 108 for Los Angeles, and 223 for Indianapolis.

When almost as many jobs are paid for by taxes as there are jobs in the private sector providing a tax base, an inevitable economic decline is under way. It becomes harder and harder to get businesses to move into that kind of economic environment. At the same time the sheer power of that many public employees makes it harder and harder to reform the system. A downward spiral of economic decline begins that is very hard to reverse. Those who would fight for lower taxes and more efficient government find it easier to leave, and so the pool of reformers shrinks while the pool of those who depend on government for a living grows.

Detroit is the embodiment of this downward spiral model of bad government. From 1947 to 1967, Detroit lost 120,000 manufacturing jobs, and residents kept leaving as unemployment grew. In 1968, following riots, more affluent residents began to move out to the suburbs by the thousands. Racial divisions grew deeper in the increasingly impoverished city. The unemployment rate is now higher than that of any other major metropolitan area, and one-third of Detroit residents live below the poverty line. In perhaps the most potent symbol of the city's dysfunctional leadership, after serving nearly seven years as mayor, Kwame Kilpatrick was forced to resign in 2008 and was imprisoned after pleading guilty to several felonies.

The Failure of Detroit Public Schools

The Detroit school bureaucracy is a particularly tragic example of the human cost of protecting unionized bureaucracy at the expense of serving the public. A 2006 study backed by the Bill and Melinda Gates Foundation found that only 21.7 percent of entering high school freshmen in the Detroit public school system graduate on time.

The national average is about 70 percent. A similar 2007 study found a slight improvement to 24.9 percent. This was the lowest rate among the fifty largest school districts studied. Not surprisingly, the Detroit school bureaucracy, the eleventh-largest school district in the United States, is cited by a Gates Foundation-funded report as the worst big-city education bureaucracy in the country.

Apparently, the key metric (measure of progress) for the Detroit public bureaucracy—as it sadly seems to be for many other big-city public schools—is how efficient it is at taking money from the taxpayers and giving it to bureaucrats. But this metric is clearly not getting young people to learn or holding the education bureaucrats responsible for running schools that work.

Consider also that the Detroit public school system will spend $7,469 per pupil. Compare this to Marin County, California, which spends only $6,579 per student and yet has a four-year graduation rate of 96.8 percent. The Detroit school system doesn't fail for lack of money. And it doesn't fail because of low teacher salaries. According to the Manhattan Institute, numbers from the Bureau of Labor Statistics show that the Detroit metropolitan area has the highest average public school teacher pay of all major metropolitan areas: $47.28 per hour.

Detroit's schools don't fail for lack of money. They fail because success is not the priority. If you measure the Detroit public school system by graduation rates and the amount of learning that it packs into students, then it has a very low success rate. But if you measure the Detroit system by whether the checks arrive for the bureaucrats each month no matter how badly they are doing, then it has a 100 percent success rate.

The young people of Detroit need more learning options, but government stands in their way. Michigan community colleges, for example, are prevented by state law from chartering schools in first-class districts. (The classification of "first-class" is based only on maintaining an enrollment of at least 100,000 students; it has no merit component. Until 2000, the minimum enrollment for "first-class" status was 120,000, but this was modified to keep pace with Detroit's declining enrollment.) If Detroit were not a first-class district, both Wayne County Community College and Bay Mills Community College would be able to open unlimited charter schools. But what's the priority of Detroit's education bureaucracy? The Detroit Public School Board of Education, fearing the possibility of more charter schools, passed a resolution in 2007 vowing not to lease or sell any of its vacant buildings to the colleges.

Schools That Work

A charter school is simply a public school freed from the bureaucracy's rules and willing to hold itself accountable for producing results. And guess what? They work. We know that charter schools can work in Detroit because they already have worked in Detroit.

At the University Preparatory Academy High School, founded in 2000, the graduation rate is 95 percent, and 100 percent of its graduates go to college or a post-secondary program. Since 1991, the Cornerstone school system in Detroit has offered another pioneering model for successful charter schools. Chairman Clark Durant and president Ernestine Sanders have led the way in offering a more engaging and academically challenging K–12 school system with more than 1,200 enrolled students. The Cornerstone system is distinct for its faith-centered model. Through the common theme of Christian charity, Cornerstone has been successful in uniting corporate donors and charitable trusts. Seven schools now operate under the support of the Cornerstone Foundation, with a high school graduation record of over 90 percent.

Imagine how different the future of Detroit's children would be if they were liberated from the current accountability-denying, taxpayer-supported, failing bureaucracy. Imagine that Detroit had a school system with enough charter schools to provide every child with a proper education so that he or she could exercise the God-given right to pursue happiness. That would be real change.

Turning Detroit and Michigan around will take a fundamentally new approach to public policy. This approach must emphasize government reform, less regulation, more incentives for creating jobs and businesses, lower taxes, and a pro-jobs psychology in both the city and state governments. Until that happens, expect to see bad policies continue to lead to bad economic outcomes, and bad economics continue to drive people out of the state. It is a sad case study for a great industrial state that once led America in innovation, creativity, and entrepreneurial drive.

It is clear from the examples of Katrina, Michigan, and Detroit that the highly taxed, heavily regulated, bureaucratic world of the past is simply going to fail. Government power structures can raise enormous amounts of money, generate a great deal of publicity, and organize a lot of votes. But they can't produce good education for young people, jobs for the poor, or economic prosperity for the places they dominate.

The result is a downward spiral of destructive behavior, dishonesty about consequences, and a rigid opposition to all new solutions and new opportunities. Nowhere is this combination of past failure and rejection of change more evident than in the failed bureaucracies of government education.

CHAPTER FIVE

Failure in Education: Death Knell of the Old Order

I N A MESSAGE DELIVERED TO CONGRESS four short months after he took office, on the first Independence Day during an unfolding civil war, President Abraham Lincoln wrote about the purpose of government.

He wrote that the leading object of government is "to elevate the condition of men—to lift artificial weights from all shoulders; to clear the paths of laudable pursuit for all; to afford all an unfettered start and a fair chance in the race of life." This passage is an eloquent statement of the principles upon which the nation was founded and which Lincoln was defending in our darkest hour. It also describes the spirit that must elevate the nation today as we face the challenge of ensuring that we maximize the chance for every American child to rise and succeed in the race of life.

We must be determined to lift the "artificial weights" of a bureaucratic system of education that hurts too many of the children it is supposed to help. In its place, we must be determined to create a system of learning that provides more choices for excellence so every child can have the maximum opportunity to pursue happiness.

In the last chapter we considered the tragic history of Detroit over the past sixty years. As the most productive and creative citizens leave Detroit and other big cities in despair of ever reforming it, they leave behind those who feel threatened by change and who are the most committed to resisting change. The result is a downward spiral as services decay and citizens feel driven to flee.

It is the poorest citizens who bear the deepest burden of the failures of a city. It is the poor who have the least ability to move to a better place. It is the poor who have the least ability to send their children to private schools. It is the poor who cannot follow the jobs as they leave the city. It is the poor who find themselves victimized by the criminals produced by a society in decline.

One of the most basic measures of the success of our school system is high school graduation. A high school diploma is the minimum requirement for successful participation in American life. The failure of our high schools to graduate their students isn't limited to Detroit or to our big cities. Nationwide, it is estimated that three out of every ten students who start high school won't graduate on time. For minorities, these numbers are far worse. One of every two African American and Latino students won't graduate on time or graduate at all. So dramatic is the failure that today it is estimated that there are more African American males in prison than there are in college. If you are an African American male and you drop out of high school, you face a 72 percent chance of being unemployed in your twenties and a 60 percent chance of going to jail by your mid-thirties. This is failure on a massive scale, and the social implications are horrendous, especially for African Americans.

While the Detroit school bureaucracy has been a particularly tragic example of the human cost of protecting unionized bureaucracy at the expense of serving the public, it is sadly not the only example. The same Gates Foundation study that found that only 25 percent of entering freshmen graduate on time from Detroit public schools found that school districts in Cleveland, Los Angeles, Miami, Dallas, and Denver also graduate fewer than 50 percent of high school students on time. In addition to Detroit, two other districts graduate fewer than 40 percent of their students on time: in New York City, the rate is 38.9 percent; in Baltimore, it's 38.5 percent.

Consider these findings for a moment. If only 50 percent of students graduate from these big-city public school districts on time, that means that a full 50 percent of students—one out of two—are failed by our educational system. Cheating the children is wrong. Why do we tolerate this level of failure? If a private company took money from its customers and then failed to serve 50 percent of them, it would be closed in a day.

If the purpose of a big-city school system is to provide jobs for members of a unionized bureaucracy—to pay them well and pay them on time—then these school systems are stunning successes. If, however, the purpose of our school systems is to provide our children with the learning, the knowledge, the tools, and the motivation to succeed in the real world, then many of our public schools, especially in our big cities, are abysmal failures.

There is ample evidence of what works in education, but the bureaucracies have systematically ignored all of it. Innovations that work include merit-based pay, increasing teacher-student ratios, revamping union rules to reward the best teachers, bonuses and incentives for new teachers, charter schools, and offering parents a coupon giving them the opportunity to send their children to the school that works best for them. I've even suggested rewarding students in the poorest neighborhoods by paying them if they get a B or better in math and science.

But real change requires real change, not new rhetoric while doing more of the same old thing. Propping up the failed past at the expense of future generations leads to prison and poverty for too many of our children.

In city after city across the country, education bureaucrats and unions make it quite clear that they put the union's interests ahead of the children. In city after city they insist on trapping the children in failing schools and reject the demands of parents to be allowed to choose better schools, whether charter schools or non-public schools partially funded by government coupons. In all too many cities, the unions have focused on politics and control of the school boards and the state legislatures, so the parents are crushed by the organized power of the people who are failing to educate their children.

The arrogance of the unionized bureaucrats who allow such failure was illustrated when Robert Thompson, a successful businessman and philanthropist, offered the city of Detroit $200 million to build fifteen charter schools that would have goals of a 90 percent graduation rate and 90 percent college matriculation rate. Thompson's plan had been approved by Michigan's Republican state legislature and Democratic governor. But the Detroit public school bureaucrats lambasted Thompson for attempting to interfere with their system. The Detroit Federation of Teachers threatened to strike if the school district accepted his donation, and Thompson found himself smeared as a racist because he is white and is trying to save black children. The unionized bureaucracy, in desperation to avoid competition, rejected the money and rejected the proffered help to Detroit's children. This is a sad example of how government "works" today. It is driven by inexcusable special interest selfishness, it is destructive of the best interests of the people, and it is even willing to sacrifice children to protect the bureaucracy.

Another example of this conflict is the current fight in Washington, D.C., between parents, who want to continue to have the choice of effective private schools with a coupon from the government, and the unionized bureaucracy, which is insisting on forcing the children back into failing government schools. Virtually all the parents who want to keep getting government coupons are African American. Yet Democrats in Congress are trying to kill the program in order to appease school union bureaucrats. In fact, even before Congress could end the program, in April 2009 Education Secretary Arne Duncan decided not to admit any new students to the D.C. voucher program. Two hundred low-income families received notice that their children's scholarships were being rescinded due to Duncan's decision. It seems to matter little to those defending the status quo when poor families are being cheated. The political power of the cheaters is simply too great for the poor and their allies to take on.

These examples of the devastating impact on poor children and their families of failing bureaucracies and the interest groups that protect them remind us that the poorest and most helpless Americans need our help in reforming the system. Americans with means can flee destructive government education bureaucracies by moving to a better school district, sending their children to private schools, or homeschooling them. The poorest and least-educated Americans are most victimized by government monopolies that fail. We must see these Americans as neighbors in need and organize to help them take on the unionized bureaucracies that help themselves before they help children.

The next time you hear someone talking about compassion and the need to help the poor, ask them where they stand on parental choice versus union monopolies. Then see how serious they are about compassion. The next time you hear someone talking about income inequality, ask them how willing they are to give poor families access to the kind of educational choices the wealthy have, so their children get the best possible start in life. Then see how serious they are about income inequality.

We have a moral obligation to engage together in replacing the current failures and insisting on real change on behalf of our fellow Americans who can least help themselves. We assert in our Declaration of Independence that we "are endowed by [our] Creator with certain unalienable rights, that among these are life, liberty, and the pursuit of happiness." Dr. Martin Luther King Jr. came to Washington and gave his magnificent "I have a dream" speech on the steps of the Lincoln Memorial, trying to mobilize the entire nation to ensure that every American was able to pursue happiness.

The greatest tragedy of these failed government bureaucracies is that with their "artificial weights" they cripple, weaken, and limit the poorest Americans whom Dr. King was seeking to lift up and advance. The effect of this failure is devastating to entire communities. For when there is no effective local school, there is no safety zone to protect the innocent and no profitable local businesses to create jobs. There is, in effect, no chance to pursue happiness.

Too often today we have government of the unionized bureaucracies, by the unionized bureaucracies, and for the unionized bureaucracies. We must return to government of, by, and for the people, and especially for our children, if we hope to help everyone win the race of life.

The time for excuses is over. The crisis is not about money. The crisis is a failure of responsibility, accountability, honesty, transparency, and determination to protect the children from the bureaucracies that are crippling their lives. Who will the people of our great cities save, their failing bureaucracies or our American children?

Our Never-Changing
Educational Bureaucracy

In 1983, the Reagan administration published *A Nation at Risk: The Imperative for Educational Reform*. This extraordinary report warned that the decay of American schools was becoming a threat to the very survival of the country.

Then secretary of education Terrell Bell toured the country trying to mobilize leaders and citizens to insist on reform. He warned that both our economic leadership and our national security strengths were in danger of decaying as young people simply did not know enough to perform effectively in the modern world.

After eighteen years of talk without much change, the Hart-Rudman Commission on National Security in the Twenty-First Century reported in 2001 that the second greatest threat to American security (after a terrorist attack with a weapon of mass destruction) was the failure of math and science education. The commission went on to warn that the danger from the failure of math and science education was greater than any conceivable conventional war.

Despite efforts by presidents, governors, mayors, Bill Gates, and a host of other leaders, the entrenched education bureaucracy managed to avoid change. The powerful combination of tenured unionized faculties, state bureaucracies of education, and increasingly federal bureaucracies of education simply ignored or ridiculed most of the demands for change.

A New Contract with Younger Americans

The problem of education in America goes far beyond the current collapse of education bureaucracies. It is obvious that something is fundamentally wrong with our current approach to being young in America. Consider some stories about the current challenges young people face.

Recently two administrators talked with me in a matter-of-fact manner about the number of young people in their two colleges who cut themselves. This modern problem of young people who cut themselves in order to mask emotional pain is something I had only read about in novels.

Early last year a friend had driven across America and reported that her biggest surprise was the number of small towns in which the number-one concern was methamphetamines and the number of meth labs. Imagine facing such lack of purpose that using methamphetamines and creating a market for criminals seems a good way to spend your life.

At the same time, an epidemic of obesity and diabetes among young people is an emerging disaster for the country. A number of public health experts have warned that our children and grandchildren could be the first generation in American history to have a worse health pattern than their parents and grandparents. Type 2 diabetes (which used to be called adult onset diabetes) among young people is a cultural disease. It is a result of eating too much and exercising too little. It is a result of passive lives without engagement in active pursuits.

Turning these patterns around will require real change. Many years ago Daniel Yankelovich described what he called a giving and getting contract. He suggested that people intuitively had a sense of what their society wanted from them and what they would get if they did their part. The giving and getting contract we have created with young Americans may be so profoundly wrong that it has become a fundamental cause of the various problems described above.

Traditionally, societies defined the time children left childhood and entered young adulthood. They became young men and women. They had real responsibilities and they interacted routinely with adults. Their mentors were older people who had lived a whole lot longer and knew a whole lot more. There was a sense that young men and women should be doing real things in the company of real adults so they could transition from childhood to adulthood within a healthy, responsible framework.

No healthy society abandons thirteen-year-old males to be mentored by fourteen- and fifteen-year-old males. That is a path to disaster, and it is the path we are on.

Imagine a twenty-first-century America in which young people learn as rapidly as they are capable, in which real achievement leads to real rewards, in which young people identify with, work with, and learn from responsible adults, in which real knowledge is more important than procedural protocols, in which the hardest-working and most responsible young adults earn higher incomes and have a better future than those who turn to drugs or refuse to do their work. This will require fundamental changes in our contract with young people and fundamental changes in everything from employment laws to learning systems to the expectations we have of young people.

A Different Future Is Possible for Today's Poor

With the right changes in our attitudes and new changes in our obsolete employment and education laws, young people could have much more exciting and rewarding lives. This change would be particularly helpful for young people born into poverty. Our current education and employment laws trap poor children into poverty by providing too many of them with failing educational systems, and by limiting their ability to start work at an earlier age.

If you have no money and you have no one in your neighborhood to learn from, then being trapped in a bureaucracy of frustrating rules and no chance to acquire wealth cripples your life.

The poor especially need the power of compound interest over time to help them grow out of poverty and into prosperity. The earlier you start working and saving, the more likely you are to rise. The earlier you learn how to make a living and how to spend less than you earn, the more likely you are to move out of poverty.

Ironically, the very liberals who are most concerned about the growing income and wealth gap find it hard to understand how their bureaucracies trap the poor into poverty. I support eliminating the gap between rich and poor, but doing so by helping the poor learn how to earn their way to higher incomes.

This model of young people starting early is at the very heart of early American history. George Washington was already a successful surveyor at eighteen. (Go visit Washington, Virginia, to see a town he surveyed in his teens.) At the time of the Founding Fathers, the average age of admission to Princeton was thirteen. Benjamin Franklin moved from Boston to Philadelphia to apprentice himself to an uncle and learn the printing trade at thirteen. He went on to become a very wealthy businessman, a very successful writer, a political leader, and one of the world's leading scientists.

This connection of early effort to lifetime success is not an obsolete eighteenth-century model. It is still true today. The key characteristics of great success are starting early, working hard, learning every day, and being prepared to bounce back from failure and enthusiastically to work your way through setbacks and frustrations.

Jim Clifton at Gallup has pointed out that the key character trait among successful entrepreneurs is not imagination or intelligence but determination to succeed. He estimates that in any given community about 10 percent of the people have the drive and determination to be successful entrepreneurs.

Tragically, some of the most successful entrepreneurs in our poorest communities work outside the law. They make money at drugs, gambling, prostitution, or a variety of other profitable but illegal functions. They represent talent we need in legal society creating jobs and wealth.

Far more common is the potentially ambitious, potentially creative person whose spirit is dulled and then broken by the experience of a bureaucratic system. Alvin and Heidi Toffler pointed out in *Future Shock* (1970) and *The Third Wave* (1980) that classrooms with students sitting obediently in a row and passively watching the teacher for fixed periods of time are throwbacks to the textile mill factory requirements of the 1840s, when modern public education bureaucracies first began. As a result, our children's learning experience is dramatically out of sync with the information-age lifestyle they experience in the rest of their lives.

Today we have bureaucratically defined teachers imposing controls and norms on bureaucratically controlled learners. The system is simply deadening. It is time to rethink the bureaucracy rather than blame the victims. It is time to create a system of learning that attracts and engages the full energy and imagination of young people. It is time to develop a system of learning and earning that helps children make a healthy transition to young adulthood without taking a detour into drugs or irresponsibility.

We need to focus on what we value and on a new vision of achieving those values. We need to focus on a new set of metrics for learning and young adulthood in America. We need to ask what we would really value among our young, create a vision of successful youth, and then develop metrics so every young person, every parent, and every citizen can understand whether we are achieving breakthroughs. We need to be honest about the disasters of our worst school bureaucracies and the damage they are doing to young Americans who come into their grasp.

A Renaissance of Learning

When younger Americans are being condemned to illiteracy, unemployment, poverty, and prison by highly paid, self-serving bureaucracies, it is time for bold experimentation to find models that save lives and create healthy, productive, prosperous futures. With the courage to do what it takes to save the next generation of Americans by creating a new opportunity for them to earn, learn, be productive, and have lives of responsibility and engagement, we could have a renaissance of learning and work in America.

We are on the edge of scientific breakthroughs that will lead to this renaissance of learning. Brain scientists are developing new insights into how people learn and how they can identify the best way for each individual to learn. Modern learning systems can be available around the clock so people can learn at an extraordinary rate. It is possible to imagine fourteen-year-olds who will have learned more than today's college graduates. (To see one early example of these changes, look at Scientific Learning [www.scilearn.com], a company founded by brain scientists at Berkeley.)

If we achieve a renaissance of learning and work among the next generation, there is no possibility that China, India, or any other country will surpass America as the most productive and most exciting country in the world. Together we can break free of the deadening hand of incompetent and disengaged bureaucracies and create a better future for all Americans.

PART TWO

Real Change
Is Possible

CHAPTER SIX

Replacing the Old Order: America Has Done It Before and We Can Do It Again

I T IS IMPOSSIBLE TO ADDRESS America's challenges within the current structure of government and politics because both are broken. And since President Obama accepts the principles of these structures and looks for solutions to America's great challenges within them, he has little hope of a successful presidency.

The current system of self-reinforcing power will never be reformed from within, but this should not lead to despair. The Founding Fathers understood that it was possible for the machinery of government to become broken, and they recognized the right of the people fundamentally to overhaul it. Thomas Jefferson wrote that "whenever any form of government becomes destructive to these ends [of life, liberty, and the pursuit of happiness], it is the right of the people to alter or abolish it, and to institute new government, laying its foundation on such principles and organizing its power in such form as to them shall seem most likely to affect their safety and happiness."

Today we are at a decisive turning point in American history. Americans face a fundamental choice: whether or not to break the power structures that represent the interests of the past. As in the key reform movements of the past, we have reached that moment when anything less than fundamental change will lead to decay and ultimately a dramatically weaker and more vulnerable America. Happily for America, with the exceptions of the Revolutionary War and the Civil War, every reform movement fundamentally to alter government has been peaceful.

Our Founding Fathers led a revolution against the most powerful empire in the world. It took them eight years to achieve success. But when it was over, they had changed the very structure of government from the British imperial model to a loose confederation of independent states.

The second transformation happened when the Federalists decided that the Articles of Confederation were not working and launched a campaign for a stronger government. They called a constitutional convention, wrote the Constitution over a four-month period at a closed meeting in Philadelphia, developed a nationwide campaign to adopt it (the *Federalist Papers* are the most elegant campaign brochures in history), and then ran the new federal government for its first twelve years. They had decisively changed the shape of government in America.

The third transformation was achieved by Thomas Jefferson and his allies when they decided that their vision of America was very different from the Federalists'. They favored smaller government, less spending, popular authority to limit the power of judges, and limited authority for the bureaucracy. They created the world's oldest continuing political party (initially called the Democratic-Republican Party and now simply the Democratic Party). They won control in 1800 and gradually became so popular that the Federalist Party disappeared. Gerrymandering was invented in Massachusetts by Eldridge Gerry in a last-ditch effort to draw a new map to protect Federalists. It failed, and the Federalists became extinct. The Jeffersonians had won a peaceful revolution that transformed the power structure of America.

In 1824, after twenty-four years of Jeffersonian domination, Andrew Jackson and his supporters began the next great transformation of American government, a populist rebellion of the frontier against the Eastern establishment. Jackson established the "spoils system" of giving government jobs to political supporters. While the Jacksonians never won the overpowering level of control the Jeffersonians acquired, they were the dominant force in American politics and government for a generation. Their spirit of domestic populism and foreign policy assertiveness has shaped America to this day.

The crisis of slavery led to the collapse of the Whig Party (which had grown as the opposition to the Democrats) and the emergence of a number of splinter parties. In a remarkably few years the Republicans emerged as the new alternative party and effected the fifth great transformation of American government. The Lincoln Republicans fought a civil war, radically strengthened the national government, shifted the focus of American political philosophy from the Constitution back to the Declaration of Independence, and encouraged the growth of modern America by a combination of the Homestead Act, the land grant colleges, and the transcontinental railroad. The power of the Lincoln Republican majority can be seen in the fact that they held the White House for forty-four of the next fifty-two years. (Only Grover Cleveland won the presidency as a Democrat between 1860 and 1912.)

The sixth great transformation, the progressive movement, represented change of a very different kind. The corruption of big-city political machines combined with the cynical lobbying power of large corporations led to a popular outcry for reform. There was a general consensus that the emerging technological revolution (electric lights, telephones, electric trolleys, automobiles, motion pictures) called for a parallel modernization of government. The result was a bipartisan wave of reform from 1896 (with the emergence of Republican congressman, governor, and senator Robert M. LaFollette of Wisconsin) to 1916 (when reform was ended by World War I). In this twenty-year period power was changed in many states as the referendum, the initiative, and a host of other reforms were passed. In Washington, Presidents Theodore Roosevelt (a Republican) and Woodrow Wilson (a Democrat) came to personify the reform mood of the era.

The Great Depression led to a consolidation of federal power under the leadership of President Franklin Delano Roosevelt and the New Deal Democrats, who achieved the seventh great transformation of government. Their formula of tax, spend, and elect was so powerful that Democrats controlled the U.S. House of Representatives for sixty years (except for four years, after the elections of 1946 and 1952).

The eighth great transformation came in 1980, when Ronald Reagan was elected president. President Reagan represented a fundamental break with the liberal model of high taxes, bureaucratic government, a welfare state that didn't work, and a foreign policy of appeasement that had resulted in humiliation. Government had deteriorated from Franklin Roosevelt's New Deal to Lyndon Johnson's Great Society to the manifest failures of President Jimmy Carter. Reagan stood for deep tax cuts to encourage investment in jobs and new companies, deregulation to liberate America's entrepreneurs, a sound endorsement of American civic culture, and a firm policy of defeating the Soviet Union and ending the Cold War with a victory for freedom. In many ways the Contract with America and the Republican victory of 1994 stood on President Reagan's shoulders and were based on his philosophy and his policy proposals.

These eight waves of change demonstrate that Americans have successfully demanded and achieved very large-scale change in our politics and government to design a new system that works for the American people. We can do so again.

Achieving the Ninth Great Wave of Reform

A system that works for the American people—and embodying the hallmark of any reform movement of this scale—must address three core questions: Whom do we serve? What do we value? How do we measure achievement? It is clear today that those invested in permanent government do not serve us but serve themselves. It is clear that they value getting our money for their own purposes, not for the common good. Their measures are always designed to excuse failure on their part. They spend their time conveying to the American people that we must accept failure.

When a cabinet secretary charged with protecting our safety says we must accept a deeply flawed immigration proposal because it "bow[s] to reality," we must inform him that bowing to reality is contrary to American tradition. All those who are willing to bow to failure after failure have a current system they can work with. It will fail and they can bow. But for most Americans, this is not an acceptable future. Most Americans believe that we hire leaders to change reality to fit our values, not to change our values to fit the newest failed reality.

By contrast, the American can-do spirit is to confront the failure of the border and say, "We refuse to bow." It is to confront the failure to rebuild New Orleans and say, "We refuse to bow." It is to confront the holding of American hostages by Iran and say, "We refuse to bow." Refusing to bow and insisting on real change will be very hard. Refusing to bow to King George engendered an eight-year war. Refusing to bow to the Japanese attack on Pearl Harbor led to the demand for total victory and required the most extraordinary four years of effort in twentieth-century America.

To do better, to defend our values and our country, we will have to roll up our sleeves and prepare to engage in whatever level of struggle it takes to reclaim a government of the people, by the people, and for the people, and replace the current government that serves the special interests, the elite establishment, the bureaucrats, and the lawyers.

In rededicating our nation to preserving government of, by, and for the people, President Lincoln said at Gettysburg, "This nation, under God, shall have a new birth of freedom." To achieve a new birth of freedom for this generation of Americans, a movement for real change must follow the prescription of the Founders and lay its foundation "on such principles and organizing its power in such form as to them shall seem most likely to affect their safety and happiness."

There are three core principles that will guide this effort to secure all Americans' right to pursue happiness. First, we must move from the politically-correct values of our elites back to the core values of the vast majority of Americans. Second, we must move from an increasingly ineffective and incompetent system of bureaucratic failure and destructive government policies toward an effective twenty-first-century system of elections and government that works for the country and for the individual. This system will define and then implement an agenda of prosperity that rewards the achievement of working people. And third, we must move from uncertainty about danger in the world and confusion about the value of public safety to a clear recognition that the world is dangerous, and that the first obligation of government is to defend America and her allies by defeating our enemies and enforcing the key principles of the oath of American citizenship: to "support and defend the Constitution and laws of the United States of America against all enemies, foreign and domestic."

And there is an opportunity for either the Republicans or the Democrats to forge a governing majority in accordance with these three principles. The Democrats appear strong right now, having gained from the public's disenchantment with the Republicans' governing performance. But at the same time, the Democrats' core supporters are less likely to champion the government reforms needed. If the "change" Obama promised turns out to be a massive expansion of government programs that are already failing, the Democrats' current period of political dominance could turn out to be short-lived.

The Republicans' opportunity lies in the lesson of the election of President Nicolas Sarkozy in France, described more in Chapter Eight. He demonstrated that it is possible to produce a decisive election victory in favor of conservative reform—in spite of the performance failures of the previous conservative administration—when voters are given a choice between ideological failure on the left and bold solutions and leadership from a newly defined right.

It remains to be seen if either political party can create the next governing majority. Great challenges come with great opportunities. The time is right for bold leadership that recognizes that in order for America to succeed, the entrenched permanent government in Washington can and must be defeated. This will happen only with the help of an overwhelming majority of Americans who demand the reassertion of core American values and principles and a bold set of solutions that protects American safety, rewards achievement, and works for the interests of the self-governed.

CHAPTER SEVEN

Becoming a Citizen Leader

For America to truly change, we must convince a lot of citizens that citizen leadership, rather than citizen passivity or citizen complaining, is the key to a successful country. The interest groups, bureaucracies, and ideologies of the past will all fight against real change. All will prefer decay as long as their special interests and their special deals are protected. Only we, the American people, can insist on the change in politics and government necessary to create a better, more prosperous, safer, and freer future.

To change government for the better, all we really need to do is one simple, yet extraordinary, thing: force our government to act on facts and evidence and adopt commonsense practical solutions. It sounds obvious, yet that's exactly what government doesn't do now. That will mean electing leaders—mayors, governors, presidents (and also congressmen, senators, police chiefs, and school board members)—who share our values and our commitment to effective change. But more than anything else, it will mean that all of us, we the people, need to be leaders if we're going to transform our government from the world that fails to the world that works.

Our choice is simple: accept the failures in government we see all around us or work to change things. Working to change things requires leaders. The forces of the old order are not going to provide leadership to change themselves. Therefore, if we are to change our country, we have to accept the challenge of leading.

Leading can be done at any level that interests you and to whatever degree you are willing to devote your time and energy to saving your community and your country.

Not everyone can become president. But everyone can become an effective citizen.

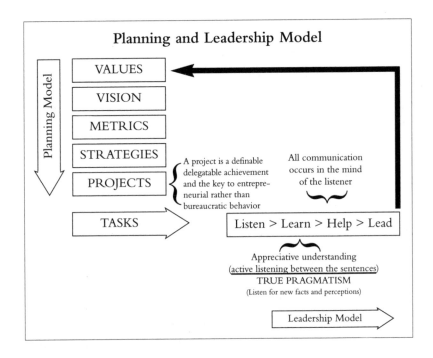

All readers of this book should become leaders in their neighbor hoods, in their civic groups, in every aspect of their lives where they can help drive the demand for change. Fortunately, you don't have to be a natural to be an effective citizen leader. You can learn to become one. Here is some practical guidance to get you started.

My role as an effective public leader began in 1969, when I read Peter Drucker's *The Effective Executive*. It is only 174 pages long. The Kennedy administration had invited Drucker to Washington to give a lecture on effectiveness. That lecture grew into a book, and this book changed my understanding of effectiveness so decisively that for the last thirty-nine years I have been recommending it to audiences. I always suggest that they buy it in paperback, underline it, and reread it every year until they thoroughly understand it. I have read it repeat edly, and its basic principles still shape the way I lead organizations and work with people.

Drucker begins by asserting that effectiveness can be learned. He insists that effective leadership is not a function of intelligence or looks or charisma. In Drucker's model, effective leadership is the learned habit of a set of skills and insights that enable the leader to develop a mission, recruit and organize a team, and focus on performance.

For thirty-six years I applied Drucker's system to looking for best practices and learning from systems of excellence. There is a learnable pattern of effective governance, which can be explained by the chart at left.

Nancy Desmond and I outlined in great detail how to use this approach in two books, *The Art of Transformation* and *Implementing the Art of Transformation*. This chart began to be developed in 1979, when I first started working with the Army Training and Doctrine Command. It evolved from 1993 to 1995 when I worked with more than 375 candidates to develop the Contract with America and then to run the House of Representatives with a new majority. It evolved further as I studied leaders who applied metrics and developed evidence-based government.

To help you understand how this works, try this thought experiment. Take any area of interest (as an example, try the area of learning for young Americans) and go through the following key planning steps:

1. What do you **value**?
2. What **vision** of success do you have for achieving what you value?
3. What **metrics** would tell you whether you are making progress toward your vision?
4. What **strategies** would enable you to achieve your vision?
5. What **projects** would enable you to implement your strategies successfully? (A project is a definable, delegatable achievement and the key to entrepreneurial management.)
6. What **tasks** have to be done well to complete each project?

When you understand how to work through these six questions, you will be ready to lead. Leadership is very different from planning. Leadership requires convincing people to help you implement your plans. Effective leadership requires that you learn to listen to those you would lead. Effective listening requires asking questions and trying to understand what the other person is saying and why it makes sense to him or her.

If you will listen to people thoroughly enough to understand what they are saying and why it makes sense to them, you almost always help them.

In addition to helping by the simple act of listening, you may also be helpful by the perspective you can bring to the situation, the questions you ask, the information you have, and the authority and resources you may be able to utilize.

When people know you will listen to them, learn from them, and help them, they will often ask you to lead. When they ask you to lead, share with them your values, your vision, your measurable standards of success, your strategies to achieve success, and the projects and tasks that can begin the process. Then immediately loop back and ask them what they think of your plans, and go back to listening carefully and learning.

If you can discipline yourself to follow this process systematically, you will have turned everyone around you into a consultant and the flow of ideas and information will be continuous. This model does work. It creates more solutions and more energy than any other model I know. The challenge is that it takes time, patience, discipline, and hard work. Most people want to take shortcuts and find gimmicks to avoid the time and effort. But there are no shortcuts to effective leadership.

Where It Begins

Leadership begins with values and vision. The solutions we want will have our values as their base, our vision for the future as our goal, and evidence (metrics) as our standard for measuring our progress.

It was confusion about our values, vision, and metrics in Iraq that allowed Ambassador Paul Bremer to get so off-track in summer 2003.

It was confusion about our values, vision, and metrics in New Orleans that allowed the city, state, and federal governments to get so off-track in 2005.

It was liberal confusion about citizenship and the pursuit of happiness that led us to create systems of welfare dependency, to accept and tolerate schools that fail to teach, to tolerate criminal predators in our neighborhoods, and to accept ineffective law enforcement.

That confusion has now hardened into the current entrenched bureaucratic government. We have a lot of work to do to turn it around, and it will require all of us to be leaders, to take power back from the system, and to demand dramatic, transformational change. Any citizen leader who thinks we can get different results without dramatically different policies is kidding himself. He should turn to Albert Einstein for leadership advice.

Einstein's Rules for Change

Albert Einstein had a firm rule for thinking about new solutions. He asserted the following: thinking that doing more of the same will lead to a different outcome is a sign of insanity. As Walter Isaacson reports in his extraordinary biography of the greatest physicist since Sir Isaac Newton, Einstein's great breakthroughs came from being able to think differently, to stand outside problems and visualize their solution in very practical, simple, human terms.

Einstein had been helped in his creativity because he had a very hard time getting an academic job. He asserted in later years that if he had gotten a junior teaching position directly out of school, he would never have had the freedom to be as radical as he was. Any academic environment would have socialized him into limiting his thoughts to conform to his colleagues'.

Ironically, it was Einstein's inability to find work in a university, along with financial necessity, that led him to become a clerk in the

Swiss patent office, a job that liberated him to be the most radically innovative physicist in history. As no one in the patent office had the intellectual and academic standing to limit what Einstein could think, he began following his instincts and allowing questions to carry him wherever logic and insight led. The result was a series of three papers in 1905 that changed physics in revolutionary ways. The settled world of Newtonian physics, dominant for more than two hundred years, was suddenly superseded by new models based on quantum mechanics (Max Planck) and relativity (Einstein).

As Thomas Kuhn points out in *The Structure of Scientific Revolutions*, the initial reaction of senior scientists to truly bold new ideas is rejection. The greatest senior physicist of 1905, Ernest Rutherford, never accepted Planck's or Einstein's theories. He thought they were simply wrong and could not understand their underlying reasoning.

When we fight for change, we need to remember the Einstein principle. When people tell you failure is acceptable and you should be patient while the current system continues to fail, cheerfully tell them that thinking that doing more of the same will lead to a different outcome is a sign of insanity. You prefer to behave sanely and focus on real change because that is what real change requires.

The Eisenhower Principle

Because our task to achieve real change is big, we need to think even bigger. This principle of effective leadership was something practiced by General Dwight David Eisenhower. Eisenhower had a remarkable career. He was a lieutenant colonel as World War II began and eighteen months later he was a three-star general in charge of the first great Allied offensive in North Africa.

As the head of an American–British coalition with many other allies (the Free French, the Canadians, the Poles, and many other countries), Eisenhower constantly had to adapt. He faced an amazing range of problems in first developing American forces in Great Britain, then leading the Allied effort in North Africa, Sicily, and Italy, and finally being given command of Overlord, the invasion at Normandy.

Overlord was the most complex and difficult venture ever undertaken in the history of war. It involved control of the sea and air and landing more forces more rapidly and with more effectiveness than the Germans could handle. Two years earlier there had been a disastrous trial run at Dieppe; the Germans had mauled a Canadian landing force. Then there had been an inadequate landing at Anzio in Italy; the Allied forces had been contained by the Germans.

Eisenhower decisively expanded and deepened the commitment of resources to ensure that the Allies could successfully land at Normandy despite all the problems of weather and of German resistance. After the successful landing, Eisenhower led the Allied forces across France and Belgium and defeated the German forces. On May 8, 1945, he was able to wire home, "Mission accomplished."

In working his way through all the extraordinary challenges, including coping with the demands of President Roosevelt, Prime Minister Winston Churchill of Great Britain, and Free French leader General Charles de Gaulle, Eisenhower learned one lesson that strikes many people as counterintuitive: "Whenever I run into a problem I can't solve, I always make it bigger," he asserted. "I can never solve it by trying to make it smaller, but if I make it big enough I can begin to see the outlines of a solution."

Peter Drucker had a variation on this theme when he wrote in *The Effective Executive* that effective leaders always consider the visible problem to be a symptom of a deeper underlying problem. According to Drucker, truly effective leaders understand that any problem is probably tied to a class of difficulties. They try to spend their time solving entire classes of problems and developing solutions that—instead of solving one problem at a time—move the entire system forward.

This is hard to do because very few people focus on the deeper issues. News coverage of politics and governments tends to focus on the sensational and the shallow, on personalities rather policies. Campaigns are just as bad or worse. And congressional hearings are usually amazingly shallow.

Yet focusing on the underlying, fundamental problems is precisely what those of us who want real change have to learn to do. It is also what the American people want. When American Solutions did a survey in summer 2007, we found that the American people said, by 92 percent to 5 percent, that they preferred long-term to short-term solutions. It is the politicians who lack patience, not the American people. Clearly there is support for a more mature, more solutions-oriented approach to public policy. We need citizen leaders who will turn that support into effective action.

Achieving Long-Term Change

As a political volunteer for fourteen years (1960–1974) and then as a candidate for five years (1974–1978), I wanted to make the Republican Party the dominant party in Georgia and to win a congressional seat. It took a long time, after years of frustration and defeat. Republicans did not win the governorship of Georgia until Sonny Perdue's victory in 2002. In my own political career, I lost two congressional races—in 1974 and 1976—before succeeding in 1978.

As a congressman, I committed my time and energy to creating a House Republican majority. It was a sixteen-year project. It began in December 1978 when I visited Congressman Guy Vander Jagt, chairman of the National Republican Congressional Campaign Committee. I told him we needed a plan to become the majority party in the House. He agreed and immediately made me chairman of a committee to come up with and implement the plan, before I'd even officially been sworn into office.

In 1979, we studied the Thatcher campaign, which had won a decisive victory for conservative values in Great Britain. Republican National Committee chairman Bill Brock brought over key members of the Thatcher campaign and we examined how they had developed messages to demolish the Labour government and make conservatism popular. In fall 1980, the Republicans picked up thirty-three House seats, and to everyone's surprise we won six seats in the Senate, giving us a Republican majority in the upper house.

Then we began a long, difficult period. We lost ground through a combination of economic recession and political reapportionment (the Democrats controlled most state legislatures and gerrymandered districts in their favor). In 1984, President Reagan won a huge victory but House Republicans gained only fifteen seats. It wasn't until 1994 that we finally succeeded in electing a House Republican majority, the first in forty years, and in 1996 kept that majority for the first time in sixty-eight years. Those were two efforts in which I was able to help plan and effect long-term change: creating a Republican Party in Georgia that could elect a governor (and me) and creating a Republican majority in the House.

The third long-term project began when I visited Army chief of staff Edward C. "Shy" Meyer in 1979 and told him I wanted to help shape America's strategic doctrine. He put me in touch with the Army

Training and Doctrine Command and the Army War College. That began a journey that has led to my working with all five military branches (Army, Navy, Marines, Air Force, and Coast Guard), the intelligence community, the State Department, and the National Security Council in the White House.

And finally, after I stepped down as Speaker, I became involved in another long-term project: reforming the nation's health system. Health is the largest sector of the economy, it is literally a matter of individual life and death, and in the case of a pandemic or an engineered biological or nuclear attack, it could be a matter of America's life and death. I began studying health issues in 1999, and since then I have not only written and lectured extensively on health, but I also helped create the Center for Health Transformation, which has become an internationally recognized leader for rethinking health policy and seeking health solutions. I believe it will contribute significantly to a great transformation of our health system, focusing on health as a moral issue and bringing together the public and private leaders in the health field to achieve the changes the system needs.

I tell you all this simply to assure you that I know real change is possible. I've worked at it. I've seen it happen. I know the pitfalls that can stop it. And I've learned some lessons on how to make it happen. For example, in Appendix 3, you can read more about the lessons I learned during the long-term successful effort to achieve real change in our welfare system.

American Solutions and the Prospect of Real Change

Real change requires a citizens' movement dedicated to transforming both politics and government.

I helped found American Solutions for Winning the Future to develop solutions, advocate change, and train and empower citizens and elected officials to be more effective across the country. If you go to americansolutions.com, you can see all the many developments, including the Platform of the American People that we developed to offer the country a red-white-and-blue platform to replace the red-versus-blue partisan split. You can read the Platform of the American People in Appendix 1.

We at American Solutions believe it is essential to support fundamental, long-term solutions, not mere quick fixes. We also believe it is important to develop solutions at the local level through local leadership. Therefore American Solutions focuses on educating, mobilizing, encouraging, and empowering, but is not an attempt to organize or direct in a centralized fashion. Please take a few minutes to review americansolutions.com for a starting point in local leadership. (See Appendix 2 for a description of the "Solutions Lab," an online tool we developed at American Solutions to create innovative new policy solutions.) My own thinking changes and evolves over time as we learn more, and I try to capture that evolution in a free weekly electronic newsletter called the "Newt Gingrich Letter."

Cheerful Persistence for Change

If we truly believe in our goals, if we understand that we're going to have to fight for them and that the fight might be long and hard, then there is every reason to approach the task with persistence—and with more than persistence, with a cheerfulness that keeps us from becoming depressed or irritated by inevitable setbacks. We need to keep our eyes on the prize.

We will have to remind ourselves every day that we are not guaranteed success, that the entrenched bureaucracy and special interests will pull out every stop to thwart us. But they can't stop us from working, every day, to achieve our goals. To do something serious and new means overcoming frustration, confusion, opposition, and indifference. It means being a leader. And a leader has to keep the long-term vision in mind and cheerfully persist no matter the obstacles.

I learned the value of cheerful persistence in part from studying Eisenhower and Reagan. They both had wonderful smiles and a remarkable ability to work through opposition, frustration, and exhaustion. So did Franklin Delano Roosevelt. This was driven home to me by Michael Barone after he wrote *Our Country*. It is a marvelous history of America with a very large section on President Roosevelt. Barone told me, "There was not a single occasion where Roosevelt was down or depressed during his presidency. That is not natural endowment. That is iron will."

Barone pointed to Roosevelt's long struggle with polio, which forged the steel of his character that made him so formidable. In that era it was expected that polio would force you into retirement. Roosevelt's friends and family expected him to live off his income and hide on family estates. Instead, he drove himself to recover, to build his strength as best he could so that he could simulate walking in heavy iron braces. His appearance walking to the podium of the 1928 Democratic National Convention (propped on the arms of his son and his closest aide) is one of the most personally heroic moments in American politics.

Yet even FDR got tired. Barone told me, "You know, there is one time in 1944 when FDR was touring military hospitals in Hawaii and he sat in the hallway between rooms and seemed totally exhausted, but then he pulled himself together, got that jaunty smile, and entered the next room to raise the morale of wounded soldiers, sailors, and Marines. Of course by then he was dying and had extraordinarily high blood pressure and had been president for almost twelve years." The keys are iron will, enormous discipline, and cheerful persistence. Those traits can change history.

Win with Yes:
Winning Agreement Through "Yes, If"

In my thirty-nine years of studying and collaborating to solve problems I have learned that a team that says "yes, if" is probably ten times more productive than a team that says "no, because." If you want to forge agreement, the first step is to find ground on which to agree. If you say, "Yes, we could do something if we could solve X," you allow the other person immediately to start thinking about how to solve the missing component. On the other hand, if you say, "No, because," you invite the other person to quit or to argue with you.

Those of us who believe in real change must approach every problem with a "yes, if" mentality. It is only through our own efforts, combined with cheerful persistence, that we can achieve the enormous shift from the world that fails to the world that works.

Who Will Deliver Real Change in the
Twenty-First Century, the Bureaucrat
or the Entrepreneur?

The heart of our citizens' movement is a belief that entrepreneurs are far more creative than bureaucrats and that learning to think and work like an entrepreneur can be learned by anyone who is interested in greater creativity and productivity.

We can make enormous gains in productivity by moving government bureaucracies from the world that fails to the world that works. We as citizens can make even bigger gains by thinking of ourselves as customers instead of passive government recipients. Customers are central to the world that works, and yet traditional bureaucracies have no concept of "customers."

In the twentieth century, the professional bureaucracies developed a modus operandi in which they were powerful and citizens were passive. Bureaucrats told parents they were not qualified to be involved in their children's education. They told poor people they should accept welfare and wait for the next check, and that housing would be provided for them but they would have to obey the rules of the local housing bureaucracy. They told senior citizens that the government would cover their health care but bureaucrats would set the prices, determine the paperwork, and establish all the conditions.

Compare this dictatorial bureaucratic model with the free market model. In free markets, customers define the value of goods and services and make their own decisions. They are always free to look for better or cheaper alternatives. Entrepreneurs must know their markets and provide customers with goods and services they will voluntarily purchase. When new entrepreneurs develop new ideas, new goods, new services, and new techniques of productivity, customers' range of choices increases. And when a company fails to provide a competitive good or service, it goes broke.

In bureaucracies, by contrast, bureaucrats define the rules and make the decisions. Recipients must wait for bureaucrats to decide to pay attention to them, and they must accept the bureaucrats' conditions to get the goods or services they want. One of the bureaucrats' highest values is establishing a monopoly and tolerating no competition; recipients have no alternative but to accept things on their terms. In the bureaucratic model, failure is simply a reason to raise taxes and give even more money to those who are failing.

Medicruise

In fall 2005, many people, left-wing politicians among them, were complaining that Medicare Part D featured too many choices. Apparently, these people feared that senior citizens could not understand the system's complexity. Suggestions were made that the government should limit the choices to just one or two.

Now imagine a new federal program that would surely be championed by those who fear unlimited choice: Medicruise. This program selects cruises most appropriate for America's senior citizens, much the same as Medicare bureaucrats select their health care options. The cruises are paid for by the federal government, with only modest co-pays by seniors.

The government will negotiate with cruise lines to rebuild the ships, designing them so that every cabin is of exactly equal value. The higher up you are and the better your view, the smaller your cabin will be. The government will approve the menus and appropriate beverages, and will review proposed entertainment to make sure nothing is so exciting as to cause heart problems for frail seniors.

It will be illegal for senior citizens to spend their own money on vacations. That way they will not be tempted by inappropriate opportunities—like non-government-approved side excursions or eating at local restaurants. I hope to convince Senator Harry Reid and Congressman Pete Stark to introduce Medicruise as a bill in Congress.

The whole concept of Medicruise seems absurd until you realize that I have just described the core provisions of Medicare. Medicare is more restrictive of seniors' rights than the British national health service. It is an example of how we have taken rights away from people and have given them to bureaucracies. These bureaucracies do not know who the people are, what they want, or what they need. It is an example of why third-party-payment bureaucracies are inherently destructive.

Bureaucracies contain inherent patterns of decay; over time, the bureaucrats think more and more about their own positions, their own prerogatives, and their own incomes. Eventually the bureaucracy's concerns turn toward the bureaucrat and away from the citizen. Taxpaying citizens dealing with such bureaucracies are trapped in the world of the bureaucrats, on bureaucrats' terms. In the free market, customers simply stop patronizing companies that fail to meet their needs.

Moving from the world that fails to the world that works requires different modes of thinking. It requires moving from bureaucrats to entrepreneurs, from recipients to customers, and from no choice to real choice. It also requires bold new organizational models for an entrepreneurial, twenty-first-century government that actually gets things done.

CHAPTER EIGHT

Replacing the Old Order: Lessons from Britain and France

IN 1979, THE CONSERVATIVE PARTY LEADER in Great Britain, Margaret Thatcher, ran a compelling campaign for real change. She promised fundamentally to change the social contract away from unionization, high taxation, and welfare state subsidies that were undermining the economy and toward lower taxes, more entrepreneurship, and a market-oriented system of greater competition and greater creativity.

The British Labour Party had pursued a series of policies that raised taxes, increased bureaucracy, strengthened the unions, and weakened the private sector and the entrepreneurial spirit. The result was an economy so bad it led to a winter of discontent with high inflation, strikes, and a general sense of misery. The British people had been forced to conclude that the model of big government, high taxes, big bureaucracy, and strong unions simply was not working. The results of the Thatcher Revolution—lower taxes, free markets, low inflation, and entrepreneurial energy—are clear and uncontestable.

As French president Nicolas Sarkozy pointed out in his 2007 campaign, the French economy was 25 percent bigger than Great Britain's prior to Thatcher, and now it is 10 percent smaller. Today, some 250,000 to 300,000 French men and women work in London rather than Paris because they can get better jobs and have a higher standard of living in London.

The Thatcher Revolution made a big impact in Britain, but it was generally scorned on the European Continent as a viable model until 2007. I encountered the French anti-Thatcher attitude toward work in 2004 when Merrill Lynch asked me to make a series of speeches around Europe explaining the American presidential campaign.

One beautiful September afternoon I found myself in an elegant reception at the George V Hotel in Paris. While talking with two French businesswomen and a businessman, I commented that the city was beautiful. One woman replied, "You should come in the summer, the city is virtually vacant. Everyone is on vacation."

Being an old-timer who had spent several years in France as a child, I replied, "You mean the August vacations."

"Oh no," she said. "We now have a thirty-five-hour work week. The way it is enforced, you have to take eleven and a half days' vacation, in addition to the five weeks' vacation we have always had, in addition to the national holidays. Everyone lumps all this into the summer. The result is Paris is two-thirds empty virtually all summer."

The woman next to her leaned forward and said, "I am an entrepreneur."

Silicon Valley, eighty hours a week, build the company, pursue opportunity: all these examples of American entrepreneurial behavior ran through my head.

"It is even better," she continued. "As long as my company is profitable, I never leave my vacation home in Spain."

The Frenchman next to her, seeing my confusion, said, "You should understand that the best-selling book on French Amazon in the summer of 2004 was *Bonjour Paresse* [Hello Laziness]. This is a manual on how to draw a paycheck without work by exploiting every loophole in French law to prevent your company from firing you. The author's thesis is that France is run by an oligarchy that exploits us, and we have a moral obligation to counter-exploit them by taking their money without doing any work.

This concept of minimum work for maximum payment as a moral virtue was so far outside the American model that for two years I cited this story as an example of why the French attitude would doom the country in the world market. The Chinese and Indians, working hard for long hours with an attitude of achieving and succeeding, were simply going to outproduce the French, working thirty-five hours a week with an attitude of entitlement.

Amazingly, along came Nicolas Sarkozy who, in the Thatcher tradition, sought first to win the argument and then to win the vote. We can learn a great deal from Sarkozy's victory in the 2007 "change" election in France—and Republicans have the most to learn from it.

In 2007, France had an unpopular incumbent president and a desire for change. Incumbent president Jacques Chirac had been elected twice, had served a total of twelve years in office, and had become very unpopular. Coming into the 2007 election, people were tired of the Chirac government, and there was a sense that change was necessary. However, the opposition on the left, the Socialist Party, failed to capitalize on the popular desire for change. They nominated a candidate of great achievement, Ségolène Royal, but she proved herself to be the candidate of the status quo, not the candidate of change. She was committed to keeping all the failing bureaucracies and all the policies that were creating unemployment. She was clearly unwilling to take on the unions, even if their policies were crippling the French economy. She was committed to avoiding the changes necessary for a French future of prosperity, opportunity, and safety.

Normally, with the incumbent conservative government so unpopular, the Left would have been expected to win the election, probably by a significant margin. But conservative candidate Sarkozy won decisively because he is an aggressive, different kind of French political leader. As minister of the interior, he was a member of the Chirac government. But not only was he willing to stand up and fight his own party for what he believed in, he is also a man who didn't follow the normal French path to success by going to an elite university, becoming part of the ruling elite, and fitting in.

Instead, Sarkozy is just the opposite of the stereotype of the French governing elite. He was born to a Hungarian father who had fled Communism. That makes him the first president of France who is a second-generation immigrant. His name doesn't sound very French. And his style certainly isn't very French. He is a tough, confrontational leader—a man who has been preaching things that don't sound very much like the French establishment.

In the campaign, Sarkozy argued that the French have to work more to earn more. To give them an incentive to do so, he argued that they shouldn't pay taxes when they work overtime. He called for tax cuts to encourage investment so the private sector could create jobs. And critically, Sarkozy has said that people must obey the law—that the creation of law and respect for the law is a central part of any civilized society.

Remember, this is a jarring message for a country that routinely accepts the burning of up to 15,000 cars a year by hooligans who, according to the elites, are simply expressing their desire to disrupt society. It's jarring for a country that was proud a few years back to have the first mandatory thirty-five-hour work week in history. Yet an increasing majority of the French believe that without the kind of changes Sarkozy is calling for, France will disappear in a wave of lawlessness and economic decay.

Sarkozy won an argument that the failure to compete would lead to a loss of purchasing power, the loss of purchasing power would lead to a decline in tax revenue, and the decline in tax revenue would lead to a decline in the French government's ability to sustain the health system and the pension system.

Like Prime Minister Thatcher, Sarkozy was able to convince a majority of his countrymen that their personal future and France's future were inextricably linked and that without fundamental change both would be worse off.

As for the opposition in the French election, much like the Left in the American Democratic Party, it was trapped by its commitment to big labor, big bureaucracy, high taxes, and social values people don't believe in. When the French voters looked seriously at Ségolène Royal and the kind of politics she represented, she lost. She simply couldn't make the case that left-wing Socialist policies would work. The result was a surprising and powerful upset by Sarkozy—a victory by a center-right reformer, a member of the unpopular ruling party, who came to personify change.

Here's where American Republicans really need to pay attention: in France, voting for change meant voting for the party in office, but not the personality in office. And voting to keep the old order meant voting for the opposition, not for the incumbent party. If Republicans had made this case in 2008 and nominated a candidate who stood for bold, dramatic, and systematic change in Washington, perhaps the election would have turned out differently. Not only that, but Republicans failed to make the case that Obama, contrary to his promises of "change," really represented the failed status quo: the bureaucracies that are failing, the unions that are resisting change, the trial lawyers whose litigation is driving jobs out of America, the social policies that are failing, the high-tax policies that are failing.

While the GOP may have missed an opportunity in 2008, another one has arisen. Now that Republicans are in opposition, it's easier for them to make the case for effective change for a better, safer, and more prosperous future, and to convince voters that Republican change is real change, whereas Democratic "change" really means more of the same failing unions, bureaucracy, and big-government programs.

However, this book is dedicated to a much longer perspective than the current political moment. Independents and Democrats who want real change need to recognize that in Thatcher, Reagan, and Sarkozy, there are some messages for a broad movement for real change. They also need to recognize that the change will not come from the power brokers, the interest groups, and the establishment.

Real change will come from the American people. That is the way it has always worked in America. It is how it worked in Britain. And it is how it is beginning to work in France.

CHAPTER NINE

An Example of Real Change and a Failure to Change: Giuliani's New York City versus Iraq as Contrasts in Change Leadership

REAL CHANGE IS POSSIBLE. We saw its principles at work in New York City during Rudy Giuliani's time as mayor in the 1990s. Giuliani implemented fundamental change in policing against enormous resistance and succeeded only because he, his team, and the citizens who supported his effort to lower crime absolutely insisted on it and were cheerfully persistent in doing so.

In Afghanistan in 2001, the United States undertook a fundamentally different type of military campaign to defeat the Taliban within five weeks. And just five weeks later we had installed a provisional government there under Hamid Karzai, who has ruled for a five-year term under a democratic constitution.

In contrast, following a brilliant three-week campaign to topple the government of Saddam Hussein, the U.S. government failed to adopt the lessons from Afghanistan and failed to employ the principles of real change that had served the citizens of New York so well.

Instead, starting in May 2003, the United States suffered a protracted four-year insurgency that was finally brought under control thanks to a real change in strategies and operational assumptions. Let us examine the lessons about change to be learned from both the success in New York City and the protracted failure in Iraq.

New York City

In the early 1990s, New Yorkers had good reason to be afraid. Street gangs, vandalism, and petty violence were on the rise, and longtime residents could see clearly that the city would soon return to the New York of the 1970s, when criminals were in charge and smart people just kept their eyes down and stayed in after dark. By 1993, many neighborhoods already had become war zones. New Yorkers felt under siege, as they had been for the last two decades. The level of crime and the sense of disorder and decay were driving jobs and people out of the city.

But things started to turn around in 1993 after the election of Rudy Giuliani as mayor. When Mayor Giuliani interviewed each of his potential police commissioners, he began with a simple question: "Can you reduce crime?" He asked this question against the backdrop of the dominant sociology and criminology belief of 1993, which was that policing had little ability to affect crime. Applicant after applicant repeated the accepted wisdom and refused to promise any specific results. But when Mayor Giuliani asked Boston police chief Bill Bratton the same key question, Bratton replied confidently, "It can be reduced 10 percent the first year."

Bratton appreciated Einstein's rule that simply doing more of the same would not produce a different result. New York needed to try something new, and Bratton was determined to do something new as the next police chief. Together, Giuliani and Bratton acted on insights about lowering crime, known as the broken-window theory, developed by two political scientists (not criminologists), James Q. Wilson and George L. Kelling. This theory contends that disorder, such as broken windows that go unrepaired, lowers the psychological-cultural barrier to crime, and that a police force focused on creating order would actually reduce crime.

Giuliani and Bratton combined great determination with great flexibility and innovation as they carried out their mission to reduce crime. The first great breakthrough was the development of the right metrics for reporting. The science of metrics is the use of data to chart solutions and measure progress. The proper use of metrics might offer the single most powerful way for government officials to identify clearly what matters, track it accurately, and shift strategies and resources to achieve necessary solutions.

Metrics are not the same thing as statistics. Every bureaucracy can churn out lots and lots of statistics. They are mostly not timely, not meaningful, and not used. They are simply reports that sit there and get old. In New York, metrics was a fundamentally different proposition. Metrics was the systematic thinking through by senior leaders of what really mattered and the careful definition of how to measure the things that mattered.

Police forces had historically measured how fast they could answer a 911 call and how many arrests there had been the previous day. The Giuliani-Bratton team believed those were the wrong questions. They wanted to know how many crimes had occurred, where they had occurred, and what time they had occurred. They wanted to see if there was a pattern of activity that could be used to develop new strategies and to focus resources in new ways. They knew that thanks to the efforts of Mayor David Dinkins, there would be 4,000 more policemen joining the force, and they wanted to know how to use them to achieve the maximum improvement in public safety.

Many traditional precinct captains rebelled against using metrics. They did not understand why the new information mattered. They did not see how it would help their precincts to spend time gathering the data. They did not want their officers to sit at computers and process data. Finally, they did not like to give police headquarters new information with which to reach in and question their authority in their own precinct. This wasn't the kind of police system they had grown up with, and they had no intention of implementing it. No precinct captain could publicly prefer comfortable routines to stopping crime. Yet in reality, many opposed changes that worked. In the first year, three out of every four precinct captains retired or were reassigned.

My favorite example of how metrics revealed the best use of resources is that headquarters discovered that anti-drug units tended to work from 8 AM to 6 PM during the week, and drug dealers tended to work at night and on weekends. Bratton pointed out the only two possible responses: either the precinct captains would have to convince the drug dealers to work from 8 to 6 during the week, or the anti-drug units would have to work at night and on the weekends.

One of the keys to the Giuliani-Bratton success was a relentless determination to implement the system they believed in. They believed the people of New York had voted for real change because they wanted real change. They thought they had the moral authority of the city's voters to insist upon and impose new ideas and new procedures on a very entrenched, old-fashioned system.

In New York the results spoke for themselves. From 1993 to 2005 the city enjoyed a 75 percent reduction in crime. Today, New York is the safest big city in the United States—and getting safer. In 1990, there were 2,263 killings. In late November 2007, NYPD figures showed that New York City was on pace in 2007 to have fewer than 500 homicides—the fewest in four decades. In the first decade of the new system, thousands of people are still alive who would have been killed under the old system.

This is real change—proof of both the human cost of bad government and the tantalizing possibility for good government to improve our lives. This was a victory for an evidence-based system of government and policing. We know this is true because when Chief Bratton took the same system to Los Angeles, the City of Angels became the second-safest city in America. Bratton achieved these results in Los Angeles with fewer police officers per capita and per square mile than he had in New York.

While there is something powerful and productive about the concept of evidence-based government that uses metrics developed by senior leadership to measure progress, identify problems, and lead the team in developing new strategies and new solutions, it's not magic. It simply takes a combination of political leaders with determination and courage and professional experts with deep knowledge of their subject and of the system they are trying to improve.

It also requires a profound commitment to the principle that the mission of the system defines its shape and its habits. Traditionally, bureaucracies replace the original mission for which they were founded with a new mission of protecting the structure, the budget, the habits, and the culture of the bureaucracy as it has evolved. That is why it's so difficult to achieve real change when a bureaucracy is no longer achieving its original mission. In such cases, it takes tremendous leadership and cheerful persistence to insist on real change. It also makes effective use of metrics critical. This allows senior leaders to shine the light of reality on the areas in which the bureaucracy has substituted its own comfort and self-protection for achieving the mission for which it exists and for which it is being paid.

There is no better way to see the difference between real change and ineffective change than to contrast the metrics-based crime-fighting approach in New York and Los Angeles with our failure to use proper metrics in Iraq after our three-week campaign to defeat Saddam Hussein.

How Iraq Went Wrong

After twenty-four years of work with the American military, I had a pretty good basis for judging the information I was getting about performance and implementation failures in Iraq in 2003. I first began working with the Army Training and Doctrine Command in 1979. Since then I have become the longest-serving teacher in the senior military. In addition I had spent years talking with the staff and students of various war colleges, command and staff colleges, and other military institutions. In 2003, I was serving on the Defense Policy Board and the Transformation Advisory Group of the Joint Forces Command. Beyond the Pentagon I was known in the intelligence community as the only person who had insisted on a billion dollar–plus increase in funding in the 1990s (a point the 9-11 Commission made in its report; it called it the "Gingrich plus-up").

As a result of all these long-standing contacts I had with the military and the intelligence community, I received a steady stream of

information about how things were going wrong in Iraq. The problems we were experiencing were of two kinds. The first was bad policy. The second was poor implementation of bad policy by the
bureaucracy and an inability to learn quickly from our errors.

The Policy Problem in Iraq

The initial campaign in Iraq in 2003 was stunningly successful. In
twenty-one short days the coalition forces defeated the armies of Saddam Hussein and occupied Baghdad. But that's when the problems
began.

General Tommy Franks's model of swift, decisive victory with limited forces was a great military strategy, but as a postwar approach it
would work only if we intended, after we toppled Saddam, to use Iraqi
forces to police the country and Iraqi leaders to provide an interim
government. Instead, there was a shift of policy and the Bush administration decided to govern Iraq via a temporary American administration. To do that effectively required a vastly bigger force. Then Army
chief of staff General Eric K. Shinseki testified it would require several hundred thousand American troops to occupy Iraq. He based that
number on his peacekeeping experiences in the Balkans. But the Bush
administration insisted, on the basis of no evidence, that it could govern Iraq on the cheap, with a minimal force.

The problem was even bigger than sheer numbers. We not only
needed more boots on the ground; we needed law enforcement and
intelligence officers. If the United States was to carry the primary burden of pacifying postwar Iraq, we needed to have a vast increase in our
military intelligence capabilities. Instead, the Bush administration actually drew down our intelligence capabilities in Iraq and left General

Ricardo Sanchez (the three-star general in command as Franks withdrew his team) with totally inadequate sources of information about what was going on in the country.

No one in the initial war planning expected the United States would try to run Iraq after defeating Saddam. There was a general belief that the non–Republican Guard portions of the Iraqi army could be converted into a policing force, and General Petraeus was actually doing that in 2003 in his area of responsibility by hiring 15,000 former Iraqi soldiers.

The even sadder part is that White House envoy Zalmay Khalilzad was headed in the right direction. Days after Hussein's government was toppled, Khalilzad led efforts toward organizing an interim Iraqi governing authority, so that the public face of the new regime would speak Arabic, worship on Friday, and be Iraqi. It was vital from day one that the United States be seen as a liberator and not as an occupier. Khalilzad was the perfect ambassador for this difficult job because he had done precisely the same thing when he served as ambassador in Afghanistan.

For some reason the lesson learned in Afghanistan—of liberating and not occupying—did not get across to Ambassador Paul Bremer, head of the U.S.-led occupation government, the Coalition Provisional Authority (CPA), and to the people he took with him to Baghdad. Nearly one month after Saddam's toppling, Bremer was appointed the top civil administrator in Iraq. Suddenly the effort by Khalilzad to organize the Iraqi interim political leadership was cut off. Suddenly the efforts to recruit and reorganize Iraqi security forces were suspended. Suddenly the new American regime put the brakes on military commanders using reconstruction money in a quick and practical fashion. In short, an American bureaucracy had arrived.

Like most bureaucracies, this one looked after itself. It created a green zone of protection and comfort to shield the bureaucrats. By creating a green zone, it acknowledged that the entire rest of the country was a red zone, a danger zone. Worst of all, the decision to have an explicitly American administrator of Iraq guaranteed that America's role would change from liberator to occupier.

General Sanchez, who commanded U.S. forces in Iraq during the first year of the occupation, later said the administration "has not accepted the political and economic realities of this war." He went on to assert, "The administration, Congress, and the entire interagency, especially the State Department, must shoulder the responsibility for this catastrophic failure." Sanchez charged, "There has been a glaring unfortunate display of incompetent strategic leadership within our national leaders."

Sanchez stressed that "from a catastrophically flawed, unrealistically optimistic war plan to the administration's latest surge strategy, this administration has failed to employ and synchronize its political, economic, and military power."

I had reached similar conclusions four years earlier. For months—from June 2003 on—I had tried to warn close friends and colleagues in the administration that things simply were not working and that we had to have a much more realistic and tough-minded review of what was going on.

By December 2003, things were so bad and the mismanagement of the Iraqi system was so great that I went public and declared that we had "gone off a cliff" in the June decisions, and that until they were reversed things were just going to get worse. To be fair to Ambassador Bremer, the policy failure was not ultimately his mistake. He worked for the commander in chief and he reported to the commander in chief. Any policy mistake was implicitly attributable to the White House or it would have been reversed.

The Implementation Problem

The implementation problems in Iraq were parallel to the implementation problems I had been studying in Afghanistan. The fact that they were occurring in both countries led me to believe we faced a systems problem and not a personnel problem. First, allow me to take a brief detour to describe implementation problems in Afghanistan, Haiti, and Panama.

In 2002, I learned that the United States had been unable to pave a single mile of road in Afghanistan during the summer season. Plenty of time had gone into the planning, paperwork, and red tape of the president's Afghanistan Road Initiative. The civilian bureaucracy had been busy. It simply had not been productive. Experts with experience in Afghanistan began telling horror stories about the inability of the State Department and the U.S. Agency for International Development to get work done.

This failure of the non-military components of our national security system came as no surprise. It was consistent with lessons I had first learned eleven years earlier. In 1991, General Max Thurmond, who had commanded the liberation of Panama, came by the House of Representatives to tell me that the process by which national policy is coordinated among all agencies of national government, military and civilian, was broken. He said it was simply impossible to get the various civilian elements of the federal government in this interagency process to move at anything like the speed required by modern war.

Four years later, General Bill Hartzog, who had helped plan the Panama Operation and had been responsible for the occupation of Haiti, told me a similar story of civilian non-performance. Despite direct orders from President Clinton, the Justice Department could not find lawyers to send to Haiti to help build a Haitian criminal justice system and court system. The inability of the civilian instruments of our government to support national policy objectives was placing an impossible burden on our military, which was being forced again and again to fill the vacuum so that such objectives could be achieved in a timely and effective way. This continuing reliance on the military to achieve both military and non-military objectives was unsustainable and was very dangerous for American foreign policy.

Seven years later, in 2002, I found myself witnessing another costly example of the failure of the obsolete interagency process and the absolute inability of the State Department and other civilian government agencies to move at the speed of modern war—this time in Afghanistan.

The First Implementation Failure in Iraq: Infrastructure and Jobs

The inability of the military and non-military organizations to act together led to the extended breakdown of infrastructure and stagnant economic activity in Iraq. The main goal in Iraq in the summer of 2003 was to establish enough economic activity to absorb people in pursuing their own interests and to give them an incentive to avoid violence in favor of prosperity. Along the way, and to accomplish these economic goals, Iraq's crippled infrastructure needed restoring.

The United States Congress did its part and appropriated $18 billion. The military commanders had lots of ideas about how to use the money to employ local Iraqis and restart the economy. But then our civilian bureaucracy took over.

And nothing got done.

The bureaucracies ground out red tape and accomplished remarkably little. Various civilian agencies developed the unproductive habit of rotating volunteers in and out on tours as short as a month, as if it were possible to learn how to do anything useful in a complex foreign country in a month.

Electricity did not go on. Jobs were not created. The Iraqi willingness to believe in America began to decline. Dangerous circumstances were converging. The willingness of young Iraqi males to accept money to participate in violence against Americans began to go up. The civilian bureaucracies in Baghdad and in Washington moved at a glacial pace, as if we had twenty years to get the job done when in fact we had about twenty weeks.

This was the first implementation problem: the failure of the Washington bureaucracies to shake off their torpor and understand the urgency of getting things done in Iraq for infrastructure and the economy. Rather than change their comfortable operating procedures, they simply refused to respond with the speed required.

Even the uniformed military elements of the Defense Department were unwilling to take seriously the requirements of winning in Iraq. There were continuing personnel problems, resource problems, and priority problems, and the peacetime bureaucracy of the Pentagon wondered why their counterparts in Baghdad were so adamant about getting more and getting it quicker. There was a bias against officers who insisted on getting what they thought they needed and a bias in favor of officers who accepted whatever Washington wanted them to have.

As the infrastructure problems persisted, so did continuing failure of the economy. It was obvious to every student of this kind of struggle that jobs and economic activity were absolutely vital to the creation of a stable, peaceful Iraq. Every serious military study indicated that while the military focused on security, restoring electricity and the economy were the top priorities that needed to be handled. The military saw these non-security issues as someone else's job, but the civilian bureaucracies did not pick up the slack. I sat through meeting after meeting in which very smart people pinpointed the problems in restoring Iraq's power grid and economic infrastructure. But they would then shift to talk about secondary issues because they had no authority or resources to deal with the most important issues.

Paul Brinkley, deputy under secretary of defense for business transformation, heroically tried to break this model of failure. He asserted his office's right to coordinate buying products from Iraqi factories and putting Iraqis back to work. At considerable personal risk Brinkley went to Iraq numerous times and visited the various state-owned factories that had been shut down in 2003. He identified more than one hundred facilities that could be reopened and would lead to hiring thousands of Iraqis.

Again and again, other parts of the Defense Department, elements of the State Department, and the White House bureaucracy stopped Brinkley's efforts, slowed him down, and threw in roadblocks, because of various bureaucratic objections. If it had not been for the resolute support Brinkley received from deputy secretary of defense Gordon England, he would have been stopped in his tracks. Even with England's backing and with his own determination and ingenuity it was extraordinarily hard to get things done to help the Iraqi people and achieve the administration's own policy goals. The Washington bureaucratic system made it virtually impossible.

When we make it hard for even the most determined and intelligent of Americans to do the right thing, we should not be surprised that the wrong things get done so often. That is the state of bureaucratic affairs today. What was happening in Iraq under the Bush administration was the exact opposite of what Mayor Giuliani and Police Chief Bratton had done for New York: the administration had failed to implement clear and proper metrics for progress in Iraq. There was no accurate and timely reporting about the status of achieving our goals. There was no senior leadership effort to rethink and change failed strategies, systems, and manners of implementation. There was no accountability. It was government operating as it normally does: wasting money, focusing on policy rather than implementation, and not bothering to use metrics to check up on how the policy and implementation were actually working or could be improved or could actually achieve necessary goals.

The domestic debate over these implementation failures followed a predictable course. The Left saw the implementation problems as proof positive that our intervention in Iraq was wrong and that we needed to withdraw immediately. The Right chanted "stay the course" because it believed in its policies and apparently feared that if implementation problems were acknowledged then that would undermine the support needed to stay the course. So the debate in Washington became a matter of politics rather than practicality. And as the politicians in Washington played for partisan advantage, things in Iraq got worse.

The Second Implementation Failure in Iraq: Reluctance to Carry Out a Counterinsurgency Strategy

In addition to the bureaucratic failure to deliver rapidly on infrastructure and economic development in Iraq, we must also add a uniquely military failure: the Army's early and deep hostility to engaging in counterinsurgency warfare in Iraq, a bitter lesson taken from our Vietnam experience. The U.S. Army fought the first parts of the Vietnam War using the wrong doctrine. Under General Westmoreland's leadership it amassed large units and sought to force the Viet Cong and the North Vietnamese to stand and fight in open battle. As the outcome of any serious fight between American forces and Communist forces in Vietnam was the annihilation of the Communist forces, the Vietnamese knew that survival required a very different strategy. They were not going to try to defeat the American army in Vietnam. They were going to try to defeat the political will in the United States. Their target was Walter Cronkite, not General Westmoreland.

With their Tet Offensive in 1968, the Communists succeeded brilliantly with this strategy, even as they were annihilated tactically and operationally. The very images of fighting in Saigon and Hue convinced Cronkite and other influential members of the elite that the war had been lost. This outcome was doubly tragic.

First, the Marines had been developing counterinsurgency tactics that were much more effective than the Westmoreland "big unit" model. The Marines had gone into the communities and sent very small units for very long tours, establishing physical safety and driving the enemy out of the villages. By protecting the villagers from the Communists, the Marines were able to establish very effective intelligence networks and then train the local Vietnamese into self-protection forces.

Second, when General Abrams took command from Westmoreland, he dramatically changed the focus of the war and started to achieve success. At his very first meeting as commander, Abrams outlined a fundamental shift from emphasizing main force units to a continuous doctrine of "one war." Abrams insisted that every element of the war, from the local village through the regional and provincial forces to the Vietnamese regular forces to the Americans, was integral to winning.

Sadly for Abrams and sadly for the South Vietnamese, the collapse of willpower in Washington was occurring at a rate faster than a decisive victory could be achieved in Vietnam. After losing more than 58,193 Americans (missing and dead) in Vietnam, Congress, at the behest of the antiwar movement, insisted on cutting off all aid and all ammunition to the South Vietnamese government even after U.S. combat forces had departed the country.

There was no reason for this except a desire to destroy the South Vietnamese government. As British counterinsurgency expert Sir Robert Thompson observed, "Perhaps the major lesson of the Vietnam War is: do not rely on the United States as an ally."

Within the U.S. Army there was a deep and bitter reaction to the Vietnam experience, as officers painfully experienced the gap that had emerged between the political elites and the military. The Army takes great pride in being the instrument of the American people, and it was frightening to see the uniform despised and military service condemned by the very people the Army was trying to protect.

A generation of Army officers was determined to avoid the counterinsurgency lessons of Vietnam. The one lesson they had learned was do not do it again. Instead, the Army turned and focused on the more traditional and more acceptable challenge of thinking through the problem of defending Western Europe against the Soviet Union.

Tragically for the Army and for America, the Army largely avoided thinking about counterinsurgency and the problem of defeating someone who does not agree to show up on a battlefield with a regular army. That is why the U.S. Army entered Iraq in 2003 determined to avoid policing and counterinsurgency. Its goal was to defeat Saddam Hussein, get out of Iraq as quickly as possible, and quickly restore the Army's prewar global security presence from South Korea to Europe without getting bogged down in Iraq. So the military bureaucracy was as reluctant as the civilian bureaucracy to devote the resources necessary to win the postwar struggle in Iraq.

On a similar note, senior Army leaders preferred to see their mission as training Iraqi security forces rather than fighting the insurgency; as a result, the Army took a short-term view of its insurgency-fighting efforts. Officers who argued for a more robust strategic engagement with the enemy were punished for lacking perspective, and those who accepted the short-term vision of senior officers were praised and promoted.

Because the Army did not want to fight a counterinsurgency campaign—it assumed that job was for the Iraqi army it was training—it did not think much about how to win a counterinsurgency campaign. This led to a disastrous lack of thoughtful analysis and planning. The center of gravity in a counterinsurgency is the people. Thus a counterinsurgency requires scores of translators and working closely with the native population, getting to know them and winning their trust. Only gradually, with gifted officers like Colonel H. R. McMaster in al-Anbar Province, did the Army begin to wage counterinsurgency warfare effectively.

The bottom line is that the bureaucracy-as-usual approach failed spectacularly in Iraq on both the civilian front and the military front. It failed because it did not recognize the nature of the enemy and its tactics, and it did not insist on metrics-based results for both civilian and military objectives. If those failures had not finally been reversed by President Bush, General Petraeus, and General Raymond Odierno, they would have inflicted enormous damage to the cause of freedom and offered dangerous hope to the terrorists that they can outlast the Americans.

In New York, strong leaders like Mayor Giuliani and Police Chief Bratton forced the police bureaucracy to change even if it meant that three out of every four precinct captains had to retire or change jobs.

In Baghdad, the federal bureaucracies—from the White House to the State Department to the Defense Department to the intelligence community—preferred failure in Iraq to change in Washington. The men and women in combat were focused on winning a war. Everyone else was focused for too long on preserving their old institutions. Only very strong systematic leadership can break through the natural self-protective patterns of large bureaucracies and force change to achieve success.

PART THREE

Real Change Requires Real Solutions

W E DELIBERATELY CALLED OUR MOVEMENT American Solutions rather than American ideas or American ideology because we know the American people want things actually to work.

The philosopher William James once asserted that pragmatism was the only genuinely American contribution to philosophy. Pragmatism in its original intellectual sense meant a focus on reality and a grounding in facts and their contextual meaning.

The American people are stunningly pragmatic. They want to know if things will work. They want their lives to be better. They largely ignore or discount ideas and ideology. They want to know if ideas and ideology can be translated into practical, measurable, certifiable achievements that will improve their lives and the lives of their children. That is why we focus on solutions that will work rather than ideas that merely sound good.

To meet this test of practical, implementable solutions let us turn to a series of specific proposals.

CHAPTER TEN

An Immigration Policy
That Makes Sense

OUR CURRENT IMMIGRATION TROUBLES are almost entirely problems of success. Our challenge is to seize that success and turn it into a boon for America, rather than allow bureaucrats to turn it into yet another failure.

Even amidst the current economic crisis, America still has the best economy in the world. America has the greatest opportunity for hardworking people to be upwardly mobile and to dream that their children can have even better lives. America creates jobs on a scale that Europe and Japan envy. In fact, America creates more jobs than there are Americans to fill them.

For four hundred years, since the first European immigrants landed at Jamestown, America has attracted energetic, ambitious people from all over the world. And even in hard economic times, America continues to draw vast numbers of immigrants seeking prosperity and freedom.

This is a good challenge. It is better to be the country people want to join than the country people want to leave. It is better to have the highest standard of living in the neighborhood than the lowest. It is better to have hardworking, energetic, ambitious people clamoring to join you than to have them seeking desperately to leave.

However, this opportunity requires a level of honesty from our political elites that they have not delivered. There has been more demagoguery and less honest dialogue about immigration than about any other topic in the last several years. The elites desperately try to ignore the needs of the American people and close their ears to demands for reform. The American people are furious at the elites because they have lied about immigration and lied about what we need to do to fix our immigration system.

In 1986 I voted for the Simpson-Mazzoli immigration bill because we were told it would solve the problem of massive illegal immigration. In his diaries, President Ronald Reagan said he was going to sign the bill because we had to regain control of our borders. The Simpson-Mazzoli bill contained three promises:

1. The government would make a concerted effort to control the borders.
2. An effective employer verification program would ensure that only legal workers were hired.
3. One-time amnesty would be granted for people illegally in the United States.

All three promises were broken. The government has made no serious effort to control our borders. Employers continue knowingly to hire illegal immigrants without any real fear of punishment. There are millions more in our country illegally today (twelve to twenty million) than there were in 1986. And we face a never-ending parade of new amnesty proposals. Today's popular anger with the elites stems from the twenty-year failure of the government to keep the promises made in the Simpson-Mazzoli bill.

There is a clear path to an effective immigration solution that is better for America and better for immigrants. The challenge is to get the elites to listen to the American people.

I owe a lot to Helen Krieble and the Krieble Foundation for their groundbreaking work in listening to the American people and trying to find a solution that meets our values and would be acceptable to the vast majority of Americans. Republican congressman Mike Pence deserves a lot of credit for working with the Krieble Foundation. Had President Bush worked with Congressman Pence and Republican senator Kay Bailey Hutchison, there might well have been a successful immigration reform bill in 2006.

Unfortunately, the Washington elites have agreed on a definition of success that is infuriating to the average American. The elites on the left oppose border control, oppose English as the official government language, oppose expanding legal immigration, and want to find a way to allow everyone here illegally to stay, all while prohibiting illegal immigration in the future. The country is convinced that this so-called solution is incompatible with American values and will weaken America's future.

In trying to force their left-wing solution on a country that rejects it, the elite have resorted to describing their critics as racist, xenophobic, unrealistic, and much worse. Those attacks are merely a sign of the elites' desperation.

Facts About the American People and Immigration

Americans strongly support legal immigration. Virtually all Americans admire immigrants and respect the work ethic they bring to America. In fact, Americans would support increasing the number of visas for highly educated immigrants and those with special technical skills, the H-1B and H-2B visas. In the American Solutions public opinion research, by 63 to 29 percent the American people support those with skills and knowledge migrating to America easily, legally, and productively. Ironically, labor unions bitterly oppose expanding the H-1B and H-2B visas even as they support amnesty for millions of people in the country illegally. The economic importance of expanding H-1B visas is explained in more detail in Chapter Eleven.

Americans are also sympathetic to the plight of those who have come to America seeking a better future. An overwhelming majority of Americans (83 to 16 percent) would support a worker visa program to make it easier for people in the United States to work legally.

Americans believe modern technology should be used to help legalize and regularize economic migration. By an even larger margin (84 to 14 percent), Americans support a system in which immigration centers in foreign countries help people find jobs in the United States and apply for worker visas. This concept was pioneered by the Krieble Foundation and reflects the developments of Kelly Services and other employment companies that have developed a remarkable ability to match people with work.

Americans also support using modern technology to fashion an effective worker program. By an enormous 89 percent to 11 percent, they support a worker visa program in which foreign workers receive a tamper-proof identification card allowing the government to track them. However, the American people have little faith that the federal bureaucracy could develop and implement such a system and protect it against fraud. By 73 percent to 20 percent, the American people would outsource the real-time verification system to companies like American Express, Visa, or MasterCard so businesses could immediately identify forged papers.

Americans are firm in their belief that foreign workers should take an oath to obey U.S. law and be deported if they commit crimes while in the United States (93 percent to 6 percent). By 88 percent to 10 percent, they favor deporting illegal immigrants who commit felonies. By 58 percent to 35 percent, they would cut off federal funds for sanctuary cities that prohibit local police from checking the immigration status of those arrested.

Americans are vividly aware that current immigration laws are not being enforced (72 percent to 21 percent). Americans also believe employers should be required to obey the law. By 78 percent to 20 percent, they support heavy monetary fines against employers and businesses that knowingly hire illegal immigrants. By an even bigger margin (83 percent to 15 percent), they favor requiring the Internal Revenue Service to conduct audits of companies that hire illegal immigrants to determine if they have paid the taxes they owed.

Forcing employers to comply with the immigration laws would clearly reduce the challenge of illegal immigration, according to 77 percent of all Americans (21 percent disagree). Furthermore, Americans disapprove of companies offering services like credit cards or bank accounts to illegal immigrants (78 percent to 18 percent). They also oppose proposals such as former New York governor Eliot Spitzer's failed effort to give drivers' licenses to illegal aliens. This would also then make it easy for people here illegaly to vote, which is apparently the goal of some liberals.

It is this desire by Americans to enforce the laws already on the books that has led to such an intense popular rejection of amnesty proposals. By 66 percent to 31 percent, Americans believe that allowing illegal immigrants to remain in this country undermines respect for the law. That is also why—by 66 percent to 29 percent—Americans prefer the term illegal immigrant to undocumented immigrant to describe people who have entered the United States illegally.

Yet Americans know that repressive measures alone will not stop illegality. A clear majority (52 percent to 39 percent) believe an incentive-based worker program is more important in stopping illegal immigration than complete control of the borders. However, Americans want a very important symbolic step from each person who is in the United States illegally. By 69 percent to 27 percent, they want people who have entered illegally to apply for their visas from their home countries and not from within the United States.

The American people would far rather see the proposed $5,000 fine turned into a round-trip ticket back home to get the worker card in one's home country and to begin again by entering the United States legally. Americans have a deep sense that any new amnesty, however disguised, would send the signal to yet another generation that it's okay to sneak into America illegally, in the expectation that in another twenty years there will be yet a third amnesty.

In effect, the American people want to draw the line on the failure of the Simpson-Mazzoli bill and create a new beginning in which everyone operates within the law. They also want people who come to America to want to become American.

Becoming American

One of the biggest gaps between the elites and the average American is on the issue of American civilization, American history, and English as the official language of government.

Elites on the left have worked furiously to eliminate American history from school curricula (or to teach contempt for a pro-American version of American history). They have opposed English as the dominant language. They have rejected assimilation into America in favor of a multicultural system with no norms. The American people reject all these attitudes as undermining American unity.

This cultural struggle over the future of America—and the very definition of America—underlies the immigration fight. The gap between the leftist elites and the rest of America could hardly be broader.

By 87 percent to 11 percent, the American people favor English as the official language of government. Even when they learn that this designation might mean no longer printing ballots or any other government document in a foreign language, they still support English as the official language by 74 percent to 23 percent.

Overwhelmingly, by 83 percent to 17 percent, Americans believe new immigrants should be required to learn English. The American people are willing to pay for their belief in English. By 83 percent to 15 percent, they would support a program offering intensive English instruction to all who need it, including stipends to help immigrants attend the program. Americans are also prepared to allow businesses to require employees to speak English while on the job (80 percent to 17 percent).

On all these topics there is a huge gap between the news media, the academic Left, and left-wing politicians on one side and the overwhelming majority of Americans on the other.

Controlling the Border for National Security

The American people overwhelmingly want to see their borders controlled as a matter of national security. By more than 7 to 1 (86 percent to 12 percent), Americans believe terrorists are trying to enter the United States illegally.

Most Americans understand the irrationality of intense security at airports and lax security at the borders. This requires the terrorist to be dumb enough that he insists on flying into the United States when he could simply ride a truck or walk into the country unimpeded. The refusal to control the border has been one of the most infuriating aspects of modern government, and one of the most inexcusable.

The American people would support more visas for technical and highly skilled workers if they could get the immigration reform they want and that America deserves: reform that establishes English as the official language of government, reform that controls the borders, reform that doesn't reward illegality, reform that enforces penalties on employers who knowingly hire illegal workers, and reform that requires illegal aliens to return to their native lands and acquire a proper visa.

If the elites would embrace the views held by the vast majority of the American people, a new law could be passed in a matter of weeks and implementation could begin within a matter of months. This is the immigration reform the vast majority of Americans want; it is the reform the officials they elect should deliver.

CHAPTER ELEVEN

Real Change to Achieve Enduring Prosperity for American Workers

IF EVERYONE WHO WORRIES about American jobs and American prosperity understood one fact, we would have a totally different and much improved national economic policy. That fact is: geese can fly.

Remember the goose that laid the golden egg? For America, that goose has been a free market economy that encourages entrepreneurs—using science, technology, and stunning increases in productivity—to create wealth that spreads throughout society.

George Washington, Benjamin Franklin, Thomas Jefferson, and Alexander Hamilton all understood this fact. They knew why America prospered, and they knew that knowledge and money can move around the world. Hamilton, for instance, studied Adam Smith's *Wealth of Nations* and worked to attract Dutch savings to fund America's national debt. Washington studied innovation in farming and husbandry in Europe and applied it to his farm at Mount Vernon. Franklin was a world-renowned scientist and a member of the Royal Society in Great Britain. He routinely communicated with British, French, and other scientists.

It was because of their belief in the power of science and the application of knowledge to creating wealth that the Founders wrote the Patent Office into the Constitution. For more than two hundred years, their free-market, pro-entrepreneur, pro-knowledge model has made America a leader in creating jobs, prosperity, and wealth for the many.

Now there are two real threats to our economic future. The first is the liberal government model of high taxes, complex regulations, expensive and destabilizing lawsuits, and rule by bureaucracies that fail to perform (especially in education). The second is the desire to hide from world competition by closing markets and "protecting" current jobs and investment at the expense of the jobs of the future. These two threats could combine to convince the golden goose to fly to other countries and create jobs and wealth there.

We have seen case after case of destructive American policies driving business and jobs out of the United States:

* Tax policy has driven the reinsurance business out of the country.
* Litigation threats are a major factor moving financial sector jobs from New York to London.
* Regulatory and tax burdens have blocked new gasoline refineries from being built in the United States for three decades.
* Energy policy, taxes, and regulations are driving chemical industry jobs overseas.

Bad policies drive entrepreneurs, knowledge, and capital away and kill American jobs while trying to "protect" them. Consider the perverse effect of limiting H-1B visas, which allow highly skilled foreign workers to live and work in the United States. Existing jobs are not protected. Future jobs are driven out of the United States, as companies hire exactly the same people to produce wealth in Canada, India, or China.

In 1960 Ghana had the same per capita income as South Korea. Today South Korea is the twelfth-wealthiest nation in the world while Ghana sits at number 100. Why? Because Ghana followed a socialist model while South Korea followed a free market model.

Forty years ago the leading Irish export was young people leaving for jobs outside the country. Today Ireland has a higher per capita income than Germany, and 160,000 temporary workers from Eastern Europe live in Ireland. As a result of a generation of cutting taxes, reforming education, investing in infrastructure, working hard, and reshaping its government to be friendly to foreign investment, the German Bundesbank has projected that Ireland is on its way to becoming the wealthiest country in Europe per capita. In fact, European Union bureaucrats in Brussels complained that Irish taxes were too low and that they were therefore cheating, which meant that in order to slow down to the rest of Europe's rate Ireland needed to raise taxes.

Bad policies lead to bad outcomes. But the reverse is true as well. If we have the right policies, policies that expand our free market system, we can create better outcomes than we can imagine.

London to Replace New York?

America's ability to win, and not just compete, in the global economy depends in part on our having the world's most efficient capital markets. We need substantial reforms in this area if America is to be the most successful economy in the world and the best source of high-paying jobs with enough economic growth to sustain the Baby Boomers and their children when they retire.

Unfortunately, a likely result of the current recession will be a slew of new, onerous regulations on businesses and the capital markets. While the stock market meltdown showed that better regulations could be useful, these must be narrowly tailored to solve specific problems, such as fraud. What's more, we should acknowledge that much of the mess on Wall Street stemmed not from deregulation, as the Left argues, but from government pressure on private companies and on government-backed mortgage giants Freddie Mac and Fannie Mae to undertake irresponsible lending policies for purely political reasons.

Even before the onset of the current economic crisis, there were already several indications that America is becoming a less desirable place to do business. In today's global economy, companies have increasingly attractive alternatives of where to locate and where to seek capital financing.

* In 2007, the U.S. financial exchanges attracted barely one-third of the volume of global initial public offerings (IPOs) that they had in 2001, while the share by European exchanges expanded by 30 percent over the same period.
* A 2005 press report by the London Stock Exchange attributed one reason for its success to the fact that "about 38 percent of the international companies surveyed said they had considered floating in the United States. Of those, 90 percent said the onerous

demands of the new Sarbanes-Oxley corporate governance law
had made London listing more attractive."

* In April 2007, Europe's financial exchanges (including the Russian and Eastern European markets) surpassed those of the U.S.
  in stock market value for the first time since World War I.

* An investment bank and institutional securities firm in Min-
  neapolis reported that companies exited public markets at a 73
  percent higher rate in 2007.

* International middle market firm Piper Jaffrey showed that in
  2006 "239 public companies either were sold to strategic buyers . . . or to private-equity groups" and in 2005 "138 companies
  left the public roster."

* Requirements that public company boards contain a majority of
  independent directors could have a chilling effect on risk-taking, a driver of economic progress. Reducing these unintended
  costs of recent regulatory reform will be essential for America to
  retain its competitive edge.

The 2002 Sarbanes-Oxley Act, which added massive new reams of
accounting red tape for businesses, clearly created a regulatory environment that has driven IPOs out of the United States. Furthermore,
the legislation is leading public companies to delist from the stock
market in order to avoid red tape (and potential criminal penalties).
Following the law of unintended consequences, the Sarbanes-Oxley
Act effectively drives businesses to be less accountable than they were
before and has done vastly more damage to the American economy
than the corporate accounting scandals it was supposed to reform. It
has had a substantial negative effect on New York as a financial center

and has been a big asset for London. It is a wound inflicted by Congress on the American economy.

Of course, all these regulations failed to prevent the Wall Street meltdown. But instead of acknowledging the key role the government played in provoking the economic crisis in the first place, opponents of the free market simply argue that the regulations did not go far enough, and that even more burdensome regulations are required to reign in "reckless" private companies.

A report by the McKinsey consulting firm commissioned by New York City mayor Michael Bloomberg in early 2007 warned that London could replace New York as the world's leading financial center. This danger has very serious implications for the American economy. The financial sector is the third-largest sector of the American economy, provides 8 percent of our gross domestic product, and has been our third-fastest-growing sector. It is the fastest-growing sector in New York City, where it comprises 15 percent of the economy. If London replaces New York as the center of world financial activities, it could mean a loss of $15 billion to $30 billion and 30,000 to 60,000 jobs.

It's not a matter of what London is doing right. The issue is what America is doing wrong. American policies are so destructive that London is competitive even though the cost of living there is actually much steeper than in New York. Substantial reform will be required if New York is to remain the financial capital of the world.

One way in which we harm our own financial sector is through our immigration policy, which makes it much harder to attract an international work force. We should address this by creating enough special work visas for high-value workers who bring specialized education, entrepreneurial talent, or capital that will grow the American economy and make America a more prosperous country.

The government currently caps the number of H–1B visas at 65,000, with an additional 20,000 allowed for "high-value" immigrants with degrees from American universities. In 2007, 123,000 applications (for only 85,000 slots) were received in the first two days of the application period. Our economy depends on these workers, not only because they meet the demands of some of our most successful companies, but also because many of these workers come here and start some of our most successful companies. Intel, eBay, Yahoo, and Google are a few examples.

To remain competitive we need massively to expand the freedom for high-value workers to come to the United States and contribute to the growth of our economy. To determine who should get visas, we ought to establish a point system that takes into account a combination of advanced degrees, technical skills, and experience in fields that require these kinds of workers to help grow our economy.

A Competitive Disadvantage: Runaway Lawsuits and Red Tape

The advocate of quality, W. Edwards Deming, once warned that litigation was one of the greatest threats to the American economy. Today, the law is being changed from an instrument of justice into an instrument of extortion and redistribution. Americans are learning to treat litigation as a lottery, to sue rather than settle, and to turn American civil life into one of conflict and suspicion. Litigation reform needs to address several factors:

* ★ making arbitration preferable to litigation
* ★ making losers pay
* ★ prohibiting law firms from bringing class-action lawsuits
* ★ banning lawyers from advertising
* ★ fixing the fraud and abuse in mass tort litigation
* ★ reforming securities litigation

The American litigation system is one more factor helping London take business from America. Why invest in America just so a trial lawyer can take your wealth from you? Almost every other country in the world has a more benign legal system. Litigation risks increasingly drive companies and investors out of the United States and kill American jobs.

Litigation reform is about more than lawsuits. We have also to rein in state attorneys general. The blackmail model championed by New York's disgraced former attorney general and later governor, Eliot Spitzer, mugs companies without going to court and kills jobs. These practices must be stopped. The Constitution is clear that the federal government sets the framework for the national economy. Congress and the executive branch have a constitutional duty to protect that role from encroachment by state attorneys general searching for headlines.

In the middle of the challenge to New York's historic importance as a financial center, the liberal answer in Congress has been to try to increase taxes on the financial community. We should oppose such tax increases. Democrats in Congress have attempted to raise taxes on publicly held private equity firms, seeking to tax them at a corporate rate rather than a capital gains rate. Private equity firms, whether held privately or publicly, generally require clients—investing institutions such as university endowments or wealthy individuals—to have a large investment of millions of dollars. So the only way for the average middle-class investor to get a piece of the private equity pie, besides winning the lottery, is to buy cheap shares of a publicly held private equity firm. However, if going public means higher taxes, private equity firms will have no incentive to go public and the average investor will be locked out of those companies. Denying the best profit opportunities to all but the very rich hardly seems like leveling the playing field.

Raising taxes on publicly traded private equity firms might not keep these firms from going public—it might just make them go public overseas. EU firms have a 26 percent tax rate. If Congress, in the name of "fairness," raises tax rates on private equity to 35 percent, it could drive new fund formation—along with jobs—overseas.

Abolish the Capital Gains Tax

As an example of how far behind economic reality American politicians are, consider the analytical gap between all three of the leading Democratic presidential candidates from 2008—each of whom advocated an increase in the capital gains tax (the tax on investment income)—and the views of President John F. Kennedy and former Federal Reserve chairman Alan Greenspan:

"The tax on capital gains directly affects investment decisions, the mobility and flow of risk capital . . . the ease or difficulty experienced by new ventures in obtaining capital, and thereby the strength and potential for growth in the economy."

—John F. Kennedy, 1963

"[The] major impact [of a capital gains tax], as best I can judge, is to impede entrepreneurial activity and capital formation. . . . I [have] argued that the appropriate capital gains tax rate [is] zero."

—Alan Greenspan, 1997

The American people agree with Kennedy and Greenspan: taxing investment is destructive. In an American Solutions survey in 2007, Americans favored abolishing the capital gains tax by 48 percent to 41 percent. That support has grown despite the fact that neither political party has made a consistent argument for getting rid of it.

The American people are way ahead of the politicians because they understand what the capital gains tax is: a tax on productivity and on their personal savings. More and more, the American people understand the importance of savings and productivity for their own livelihood. An October 2007 editorial in the *Wall Street Journal* explained why:

> Recent surveys indicate that roughly 52 percent of American adults own stock in some form, and last year 8.5 million of these investors paid a capital gains tax. The value of those assets will decline if capital gains taxes go up because financial markets instantly capitalize higher taxes on stock profits into lower stock prices.
>
> We saw this effect in May 2003 after the passage of President Bush's investment tax cuts. An analysis by the investment advisory firm Strategas shows that stock values rose by 10.3 percent in the following weeks, and over the last four years the net worth of Americans' stock holdings has increased by some $6.2 trillion. Economic growth was the largest driver of stock prices, to be sure, but a higher after-tax return on capital also played a role.

Just as the Founding Fathers would have predicted, the capital gains from increased productivity actually led to increased prosperity for virtually all Americans. The editorial cited a study by Gary Robbins, a former Treasury Department economist, who found that for the period 1946 to 1998, about "90 percent of the returns to capital investment accrued to workers in the form of higher wages."

Ironically, tax increases on productivity actually led to a decline in government revenues, a now familiar dynamic:

> For the past forty years, capital gains tax increases have been associated with a decline in tax revenues. Rate cuts have generated more tax collections. One reason is that higher rates give investors an incentive to hold their assets to avoid paying the tax. The capital gains rate was last raised in 1986. Revenues from the tax tripled in the year before the increase, as investors cashed out of assets before the window of the lower tax rate slammed shut. But in each of the five years after the rate jumped to 28 percent from 20 percent, capital gains revenues remained below the pre-1986 level, according to a study by the National Chamber of Commerce Foundation.
>
> Conversely, the 1997 capital gains tax cut had a stock market unlocking effect. Congress's consistently mistaken Joint Committee on Taxation predicted that the government would collect $195 billion from 1997 to 1999 from capital gains payments. The actual amount was $279 billion. In other words, the lower tax rate raised $84 billion more than expected—which is one reason the late 1990s produced budget surpluses. Most recently. . . the 2003 tax cut produced a doubling of tax receipts to $97 billion in 2005 from $47 billion in 2002. That's twice what Congress predicted.

Move to a One-Page Optional Flat Tax

According to the American Solutions research, four out of every five Americans would like to have the option of a one-page tax form with a single tax rate. This concept of an optional flat tax was developed by Steve Forbes when his flat tax campaign was undermined by criticisms that it would take away popular tax breaks. Steve Forbes and

Stephen Moore have both proposed giving American taxpayers an opportunity to choose simplicity versus complexity and a single rate over a lot of deductions. They call it the free choice flat tax, and it's an idea whose time has come.

The Free Choice Flat Tax

All workers and corporations would have the freedom to choose each year to file their income taxes either under the new free choice flat tax option or under the current U.S. income tax code. Anyone who strongly favors a deduction or credit under the federal government's current complex income tax system would have the choice to keep filing that way.

Rhode Island adopted an optional flat tax, and lawmakers there expect that it will make the state more competitive with neighboring states in attracting new business and entrepreneurs who create jobs.

Tax simplicity—by saving time, relieving businesses from record keeping, and relieving the budget from accountants' and attorneys' fees—is even more important than a lower tax bill. Many people are actually willing to pay a little more in taxes in return for certainty and simplicity. They feel they save so much in record keeping and compliance, which costs an estimated $200 billion a year, that they are thrilled by the optional flat tax.

The free choice flat tax option would apply one single tax rate of 17 percent to all individual and corporate taxpayers. It would also include a standard exemption of $13,200 for each adult ($26,400 for a married couple) and a $4,000 exemption for each child or dependent. The current $1,000 tax credit for each child age sixteen or younger would also apply, as would the current earned income tax credit (EITC). This would mean no federal income tax on the first $46,165 in income for a family of four.

The free choice flat tax option eliminates all loopholes that could allow higher-income people to avoid paying taxes. But the personal exemptions, the child tax credit, and the EITC would free 42 percent of taxpayers—all from low- and moderate-income households—from paying federal income taxes at all. Many tax filers would receive net tax rebates from the child tax credit and EITC.

The free choice flat tax would eliminate the death tax, the capital gains tax, and the alternative minimum tax. There would be no tax on retirement benefits or on Social Security benefits. There would be no tax on dividends because corporations would have already paid tax on that income at the corporate level.

Filing under the free choice flat tax option would require just one form on one sheet of paper. This would save taxpayers billions each year in costs of record keeping, paying for tax advice, and filling out complicated tax returns, as well as countless hours of aggravation and worry.

The free choice flat tax option is specifically designed so that no person or corporation pays more in taxes than they pay under the current system. In fact, the free choice flat tax option is intentionally designed so taxpayers will pay lower federal income taxes than they pay under the current system. When additional revenues from higher economic growth are counted, then the free choice flat tax option is expected to be revenue neutral, raising as much revenue overall as the current tax system. The free choice flat tax could be adopted immediately at little risk to the taxpayer or the government.

The Fair Tax

There is also a proposed tax system that would involve a lot more change and a bigger risk. Yet it, too, has gained momentum as people grow tired of the current mess. It's called the fair tax.

There is no more passionate group of tax supporters in America than the advocates of the fair tax. They propose replacing the current taxes on income with a tax on consumption (basically replacing income tax and the IRS with a national sales tax), arguing that the world market has placed America at a considerable disadvantage. Other countries use a value-added tax, which can be deducted on exports and applied to imports. Under the various international trade agreements, income taxes (including the Social Security tax) cannot be deducted from exports or applied to imports.

The fair tax idea is a much bigger innovation than an optional flat tax on income. However, it faces three big challenges:

First, people must learn how their personal spending habits would be affected. During every survey that portrays the fair tax as a consumption tax, people become cautious and suspicious. Americans would have to be convinced that they gain more from abolishing the income and the Social Security tax than they lose in the consumption tax.

Second, we would have to amend the Constitution to remove the right to impose a personal income tax. I would never want Congress to have an ability to tax both your income and your spending. We all know they would if they could.

Lastly, enforcement is required, because people will always be tempted to find a way not to pay. While the Internal Revenue Service would not be looking at your income tax return, it would be looking at every business as an indirect tax collector on every sale. This nuance must be more accurately explained by the fair tax supporters.

The fair tax is worth studying and debating, but for the reasons listed above, it will require a lot of work to be adopted.

However, we could do something to start phasing in a fair tax approach now. Nine states survive perfectly well with no state income tax. These include large states such as Texas and Florida and the very prosperous state of Tennessee. Studies show the states without income taxes have higher economic growth and more rapid growth in jobs and personal income.

The other forty-one states could move toward phasing out their state income taxes as well. Part of the lost revenue can be made up by increasing the state sales tax by a couple of points. The rest can be made up by restraining the growth of state spending to increase no more than the rate of population growth plus inflation. A study by Steve Moore and Peter Ferrara argues that state income taxes can be phased out in fewer than ten years through this formula.

Encourage Business Job Growth in America

As Kevin Hassett of the American Enterprise Institute has suggested, we should abolish the capital gains tax for businesses as well as for individuals. We also need a tax break for corporations that keep their headquarters in the United States. It is in our interest to keep corporate management, creativity, and power centers in the United States. Every company willing to do that should receive a substantial tax break.

We should create a tax system in which every investment in new equipment can be written off in one year. We want American workers to have the world's best equipment and best new technology so they can be the world's most productive. It is self-destructive to have a depreciation code that lasts longer than the equipment depreciating.

The research and development tax credit needs to be permanent to maximize investment in new science and new technology. When businesses have to wait for Congress to extend the tax credit to make continuing research and development investments, time and money are wasted.

The double taxation of dividends should be ended as well so the bias against investment is ended. Beyond the tax code, American business will need an enormous amount of capital to grow as rapidly as needed in the next two generations as our economy takes advantage of dramatic scientific and technological innovation.

Fortunately, there is a reform that can help younger Americans grow a dramatically bigger economy, with better take-home pay and more accumulation of resources for their own retirement. This can be achieved by giving every American the choice to create a personal Social Security savings account, which I describe more fully in the next chapter.

CHAPTER TWELVE

Real Change
for Social Security

with Peter Ferrara, director of
entitlement and budget policy at the
Institute for Policy Innovation

I T SHOULD SURPRISE NO ONE that Social Security modernization is inevitable. In 1935, when Social Security was adopted, the average American lived to be sixty-three and would not draw a Social Security pension until age sixty-five. In effect, a majority of the taxpayers would never get back their investment in Social Security. When the first Social Security checks were paid there were forty-two taxpayers for every Social Security recipient. Today there are three, and in a few years there will be two. The simple mathematics of looking at a redistribution of money from forty-two taxpayers versus a redistribution from two taxpayers is clear and unavoidable. We will have to rethink Social Security because our new ability to live longer requires a new ability to save and invest more.

Everyone knows Social Security is going bankrupt. A recent report from Social Security's board of trustees projects that Social Security will run out of funds to pay promised benefits by 2042, when most workers who today are forty or older will be in retirement. Paying all promised benefits after that time will require raising today's total Social Security payroll tax of 12.4 percent to close to 20 percent. Social Security alone would then take close to one-fifth of working Americans' incomes.

Such a tax increase would reflect the program's history of ever-increasing tax rates with ever-decreasing benefits. In the beginning, the Social Security payroll tax was just 2 percent of the first $3,000 in wages, split between employer and employee. Today the total tax is 12.4 percent of roughly the first $100,000 in wages.

By 2017 Social Security will start running cash deficits each year. To continue paying all promised benefits, Social Security will have to get the cash from the federal government by turning in some of its trust fund bonds. But the government has no cash in reserve to repay any of those bonds. So guess who will pay for them? That's right: you, the taxpayer.

From 2017 until the Social Security trust funds run out in 2042, in order for Social Security to continue to be able to pay all promised benefits, taxpayers will have to cough up an additional $6.5 trillion to pay off all the trust fund bonds. Those funds are in addition to the enormous payroll taxes workers and employers will have to pay in the same period.

This additional, enormous taxpayer liability happened because Social Security never saved and invested any of its "surpluses" (funds not needed to pay the current year's promised benefits). Instead, the program loaned the surpluses to the federal government, which used the money to pay for everything from "bridges to nowhere" to welfare to foreign aid. In short, the Social Security surpluses went to the general fund to pay for anything and everything the government pays for. In return, the government gives Social Security paper IOUs promising to pay the money back, with interest, if it is ever needed to pay promised benefits.

This process, which occurs every year, is known as The Raid on the Social Security trust funds. Every poll shows that the American people overwhelmingly detest The Raid, but it continues because Congress does not want to stop spending the money gained each year. The $6.5 trillion taxpayer liability that will begin in 2017 represents the additional accumulated cost of The Raid. So taxpayers first paid taxes to create the IOU, and then they will pay a second round of taxes to redeem it. Sounds fair, doesn't it?

Blind defenders of the Social Security status quo argue that the IOUs Social Security gets back for The Raid are official government bonds, just as reliable as any other government bond held by investment and retirement trusts across the country. But the real issue is not whether the bonds will be paid back. The problem is that it will be enormously difficult for the taxpayers to pay them back—an additional $6.5 trillion on top of what they already pay in payroll taxes. This enormous tax burden may lead the government to cut some Social Security benefits, which would effectively repudiate some of the bonds.

Indeed, savings and investment are nowhere a feature of the Social Security system. The majority of the funds paid into the system each month is immediately paid out in the form of benefits to current retired beneficiaries. Any surplus is spent by the federal government in return for IOUs sent to the Social Security trust funds. That is why Social Security is actually a tax and redistribution system, rather than a savings and investment system.

Because Social Security operates this way, it is not a good deal for working people in the long run. Even if Social Security somehow pays all its promised benefits, the real rate of return (the return net of inflation) on all the taxes paid into the system over the years would be 1 to 1.5 percent or less for most workers today. For many, it would be zero or even negative. A negative real rate of return would be like saving your money in a bank, but instead of the bank paying you interest, you pay the bank interest. By contrast, the long-term real rate of return on stocks has been over 7 percent, and the real return on bonds has been around 3.5 percent. Remember these rates are compounded every year, so they really build up income over time.

Suppose that workers were free to save and invest, in their own personal accounts, up to roughly 50 percent of what they currently pay in payroll taxes. Employers would contribute the same amount to their workers' personal accounts out of the payroll taxes they currently pay on behalf of their employees. This plan was proposed in a bill introduced in Congress by Republican congressman Paul Ryan of Wisconsin and former Republican senator John Sununu of New Hampshire. (Lower-income workers would be allowed to invest a slightly higher percentage of what they currently pay in payroll taxes, and higher-income workers a little less.)

Let's look at what would happen to the Smiths, a middle-income, two-earner family that could invest in this option throughout their entire careers. Mr. Smith earns $40,000 at age forty (roughly the average income for full-time male workers). Mrs. Smith earns $30,000 at age forty (roughly the average income for full-time female workers). Their wages increase each year at the average rate of wage growth, and have been doing so since Mr. Smith started working at age twenty-three. He earned $20,202 that year. Mrs. Smith started working at twenty-three and earned $15,152 that year.

Investing half in stocks and half in bonds, and earning just standard, long-term, market investment returns, the Smiths would reach retirement with a combined $668,178 in their accounts (in today's dollars, after adjusting for inflation). If they invested two-thirds in stocks and one-third in bonds, they would probably reach retirement with $829,848 in their accounts. This accumulated fund would be enough to pay in retirement benefits more than twice what Social Security promises to pay the Smiths under current law but cannot finance.

Now suppose that the amount workers can shift into their personal accounts from their payroll taxes is expanded over time. Eventually, the Smiths can place up to 80 percent of their original payroll tax into their personal accounts, again with their employers matching this contribution. In other words, Mr. Smith and his employer would shift ten percentage points of the 12.4 percent Social Security payroll tax into his account. Suppose the Smiths could exercise this personal account option throughout their entire careers, investing half in stocks and half in bonds, and again earning only standard, long-term investment returns. The Smiths would reach retirement with $1.2 million in their combined accounts (in today's dollars after adjusting for inflation). That would be enough to pay, out of the continuing investment returns alone, substantially more than what Social Security currently promises but cannot finance. This would allow the Smiths to leave the entire $1.2 million fund to their children. Under the current Social Security system, it is not possible for beneficiaries to leave their retirement benefits to their children.

Now let's look at a career low-income worker, Mr. Jones, who makes $20,000 a year at age forty. Suppose he exercises the

Ryan-Sununu option each year throughout his entire career (shifting up to 60 percent of his own payroll taxes and his employer's payroll taxes into a personal account). Mr. Jones does better than you might expect, for two reasons. First, because he makes less money than Mr. Smith, the Ryan-Sununu option allows him to shift more of his payroll tax into his personal account, approximately 60 percent. Second, he starts work a little earlier because he doesn't go to college. He makes early contributions to his personal account during those years that accumulate investment returns for a very long time. The power of compound interest helps him more because of his early start.

Investing half in stocks and half in bonds, at standard, long-term market investment returns, Mr. Jones reaches retirement with $271,505 in his account (in today's dollars). That is enough to pay 84 percent more than what Social Security currently promises him but cannot finance. Investing two-thirds in stocks and one-third in bonds, he reaches retirement with $347,827, enough to pay him retirement benefits twice what Social Security promises but cannot pay. If the personal accounts were expanded to allow him to put 80 percent of what is currently paid in payroll taxes into his personal account, then Mr. Jones would accumulate $463,653, enough to pay him 166 percent more than what Social Security promises but cannot finance.

With the Ryan-Sununu option, the current Social Security safety net would also be maintained in full with a federal guarantee. This guarantee would ensure that all workers with personal accounts would receive, through their personal account combined with remaining Social Security benefits, at least as much as promised by Social Security under current law. If the total benefit for someone with a personal account fell below currently promised Social Security benefits, the federal government would send that person a check each month to make up the difference. As only a few workers would fall below the guarantee, and as the taxpayers would only be making up the difference, the burden of the guarantee would be dramatically smaller than the burden of the current system.

Just think about what sweeping changes our society would experience if workers at all income levels could accumulate several hundred thousand dollars in their own personal accounts by retirement. All workers would be accumulating a substantial, direct ownership stake in America's businesses and industries, and they would all prosper while dramatically increasing the capital available to the American economy. This would be a historic breakthrough in the personal prosperity of working people.

American Opportunity

In the 1860s, the Homestead Act opened land ownership to working people. If you got your family out to open land, fenced it in, and worked it to produce crops or raise cattle, the land would be yours. Many people of little means did just that and built a family legacy of prosperity that lasted through future generations. Land ownership in America became widespread.

In the 1930s, the Federal Housing Administration and later similar agencies opened manageable mortgages and homeownership to average-income working people. With hard, consistent work to meet the monthly payments, average-income families could own their own homes. Incredibly, home ownership rates have remained above 60 percent since 1960.

Now, in the early twenty-first century, the next great breakthrough in the personal prosperity of working people would be personal accounts for Social Security. Even workers earning the lowest incomes could give their children a major financial boost with the substantial funds accumulated in their personal accounts by retirement. As a result, new private sector capital would flow into the inner city and other poor communities across the nation. This would provide a financial foundation for higher education, small businesses, the launching of professional careers, the construction of new housing, and other steps on the road to reaching the middle class.

Look at what such personal accounts would do to reduce federal spending. They wouldn't just reduce the growth of federal spending. They would shift large chunks of federal spending from the public sector to the private sector, as the better benefits of the personal accounts replace the benefits of the current Social Security system. In addition, the federal government would no longer own and control all Social Security retirement funds. This would prevent The Raid. Moreover, with future retirement benefits financed from workers' own money in their personal accounts, the government would no longer be able to reduce future benefits, as it did in 1983 and as both Democrats and Republicans discuss doing today.

Under the Ryan-Sununu option, the federal government would still sponsor a complete Social Security system. Both workers and employers would be required to contribute to retirement savings via Social Security, and workers would be guaranteed the same level of benefits the current system promises. The most significant difference is that the new Social Security system would provide workers with far more retirement money. More money with the same federal guarantee: this is quite simply a better deal for workers.

How would personal accounts work on a practical basis? The Ryan-Sununu bill stands as a comprehensive model for reform. It included substantial input from the nonpartisan chief actuary of Social Security to make it practical and workable. It also incorporated the work of G. William Shipman, formerly a principal at State Street Global Advisors, one of the largest pension fund investment firms in the world. Shipman developed an administrative framework for personal accounts that would make them workable for the investment fund companies and minimize the costs of administration.

Workers could start shifting any percentage of the Social Security payroll tax into their personal accounts at any time, and expand over time to the full Ryan-Sununu level of 50 percent of the payroll tax for themselves and their employers. Workers would choose investments for their personal accounts from a special list of investment funds composed of stocks and bonds, approved and regulated by the U.S. Treasury Department for this purpose. The investment funds would be sponsored and managed by major private investment companies, with an annual fee of less than one-fourth of 1 percent of total assets. Workers could choose to switch to different investment funds during a three-month open season each year. This would work very much like the Thrift Retirement System for federal employees. Social organizations like AARP, the NAACP, and labor unions could team up with major private investment firms to offer investment fund options for their members.

Benefits from the personal accounts would be substituted for a proportional amount of benefits payable from the current Social Security framework, based on the proportion of payroll taxes shifted to the accounts throughout the worker's career. Let's go back to Mr. Smith. If the amount of payroll taxes so shifted, on a present value basis, equaled 50 percent of Mr. Smith's share of the tax, the benefits from his personal account would substitute for about half the Social

Security benefits currently promised him under the old system. Mr. Smith's personal account, in other words, would pay half the benefits currently promised by the old Social Security framework.

At retirement, Mr. Smith would use part of his accumulated account funds to purchase an annuity designed to pay at least as much as the Social Security benefits the account is replacing, with the same annual inflation-indexed cost of living adjustments as Social Security. After paying for the annuity, Mr. Smith is free to use the rest of the funds from his account as he chooses, including leaving some or all to his family at his death.

In other words, if his personal account can pay more than the Social Security benefits it replaces, Mr. Smith gets to keep the gain. If the account is insufficient to pay for all the benefits it replaces, the government will pay him the difference, so he would get at least as much overall as Social Security promises under current law.

This plan works because market investment returns are so much higher than what Social Security even promises, let alone what it can pay. So it is very unlikely that workers with personal accounts would end up with less than what Social Security promises. The system is designed so that these workers would end up with a lot more. In any event, even if a worker had terrible timing and began collecting his retirement at a time like now, when the stock market had declined significantly, he still could not collect less than he would under the existing system. This level of security is necessary to achieve fundamental, sweeping change in a program as politically sensitive as Social Security.

Workers would be completely free to choose to stay in the old Social Security framework as is, without personal accounts. There would be no benefit cuts or tax increases for these workers, or for anyone else. Today's seniors would get all promised benefits under current law without any change, but they would forgo any gains that they would otherwise realize with the personal Social Security account option.

The chief actuary of Social Security analyzed this plan and concluded that it would achieve full solvency for Social Security, eliminating all long-term deficits. Personal accounts would pay more and more current Social Security benefits over time. The chief actuary concluded that personal accounts would be such a good deal for workers that eventually the vast majority of Americans would choose them. If the accounts grew to at least the size proposed under the Ryan-Sununu bill, the financial burden on Social Security for retirement benefits would eventually be reduced to almost nothing, with virtually all retirement benefits provided instead through personal accounts. With the remaining payroll taxes still flowing into Social Security, this would eventually leave enormous surpluses in the system, requiring large payroll tax cuts. If the accounts were eventually expanded to sufficient size, the payroll tax could be phased out completely.

As long-term market investment returns are so much higher than what Social Security even promises, let alone what it can finance, the benefits paid by personal accounts would be substantially higher than the Social Security benefits they replace, leaving workers with a substantial net gain in benefits. The bigger the account option, the more workers would gain.

If the accounts were expanded enough, middle-income families earning just standard, long-term market investment returns could retire with close to a million dollars (in today's dollars). Even low-income workers could accumulate $300,000 and more throughout their careers. The chief actuary of Social Security concluded that after just the first fifteen years, workers would have accumulated

$7.8 trillion (in today's dollars, after adjusting for inflation). This is as large as the entire mutual fund industry today. After just the first twenty-five years, workers would have accumulated $16 trillion (in today's dollars).

The widespread accumulation of such substantial wealth throughout our entire society would be truly transformative. For one thing, it would do more than any other viable reform to address the concerns some have expressed regarding wealth and income inequality. It would do so not by trying to redistribute existing wealth, which would undermine our economy, but by the creation of new wealth more equally distributed, which would reinforce the economy. All workers would have a direct share in the wealth created by America's free market economy.

Across America, new savings and investments would flow through the personal accounts, increasing economic growth. The result would be new jobs with higher wages and higher family income for working people. In addition, if the federal government were forced to stop spending the annual Social Security Raid, it would have to be honest about the budget and the larger financial picture, because it would force Congress no longer to hide deficit spending in Social Security IOUs that it cannot finance. That would force Congress to prioritize or cut spending.

Finally, a word about financing the transition to personal accounts. As Social Security operates on a tax and redistribution basis rather than a savings and investment basis, if part of the current payroll tax is used to fund savings and investment in personal accounts, funds will have to come from somewhere else to continue paying all promised benefits to current retirees.

In part, this issue can be addressed by starting the accounts at whatever size seems feasible at the beginning, and then expanding them over time. For conservatives, this presents an opportunity to drive badly needed spending reductions in the federal government. We can utilize the reductions in other government spending as the foundation for the transition financing.

Higher economic growth produced by the reform would generate new revenue that would also help finance the transition. The remainder of the necessary transition financing can be borrowed, with that debt held in a separate account to be paid out of later surpluses produced by the reform. This borrowing is analogous to taking out a mortgage to finance the acquisition of an asset, like a home, only this time the asset is an accumulation of wealth in the personal accounts.

Enduring Prosperity for American Workers

The combination of tax reform and Social Security reform described here and in the previous chapter would lead to booming economic growth and new, higher-paying jobs. American workers would have the choice to replace the current monstrous income tax system with the option of a single, flat tax rate of 17 percent (with generous exemptions excluding the lowest-earning 42 percent of Americans from any income tax at all). The death tax, the capital gains tax, the dividend tax, the alternative minimum tax, and taxes on Social Security and retirement income would all be abolished. Businesses would enjoy a 17 percent flat rate as well, with immediate deductions for all business investment and no corporate capital gains tax.

With Social Security reform, the payroll tax would be effectively phased out over time and replaced with a personal savings and investment account. State income taxes could be replaced over time by sales taxes and spending restraint.

These tax reform incentives would cause capital investment to flow into the American economy from around the world. The personal accounts would also generate huge amounts of new capital here at home. This economic vision would create a future of enduring prosperity for all American workers. But to realize this vision, politicians in Washington have to stop stealing money from American workers and allow them instead to own and invest in America with a personal Social Security savings account.

CHAPTER THIRTEEN

American History Requires Real Change in Today's Judiciary

I T IS HARD TO OVERSTATE THE DANGER of tyranny from elitist judges who believe they have the right and the power to dictate to the American people what we will do and how we will do it.

Real change in American life will occur when the American people come to understand that we do not have to sit by passively while the federal judiciary redefines American history and takes away the people's power to decide their future. The nature of judges and the power they have should be a central issue in American politics today.*

---

* In spring 2009 I was honored to be a visiting lecturer at the University of Georgia School of Law, where I taught a course entitled "Judicial Supremacy vs. Co-Equal Branches." The purpose of the course was to explore historical materials to determine whether judicial supremacy constitutes a fundamental violation of American constitutional thinking, a radical departure from the constitutional system that the Founding Fathers invented, and a dangerous model for the survival of a free society. The course also explored arguments for the benefits of returning to a more modest role for the judiciary. You can view these lectures and other course materials at www.judicialsupremacyvscoequalbranches.com.

Judiciary Supremacy and Redefining the Role of God in American History

The threat of judicial tyranny has occurred before in American history. The Founding Fathers were deeply offended by the British judges who reshaped the law to fit the king's needs. They saw judges as instruments of oppression, which is why they devoted so much attention to the right to a jury of one's peers and to protection against the courts.

The Revolutionary War generation made complaints about imperial judges a core argument for changing the system. In the *Federalist Papers*, Madison, Hamilton, and Jay promised explicitly that the judiciary would be the weakest of the three branches and would respect the judgment of the legislative and executive branches.

After the promises of limited judicial power in the *Federalist Papers*, the Federalists decided to break their own principle when they lost the election of 1800. Faced with a crushing defeat by the Jeffersonians (then called the Republican-Democratic Party), they decided to more than double the size of the judiciary (from seventeen to thirty-five) and pack it with sympathetic judges.

At that time there was a four-month gap between the presidential election in November and inauguration in March. As a result the Federalist Congress and president attempted to undermine the election outcome by a series of lifetime appointments, creating the courts and approving their own judges.

The Jeffersonians were enraged by this effort deliberately to undermine the will of the American people. They asserted that elections had meaning and that judges could not be used to repudiate what the American people had voted for. In the Judiciary Act of 1802, the Jeffersonians abolished more than half of the new federal judgeships.

Some of the judges claimed this was unconstitutional, as they had been appointed for lifelong terms. The remaining judges refused to hear the case on the grounds that if they tried to overrule Congress and the president, their own judgeships would be abolished.

The precedent of abolishing judgeships is different from impeachment. Impeachment renders judgment on an individual judge. Abolishment renders judgment on an entire court. Today's Ninth Circuit Court judges (consistently the most radical and the most overturned by the Supreme Court) would do well to study the history of Jefferson. After all, it is impossible to argue that Jefferson and Madison were not aware of the Constitution and its powers.

The next great test of the judicial branch opposing the American people came with the *Dred Scott* decision of 1857. In that case, the Supreme Court overruled the two elected branches and sought to extend slavery throughout all the new territories in America. The result of that judicial overreach was a civil war in which more than 620,000 Americans were killed.

Today the dangers from elitist judges are many, but the most vivid danger we face involves the dishonest and destructive effort to drive God out of public life. This is alien to our history as an American people.

If there is one idea that is central to America's uniqueness, it is that we are all endowed by our Creator with unalienable rights to life, liberty, and the pursuit of happiness. In order for America to remain the freest, most successful nation on earth, we must have real change that forces our judiciary to acknowledge and respect the central role of our Creator in American history, and real change to bring an end to the idea that the judiciary is supreme over the legislative and executive branches in interpreting the Constitution. That is why in 2009 I helped create a not-for-profit organization called Renewing American Leadership whose mission is to defend and advance American civilization—specifically, to preserve and protect our American history and our Godly heritage.

Our Rights Come from God

The Declaration of Independence is, and must be, the starting point for any examination of the source of our rights and God's place in American public life. It is simply impossible to understand the United States without first understanding the Declaration. The Declaration is the mainstay of our civic life; it is our rock, it is our anchor. "All honor to Jefferson," Abraham Lincoln once wrote, "to the man who, in the concrete pressure of a struggle for national independence by a single people, had the coolness, forecast, and capacity to introduce into a merely revolutionary document, an abstract truth, applicable to all men and all times."

What, then, does the Declaration of Independence have to say about the matter? When it asserts, "We hold these truths to be self-evident, that all men are created equal, that they are endowed by their Creator with certain unalienable rights, that among these are life, liberty, and the pursuit of happiness," it makes some key assumptions. It assumes that God is sovereign over the universe. It assumes that God created man. And it assumes that man must obey an order of justice God Himself has instituted.

That order of justice requires all men to honor one another's natural rights because these rights are the unalienable endowment of the Almighty. When someone violates the rights of another they are not merely breaking the law. They are violating God's grant of protection.

This conviction was echoed many times during the Founding. "The sacred rights of mankind," wrote Alexander Hamilton, "are not to be rummaged for, among old parchments, or musty records. They are written, as with a sun-beam, in the whole volume of human nature, by the hand of the divinity itself; and can never be erased or obscured by mortal power." "The right to freedom being the gift of God Almighty," explained Samuel Adams, "it is not in the power of man to alienate this gift."

The Declaration of Independence embodies the deep sensibility of the American people: our rights are God-given; we could not eradicate them, even if we wanted to; and any government that tries to annul these rights will cease to be legitimate. These are the truths of the Declaration of Independence. Americans have relied upon these truths in our times of crisis; they have been the lights that guided us through our darkest hours.

In one of America's most difficult periods, as the nation plunged headlong toward civil war, Abraham Lincoln recalled the basic assertion of the Declaration, that "nothing stamped with the divine image and likeness was sent into the world to be trodden on, and degraded, and imbruted by its fellows."

Four score years later, while the flames of war spread across Europe and the Pacific, President Franklin D. Roosevelt wrote, "Our modern democratic way of life has its deepest roots in our great common religious tradition, which for ages past has taught to civilized mankind the dignity of the human being, his equality before God, and his responsibility in the making of a better and fairer world."

FDR, the greatest Democratic president of the twentieth century, believed in good and evil, and believed his generation faced a war between what he called "our Christian civilization" and paganism.

President Roosevelt understood how hard it can be to defeat evil. On D-Day, June 6, 1944, as hundreds of thousands of young Americans risked their lives to defeat evil, FDR went on national radio to lead the nation in prayer.

Reading Roosevelt's words today as we consider our own young Americans—our sons and daughters, our neighbors in harm's way around the world—is quite moving, especially knowing that as he prayed with the nation, the Greatest Generation had launched its mightiest battle. You can find the entire prayer in Appendix 4 and can listen to it in FDR's voice at www.newt.org/FDRprayer.

It is for this reason that we made an effort in 2007 to have every American radio station play FDR's full national prayer on June 6. We wanted to remind Americans that we can be united in the face of evil, we can seek God's guidance for America, we can support our young men and women in uniform who risk their lives, and we can be determined to defeat evil. I hope that the FDR radio prayer project will become an annual event, with more and more stations taking part. This would be an important commitment to remind all Americans that we are a nation founded and sustained in history by our Creator.

FDR knew that he could call upon God for tremendous wells of strength and comfort in time of need, as did Lincoln and Washington before him. In our hours of desperation, both as individuals and as a country, we return to our founding truths time and again. Even today, these truths continue to sustain and guide us. In this age we face the Irreconcilable Wing of Islam, an enemy who does not believe that God created all men equal by right. According to their evil ideology, Islamists believe that justice is owed only to fellow Islamists—while the rest of humanity (even fellow Muslims) have no rights and can be slaughtered as a duty to God.

Americans believe that all men and women have equal rights, because that is the will of the Almighty and God has endowed them. Indeed, we believe that no person "stamped with the divine image and likeness was sent into the world to be trodden on, degraded, and imbruted by [his] fellows."

Just as in the times of the Nazis and the Communists, darkness is again falling across the earth, and it is again the calling of America to light her moral lamps and place them out for all the nations to see. Any court that does not recognize this history is in danger of losing its legitimacy and its powers.

The Challenge from a Bigoted Anti-Religious Judiciary Asserting a Doctrine of Judicial Supremacy

We are accustomed to having the truths of the Declaration challenged from without. But for the first time in nearly 150 years, those truths are now being challenged from within. A growing culture of anti-religious bigotry declares that the nation cannot publicly profess the truths on which it was founded. We are told that our public schools cannot invoke the Creator, nor proclaim the natural law, nor profess the God-given equality of human rights.

In hostility to American history, these anti-religious bigots insist that religious belief is inherently divisive, and that public debate can proceed on secular terms only when religious belief is excluded. In this contorted logic, the public square allegedly becomes more welcoming as it strips away all religious symbols and language. They seek to build a wall of separation between the historic America and the radically different America they want to create—an America without

God, an America without traditional values, and an America without knowledge of its own history.

Unfortunately, these false principles of secular absolutism have deeply penetrated the legal establishment and are called upon to justify all sorts of judicial destruction. In New Jersey, school officials prevented a student from reading his favorite story to the class because it came from the Bible. In Pennsylvania, a teacher's assistant was suspended because she wore a necklace with a cross. And in California, the nation's most persistent atheist has renewed his crusade to strike the words "under God" from the Pledge of Allegiance.

Reason and Historical Wisdom Should Guide the Courts

These relentless efforts to drive God from public life, aided and abetted by judicial elites, inevitably pressure believers to withdraw from public life and public involvement. For two principal reasons it is profoundly wrong for the courts to sanction this anti-religious bigotry.

First, basic fairness demands that religious believers have a chance to be heard. This is a democracy. We are supposed to invite all persons and all parties to the public debate. It is wrong to single out for discrimination those who believe in God. Yet today it is impossible to miss the discrimination against religious believers. We often hear the need to celebrate free secular and artistic expression—but rarely for religious expression. Too often, the courts have been biased against religious believers.

Second, we would all benefit, especially judges, from reflecting on the wisdom of the Founding Fathers. The Founders considered religion a great benefit to society. They had a very straightforward belief that the purpose of government was the protection of liberty, and that the maintenance of liberty inevitably required virtue among its citizens. The "pursuit of happiness" was a phrase borrowed from the Scottish enlightenment, meaning pursuit of virtue and wisdom.

The Founders believed that if virtue was to survive in the American experiment, it would require "true religion," which cultivates the virtues necessary to the protection of liberty. Implicit within this vision is a pluralistic sensibility. Any true religion would deserve the respect of the government, which would include the freedom to express in public the moral principles of such a true religion.

This belief that religion was an indispensable support of republican government was inherent throughout the founding generation. Its strongest and best statement can be found in George Washington's Farewell Address: "Of all the dispositions and habits which lead to political prosperity, religion and morality are indispensable supports. In vain would that man claim the tribute of patriotism, who should labor to subvert these great pillars of human happiness, these firmest props of the duties of men and citizens."

Washington's words are as true today as they were 210 years ago. The courts should recognize that the benefits of these indispensable supports cited by Washington accrue to Americans not just of one particular faith, but of all faiths, and all people of goodwill, religious or not. Washington and the other Founding Fathers feared that the weakening of these religious supports would undermine the very republican institutions under which all Americans find their liberties.

The People Must Be Prepared to Challenge Judicial Supremacy

This challenge from within would not be so troubling but for the power of the state—through the judiciary—to dictate an anti-religious agenda to a nation that is not anti-religious and approves of religious expression in the public square. For the last forty-eight years, since *Cooper v. Aaron*, the Supreme Court has operated on the fundamentally false assertion that the federal judiciary alone is supreme in the exposition of the Constitution.

The whole purpose of creating our constitutional system with three branches was to place power in the hands of the people and protect the people from any one branch having the power to dictate. The doctrine of judicial supremacy did not exist in the Constitution. When asked about it, Jefferson had rejected it, writing to William Jarvis in 1820 that "[t]o consider the judges as the ultimate arbiters of all constitutional questions [is] a very dangerous doctrine indeed, and one which would place us under the despotism of an oligarchy.... The Constitution has erected no such single tribunal, knowing that to whatever hands confided, with the corruptions of time and party, its members would become despots. It has more wisely made all the departments co-equal and co-sovereign within themselves."

Of course, if you are a left-wing lawyer who would like to impose your values on Americans who are not smart enough or sophisticated enough to agree with you, then you would think judicial supremacy is a terrific idea. If you are a judge who would like uncontested power without having to run for election or engage in the messy process of legislating with other elected officials, then judicial supremacy is just the thing.

The rise of judicial supremacy is an arrogant overreaching by the legal class to have unusual power over its fellow Americans. It should be stopped in its tracks, and judges who overreach should have their offices abolished.

Those who doubt that the elected branches have the power to reform the judicial branch need merely read the *Federalist Papers* for quite specific recommendations for how it can happen. They can also study the aforementioned Judiciary Act of 1802, which abolished more than half of the federal judges in a power struggle over the future of the judiciary branch.

We are not helpless in the face of judicial tyranny if we have the nerve to stand up to it. The need to stop judicial domination is made even more compelling by the anti-religious bigotry of the activist judges. Consider these recent examples:

* In June 2002, the Ninth Circuit Court of Appeals found the words "under God" in the Pledge of Allegiance unconstitutional. In 2004, the Supreme Court dismissed the case on technical grounds, but another lawsuit has been brought to the Ninth Circuit to remove the words.

* A federal district court in Illinois held that the federal statute that authorizes the Department of Defense to host the Scouts National Jamboree at a U.S. military base is unconstitutional because it provides federal funding exclusively to a religious organization. The government appealed that ruling to the U.S. Court of Appeals for the Seventh Circuit. In April 2007, the court dismissed the case on technical grounds related to plaintiff standing.

* A federal district court in Washington state ruled against a Christian school club receiving school recognition or funding, as its membership is restricted to Christians and therefore violates the Kent school district's general non-discrimination policy. The

club appealed to the Ninth Circuit, which ultimately ruled in favor of the school district. The ruling is now being appealed to the Supreme Court. In the meantime, the Ninth Circuit has already extended this precedent from high schools to colleges, meaning that universities can prevent Christian student clubs from requiring their members or leaders to be Christians.

★ A federal district court in California held that the City of San Diego's practice of leasing large parcels of prime parkland to the Boy Scouts of America at nominal rates was unconstitutional because the Boy Scouts are a religious organization and San Diego's leasing process was not neutral. The defendants appealed to the Ninth Circuit, which stayed the case and withdrew it from submission pending a decision by the California Supreme Court on related state law claims. As six dissenting Ninth Circuit judges later argued, the court's finding that the plaintiffs had standing to sue "creates a new legal landscape in which almost anyone who is almost offended by almost anything has standing to air his or her displeasure in court."

Real Change to Stop Anti-Religious Harassment in the Courts

These types of cases proliferate in part because our federal government effectively subsidizes them under the terms of the Civil Rights Attorney's Fees Award Act of 1976. Under this act, anybody who brings an even partially successful civil rights suit may have the defendant pay all legal fees for both parties. This is a discretionary award that is routinely granted to successful plaintiffs. Successful defendants, on the other hand, are not allowed any such fee reversals, and have to pay all their own legal fees regardless of the outcome of the case.

While this law may be sensible to help those who cannot afford to pay legal fees to prosecute a civil rights lawsuit, the problem is that it has also been applied to Establishment Clause cases. Unlike other civil rights litigation in which someone has been denied a job or been treated unfairly by the government, there are no actionable injuries in Establishment Clause cases. Part of living in a democracy means living with some things you may not like, so long as they do not actually hurt you or violate your rights.

As a result, wealthy and powerful organizations have used this advantage to strong-arm their agenda of anti-religious bigotry. Groups use the threat of enormous legal fees to force their bigotry agenda on school districts and municipalities.

And what if potential defendants don't knuckle under? For anti-religious organizations, there is no potential downside, with a potentially very lucrative upside. These organizations rely on staff or volunteer lawyers for plaintiffs' counsel. Volunteer lawyers work for free, and staff lawyers for a non-profit are paid at well below market rate. If the group loses the case, it will have lost no money; the volunteers are not paid and the staff lawyers would have to be paid regardless. But if these anti-religious organizations win the case, the defendants pay attorney's fees set at the private sector's market rate. The result is pure gravy: the groups get to collect private sector rates for deeply discounted legal work. It amounts to a taxpayer subsidy for anti-religious organizations.

Former congressman John Hostettler, a Republican from Indiana, worked hard to correct this imbalance in the law. He was a tireless advocate of the Public Expression of Religion Act, under which plaintiffs could still ask the courts to prevent governmental endorsement of religion, but, if victorious in court, would be limited to injunctive relief. In other words, the court could order the removal of Establishment Clause violations, but defendants would no longer have to pay the legal fees for both sides.

Eliminating the financial incentives for advocacy groups to take on trivial church-state cases would help restore the original civil rights law to its intended purpose. It would signal that Congress is exercising its constitutional duty to correct the judicial branch, which has gone so far astray of the plain meaning of the First Amendment. And most important, it would signal a renewed commitment to the essential American values expressed in the Declaration of Independence and honored in the Pledge of Allegiance.

CHAPTER FOURTEEN

How We Balanced the Budget and How We Can Balance It Again

A BALANCED BUDGET IS ONE OF THE CLEAREST examples of the world that works. One of the key pledges in the Contract with America was a balanced budget amendment to the Constitution. We passed it in the House but lost it in the Senate by one vote, which prevented it from going to the states for ratification. The House Republicans of 1994 then did something truly unprecedented. We decided to balance the budget even if we did not pass an amendment to do so. We were going to balance the federal budget and prove it could be done while lowering taxes, increasing defense and intelligence spending, and increasing investments in scientific research. The meeting of senior elected leaders in April 1995 to discuss this key commitment was one of the most important of our time in the majority. We were going to do what we thought was right for the country, even though we knew it would lead to tremendous conflict with entrenched interest groups and bureaucracies.

The constitutional amendment had specified a balanced budget in seven years. We accepted that challenge. Shortly after we began, we ended up in a deadlock with President Clinton and a government shutdown ensued, lasting for several days. The elite news media became hysterical. Rather than focusing on the fact that no essential services were interrupted, they instead interviewed tourists disappointed that the Smithsonian and the national monuments were closed.

The news media are still convinced that shutting down the government was a major mistake. Yet the reelection of the first Republican House majority since 1928 occurred after the shutdown. The balanced budget bill, which paid off $405 billion in federal debt, occurred after the shutdown. The budget was balanced for four consecutive years for the first time since the 1920s.

What we learned in 1995, and what we must recognize today, is that there are four key principles to achieving a balanced budget:

1. Cut taxes to increase economic growth and therefore increase revenues. It may seem counterintuitive—and it certainly is to elite editorial writers—but cutting taxes to increase economic growth is the best long-term strategy for balancing the budget. Tax hikes retard economic growth and depress revenues.

2. Set priorities and increase spending in key areas while reducing it in non-essential areas. Setting priorities was very important. Historically, balanced budget conservatives had tried to be cheap on everything. This created such a wave of resentment across the board that they could not sustain their effort. We felt strongly that some investments needed to be increased even while others were dramatically reduced. We doubled the investment in

biomedical research at the National Institutes of Health while cutting less essential spending elsewhere.

3. Eliminate pork barrel spending. One of the reasons I strongly favor a balanced budget commitment is because it disciplines politicians. If there is a limited amount of money, then elected officials have to learn to say no. Pork barrel special legislation has gotten much worse in the last few years. In 1988, President Reagan vetoed a transportation bill because it contained eight earmarks. In 2005, a $286 billion transportation bill signed by President Bush included 6,200 earmarks costing more than $20 billion. As the balanced budget fervor declined after 1998, so did the control over such indefensible pork barrel spending.

Consider some recent examples:

* $2 million to establish the "Charles B. Rangel Center for Public Service" at City College of New York (sponsored by Democratic congressman Charles B. Rangel of New York). One obvious rule should be that nothing paid for with tax dollars can be named for a living political figure, let alone a serving member of Congress.

* $1.2 million to create a museum in Kansas about prisons (former Democratic congresswoman Nancy Boyda of Kansas)

* $500,000 (on top of $2.5 million in previous earmarks) to spruce up a Washington, D.C., neighborhood where Republican congressman Jerry Lewis of California recently purchased a townhouse. When this earmark was challenged, the House voted 361–60 in support of Congressman Lewis, the top Republican on the Appropriations Committee.

As the public began to complain about special pork barrel spending, the politicians responded by trying to hide it. Democrat David Obey of Wisconsin, the chairman of the House Appropriations Committee, announced that earmark requests will be removed from bills working their way through Congress. Instead, they will be added as last-minute surprises in conference committees.

Democrats have also moved earmarks into emergency supplemental bills, like the one to support U.S. troops in Iraq and Afghanistan, including provisions such as $75 million "to ensure proper storage for peanuts." Democratic senator Robert Byrd of West Virginia inserted $125,000 for the International Mother's Day Shrine building in Grafton, West Virginia, in the fiscal 2008 interior appropriations bill. In 2007, Congressman John Murtha of Pennsylvania, chairman of the Defense Appropriations Committee, inserted $163 million in pork barrel projects. This is the highest total in Congress and twice his total for 2006.

One project, $1 million for the "Center for Instrumental Critical Infrastructure" in Murtha's district, was challenged by Republican congressman Jeff Flake of Arizona when his staff could not verify the center's existence. Democratic congressman Pete Visclosky of Indiana, who chairs the spending subcommittee responsible for the project, admitted he didn't know whether it existed. Despite this, Flake's challenge failed by a vote of 326–98.

When the then director of national intelligence recommended that the National Drug Intelligence Center (NDIC), a longtime pet project in Murtha's district, be closed due to poor performance, Murtha had the House Intelligence Committee approve a $23 million earmark. Murtha explained in a letter that the center "anticipates undertaking a new and vitally important mission . . . with the National Counterterrorism Center—assuming responsibility for the terror no-fly list, the terror incident training program, and the post-disaster recovery site for the National Counterterrorism Center." Yet none of these claims was true.

On May 11, Republican congressman Mike Rogers of Missouri attempted to strike the $23 million earmark for the NDIC. The next week, Rogers—in an account Murtha has not denied—said the Democrat told him, "I hope you don't have any earmarks in the defense appropriation bill because they are gone, and you will not get any earmarks now and forever." When Rogers requested that the House reprimand Murtha for this behavior, the resolution was voted down 219–189.

One step toward controlling pork barrel spending is much more transparency in government. Republican governor Rick Perry of Texas is a good example. As described by Grover Norquist, head of Americans for Tax Reform, "Perry placed all of his office's expenses online last year in a searchable form. The state of Texas has further required that any school district that cannot prove that it is spending at least 65 percent of its education budget in the classroom must publish its check register—every single expenditure—online for citizens to inspect."

4. Shift from expensive, wasteful systems to smarter spending. Modern corporations that achieve success do so by being smarter and more productive, not just by being cheaper. The same principle should apply to government. For instance, Elaine Kamarck, the

former director of Vice President Gore's Reinventing Government project, has developed new approaches to replacing bureaucracy with more effective information age systems. Stephen Goldsmith, the former mayor of Indianapolis, has developed a very dynamic record of achievement in privatization and modernization that improved government and the quality of life in Indiana substantially. Both have written books about their solutions and both have taught in American Solutions workshops. Their ideas can be found at the American Solutions Web site in the workshop archives (along with more than forty other workshops filled with solutions).

Making Government Smarter and More Productive

Businesses are forced to become more productive by the demands of their customers, the innovation and improvement of their competitors, and the pressure of recessions cutting revenue. Governments try to make competition illegal, ignore the demands of their customers, and seek to prevent recessions by simply raising our taxes or borrowing the money.

One of the great positive impacts of a balanced budget movement is that it forces government to find more productive and more effective ways to get things done with fewer and fewer resources. Under a balanced budget, politicians can spend more on one group only if they either take money from another group or find methods of cutting waste, inefficiency, and fraud so they can transfer the money saved to other constituencies. There is little incentive to insist on constant improvements in productivity if you can simply raise taxes or borrow

more money. Limited resources create enormous pressure for improvement in productivity and effectiveness.

One of my favorite areas for dramatic improvement in government
productivity—which leads to a balanced budget—is in building highways and bridges. Consider three success stories that saved a lot of time
and money and provided lots of lessons for improving government.

1. *The 1994 Northridge earthquake.* In January 1994, an earthquake in
   Northridge, California, measuring 6.7 on the Richter scale, shat-
   tered the overpass bridges of Interstate 10, the most heavily traf-
   ficked freeway in the world. Governor Pete Wilson was advised
   that the repair would take more than two years because of the
   extended public hearing requirements imposed by law. But I-10
   was restored to public use not in two years but in two months.
   How did they achieve this 12 to 1 improvement in performance?
   * Emergency powers for the governor expedited recovery. The
     California Government Code gives the governor the ability to
     invoke "emergency powers" that can suspend, for the duration
     of an emergency, any regulations and statutes that might impede
     or delay recovery. Governor Wilson promptly suspended the
     required public hearings to clear the way for rebuilding efforts.
   * Performance contracting sped performance. Governor Wilson
     required bidders on the rebuilding contract to agree to a
     bonus/penalty condition: if they finished early, contractors would
     receive a bonus of $200,000 for each day before the completion
     date. For each day past the date, contractors would incur a
     penalty of $200,000. As every day the bridge was closed cost
     California's economy an estimated $600,000, Wilson's plan was
     a cost-efficient incentive.

2. *A catastrophic tanker crash in Oakland.* In April 2007, a gasoline tanker truck crashed on a ramp in Oakland, California, that connects the East Bay to San Francisco. The closing of the ramp forced commuters to take a slower route. Bay Area residents planned for a lengthy inconvenience, as the repairs were expected to take fifty days and cost $5.2 million. However, effective incentives offered by the state led to a far more efficient outcome than anyone expected. How did they save thirty-three days and almost 80 percent of the projected cost?

* Incentives produced speed. The California Department of Transportation set a deadline and promised bidders a $200,000 bonus for every day they could finish the repairs before it, not to exceed a total of $5 million. The highest bid for the project was $6.4 million, while the lowest was under $900,000. The winning contractor, with a bid of $867,075, completed the project in seventeen days—almost three times faster than the original estimate and more than $4 million under budget.

* Serious problems merited serious response. Within twenty-four hours of the accident, the federal government approved emergency reconstruction money, and the state soon settled on a design plan. The contractor had workers and equipment on the scene fifteen minutes before the actual signing of the contract. Shop drawings were approved in hours, not months, and state inspectors were flown in to oversee quality control. From the start, crews worked twelve-hour shifts.

3. *Transportation overhaul in Utah.* In the mid-1990s, the interstate system near Salt Lake City, Utah, was in need of serious reconstruction because of the growing traffic demands of a burgeoning population. The project posed a major challenge because it

included the construction or reconstruction of 130 bridges and three major junctions with other interstate routes. It was the largest-ever interstate reconstruction project. The expected time for the project was originally ten years. However, the project needed to be finished before the 2002 Winter Olympics, just six years away. Facing these challenges, Governor Mike Leavitt and Tom Warne, the executive director of the Utah Department of Transportation, chose to use the design/build model of construction.

* Using the design/build model reduced time. In a design/build arrangement, one firm uses its own employees or subcontractors on all aspects of a project—planning, design, and construction. As a result, projects run under this model are often completed faster. The revised schedule for the Salt Lake corridor project was four and a half years.

* Incentives led to faster, better construction. The contract for the project included incentives of up to $50 million for timely completion, quality, and traffic maintenance. As a result, construction was completed in just over four years, beginning in April 1997 and ending in May 2001, before the Winter Olympics and ahead of the revised four-and-a-half-year schedule—and $32 million under budget.

The Big Bust

Compare these three success stories in saving time and money with one of the most disastrous public infrastructure projects in modern America: Boston's Big Dig.

The Big Dig highway project was the most expensive such project in U.S. history. The initial price tag was $2.6 billion (in 1982 dollars), and it was supposed to be completed in seven years. From the start, it was plagued by leaks, falling debris, delays, and other problems linked to faulty construction. On July 10, 2006, a woman was killed by falling concrete in a connector tunnel.

The Big Dig used enough concrete to build a three-foot-wide sidewalk from Boston to San Francisco and back three times. At its peak, the project had 5,000 construction workers and cost $3 million a day. In 2008, the *Boston Globe* reported that the Big Dig's total cost would hit an astounding $22 billion and will not be paid off until 2038.

That sounds disastrous—and it is. The Big Dig was a classic pork barrel project, with weak oversight, no incentives for achievement, and no innovation in management. But that's the way government programs usually work. That's why we need real change for a smarter, more efficient government.

CHAPTER FIFTEEN

NASA versus the Culture of Competitive Entrepreneurship

O NE OF THE GREAT DISAPPOINTMENTS of my life has been the hijacking of the great space adventure by the NASA bureaucracy. Space should be an area in which American innovation, creativity, and entrepreneurship are producing constant breakthroughs that increase our economic capability, improve our quality of life, and raise our prestige around the world. Instead, space has been hijacked by dull, inefficient, and unimaginative bureaucracies and transformed into an expensive, risk-averse, and sad undertaking. This outcome is a surprising failure and a great disappointment for those of us who grew up in the early days of the great space adventure.

I was in the seventh grade when the Soviets launched Sputnik and shocked Americans by becoming the first to orbit a satellite. Like many young Americans, I began reading *Missiles and Rockets Magazine* (later combined with *Aviation Week*) and devouring everything I could find about space. In 1961 President John F. Kennedy electrified the country when he proposed putting an American on the moon before the end of the decade. Eight years and two months later, we had done it. It was a time of great excitement and boundless optimism.

The combination of the space adventure and President Eisenhower's work to invest in higher education and in math and science led to a tremendous surge of energy in science and engineering. America was making real progress.

And then funds began to be cut, bureaucracies began to emerge, and everything slowed down. After the great adventure of getting to the moon, the NASA bureaucracy took over and began spending more limited funds with more red tape. We went from building and launching to studying and planning. As we did fewer things, we did them less well. When NASA took over running the space shuttle and building the space station, bureaucracies came to infect everything. They even began to spread from the federal government to private sector federal contractors.

Consider the example of Lockheed Martin, NASA's major contractor overseeing the $356.8 million Mars exploration program.

* In 1998–1999, Lockheed underwent five formal investigations alleging mismanagement and an overemphasis on cost-cutting.
* A $1.3 billion spy satellite was destroyed when a Lockheed rocket booster short-circuited and exploded shortly after launch; a $250 million satellite was destroyed when someone left sticky tape on a wiring connector; an $800 million military satellite was destroyed when someone loaded corrupted code into the computer.

* The $265 million Mars Pathfinder crashed due to Lockheed landing technology that was found to be complex, risky, and largely untested.

* The $125 million Mars Climate Orbiter was lost when Lockheed forgot to convert from English to metric units.

* In 2004, the $264 million Lockheed-built Genesis probe crashed into the Utah salt flats because its parachute trigger switches were installed backward. Lockheed skipped a critical pre-launch test that would have uncovered the fatal flaw.

How was Lockheed punished for these failures? In 2006, the company was awarded a new $7.5 billion contract to build NASA's next manned lunar spaceships. This choice was surprising given Lockheed's troubles and the fact that it has no experience with manned space flight. NASA passed on a competing bid from Northrop Grumman/Boeing, which had successfully built the Apollo, Gemini, and Mercury capsules, Skylab, and the space shuttle.

I am not picking on Lockheed Martin. There could be similar case studies in very expensive failure from other large bureaucratic companies. Part of the problem is that federal procurement is now so bureaucratic and takes so long that only a handful of companies can even apply. These cumbersome, bureaucratic companies can match the federal government's expertise in red tape. What matters is not the quality of their engineering but the quality of their lobbying.

The cost of being a major federal contractor is now so great and the contract timeline is so long that no entrepreneurial, market-oriented company can compete. The result has been a downward spiral: fewer and fewer companies, which become bigger and more bureaucratic, establish a quasi-monopoly on federal space contracting. With fewer competitors and higher costs of entry, the innovation pool has dried up. The solution is to remove NASA from the space transportation business and return it to doing research and investing in radical new technologies. We would not ask the Air Force to run our commercial airlines and we should not ask NASA to run our space line.

Prizes for Space

Americans motivated by incentives and prizes have achieved amazing things. Charles Lindbergh flew from New York to Paris in 1927 for a $25,000 prize. Economic incentives (land and money) led private enterprise to complete the transcontinental railroad dramatically faster than people had thought possible. The air mail subsidy underwrote the growth of the airline industry before World War II.

The $10 million Ansari X Prize was offered for reaching space twice within fourteen days. For a prize of $10 million, various billionaires and other entrepreneurs spent over $200 million. The winning entry spent $20 million to win $10 million.

Anyone who has watched the America's Cup competition knows that people will spend a lot of time and money competing for the prestige and satisfaction that comes from achieving something big.

Despite the motivating potential of prizes, Congress has supported red tape and disapproved of incentives, and the bureaucracies have been equally resistant. NASA's 2008 budget allocates three-hundredths of 1 percent for prizes, called Centennial Challenges. This is one–four thousandth of the total ($4 million out of $17 billion). Sadly, even this paltry amount represents a 60 percent decrease from 2007.

I propose a dramatically bolder approach. NASA currently has plans to spend twenty years getting to Mars at a cost estimated of up to $450 billion. A very significant amount of that time and money will be spent studying, planning, and thinking. We would get much further much faster if we simply established two prizes: a tax-free $5 billion prize for the first permanent lunar base and a tax-free $20 billion prize for the first team to get to Mars and back. A very senior aerospace official told me that these two prizes would accomplish both goals decades before NASA, while saving about $200 billion in projected NASA spending. That would be a 19 to 1 return on the prizes. We could call them the twenty-first-century America's Cup.

Why Prizes Get Things Done

Prizes are powerful because they allow anyone to compete, opening the door to new ideas and new players. In addition, prizes stimulate the imagination and the competitive spirits of many who would never waste their time in a bureaucratic process.

Since World War II we have become deeply committed to a peer-reviewed, lengthy application system of research grants that inherently limits the number of applicants and reduces risk-taking to the level acceptable to the reviewing panel. We should dedicate at least 10 percent of the money in every research field to funding prizes that enable people from outside the field and people with ideas too wild for peer review simply to see if they can get the job done.

It is important to remember that in 1903, when the Smithsonian Institution had an aviation project funded by Congress that attracted some of the best minds of the day, two bicycle mechanics from Dayton, Ohio, invented powered flight while the expensive Smithsonian experiments were crashing into the Potomac. Prizes will lead to more people from wider backgrounds trying more ideas. Some will lead to startling breakthroughs. The American people support the concept of prizes; in American Solutions polls 79 percent support prizes for key breakthroughs.

Private Sector Incentives

It is greatly in America's interest to create a vibrant private sector space system for near-Earth orbit. If we had invested the total cost of the shuttle and the space station in tax incentives for the private sector, we would be far further into space, with much stronger capabilities, with many competing companies, and with an enormous number of new innovations. We should return NASA to funding space science and basic research into fundamental new capabilities and focus on encouraging private sector space entrepreneurship. Three tax breaks could make an immediate difference:

1. Create a twenty-year, tax-free window for any profits from space tourism and space manufacturing. This creates a strong incentive to invest.
2. Create a 50 percent tax credit of up to $50 a year for space tourism raffle tickets. This will get citizens excited about the possibility that they could do what today only government astronauts and very rich people are doing.
3. Permit 100 percent expensing of all investments in private space developments so they can be written off in one year.

These three incentives, combined with a federal regulatory regime for private space travel as permissive as the aviation development rules of the 1920s, would create an explosion of new ideas and new achievements over the next few years. Space could become exciting once again, and as more young people explored science and engineering, breakthroughs in other fields would occur. Two of those fields would no doubt be energy and the environment.

CHAPTER SIXTEEN

Green Conservatism
Is the Real Answer to
Environmental Challenges

THE ENVIRONMENT, BIODIVERSITY, and energy reform are among the most important challenges facing America. For far too long, conservatives have allowed the Left to define the issues with its big-government bureaucracy, trial-lawyer litigation, excessive regulation, and higher tax solutions that not only erode individual freedom, but also do a poor job of protecting the environment. The failure of the Superfund Cleanup program, in which massive amounts of money and time have been absorbed in lawsuits, paperwork, litigation, and bureaucracy instead of encouraging engineers and companies to simply get it done, is a good example.

Instead of offering competitive solutions that fit our values, conservatives have been content with merely opposing the Left's destructive proposals. This passive response allows the Left to posture as the faction that cares about the environment; conservatives wind up seeming anti-environment, anti-biodiversity, and anti-energy reform.

I grew up in a family that cared deeply about nature and spent time in the outdoors. As a young professor at West Georgia College, I taught in the second Earth Day in 1971 and coordinated an interdisciplinary environmental studies program.

It is vitally important that we develop a positive, solution-driven approach within a market-oriented, non-bureaucratic model. This approach, which Terry Maple and I discuss in *A Contract with the Earth*, is called Green Conservatism. However, given that it encompasses values shared by the vast majority of Americans, it could also be called Mainstream Environmentalism.

* 73 percent of Americans believe we can have both a healthy economy and a healthy environment.
* 79 percent of Americans agree that we will solve our environmental problems faster and cheaper with innovation and new technology than with more litigation and more government regulation.
* 72 percent of Americans agree that entrepreneurs are more likely to solve America's energy and environmental problems than bureaucrats.
* 68 percent of Americans agree that we don't need to raise taxes to clean up our environment.
* 79 percent of Americans support giving large financial prizes to companies and individuals who invent new ways to successfully cut pollution.
* 90 percent of Americans support giving tax credits to homeowners and builders who incorporate alternative energy sources in their homes like solar, wind, and geothermal energy.

* 77 percent of Americans support building more oil refineries in America to lower the cost of gas and reduce our dependence on foreign oil.

* 65 percent of Americans support building more nuclear power plants to cut carbon emissions and reduce our dependence on foreign oil.

Green Conservatism combines concern for the environment with concern for freedom and economic growth. It holds that biodiversity and the environment can be better protected by a system that encourages science, technology, entrepreneurship, creativity, and free markets than the Left's system focused on big government, more bureaucrats, more red tape, more litigation, and higher taxes.

Environmental Extremism

In addition to favoring science and innovation over red tape and litigation, we must reject an approach to the environment that relies on apocalyptic warnings. When I was still teaching, *Time* and *Newsweek* worried about the coming Ice Age. Then, when I was a young congressman, there was great concern about nuclear winter. Some leading politicians were convinced that a nuclear war was going to throw so much dust into the atmosphere that the entire planet was going to freeze. Then in the early 1990s, some of the apocalyptic worry shifted to technological change. There was a movement to review all new technologies to save us from danger (and in the process probably stop most innovation in science and technology).

In every instance the danger was apocalyptic, science and technology were major threats, and the free market was hazardous. Big government, big regulation, centralized bureaucratic controls, and higher taxes were the solution.

Former vice president Al Gore wrote in his 1992 book *Earth in the Balance*, "We have tilted so far toward individual rights and so far away from any sense of obligation that it is now difficult to muster an adequate defense of any rights vested in the community at large or the nation— much less rights properly vested in all humankind or in posterity."

It is simply not possible to understand what government mechanism would institute rights vested in "all humankind or in posterity." The danger here is that private property rights and individual liberty could be taken away in favor of some collectivist and non-democratic elite's interpretation of what is needed. The level of power that this would give to international bureaucrats is almost beyond belief.

Anyone who believes in freedom and the uniqueness of American civilization has to ask just who these bureaucrats of international appropriateness are going to be, and what values they will possess. Will they be values shared by you and me?

Knut

The desire for extremism as the basis of environmental activism reaches its illogical absurdity in the case of Knut the polar bear cub. As my first name is Newt and Knut is a variation of the Danish word *Canute*, from which my name is derived, people began sending me articles about the cute baby polar bear that animal rights extremists wanted to kill.

In December 2006, Knut was born in the Berlin Zoo, and his mother refused to take care of him. He was on the verge of starving to death when the keepers intervened and began feeding him by hand. This enraged animal rights extremists, who claimed it was inhumane for Knut to live if he had to be cared for by humans.

According to German animal rights campaigner Frank Albrecht, "The zoo must follow the instincts of nature. In the wild, it would have been left to die. The zoo must kill the bear." According to Wolfram Graf-Rudolf, director of the Aachen Zoo, Knut will "not be a 'real' polar bear. . . . One should have had the courage to put him to sleep much earlier."

Animal rights activists even attempted to force German courts to impose a death sentence for Knut. It is a good thing they didn't: Knut has become a celebrity, and he has drawn record attendance to the Berlin Zoo, enriching the lives of more than a million visitors. Knut has also helped educate people about conservation and the environment. Berlin Zoo director Gerald Uhlich declared, "Knut is a fantastic ambassador," and a new children's book, *Knut: How One Little Polar Bear Captivated the World*, is designed to raise awareness about how humans can help endangered species.

Compared with this kind of extremism, Green Conservatism offers many solutions that are practical, sensible, and rely on incentives, science, and entrepreneurial leadership rather than on bureaucrats, trial lawyers, and red tape.

Examples of Green Conservatism

The Atlanta BeltLine Project is a good example of the local leadership and public-private partnership that can really improve the environment in a very practical way. Led by the Trust for Public Land, a group I worked with very successfully to save the Chattahoochee

River as a recreation area, this project will give Atlanta a twenty-two-mile pattern of parks and trails. These will enhance the environment, improve opportunities for exercise, and improve the health of the people of Atlanta.

Another tremendous example of local leadership in Atlanta is the Atlantic Station project. Developers transformed an abandoned brown field (a massive steel mill) into a very high-value and energy-efficient urban center of work, commerce, and living.

As Terry and I wrote *A Contract with the Earth* on this topic, and American Solutions has a series of workshops on Green Conservatism available online, I will not go deeper into it here. In the next chapter, I will emphasize one aspect of the environment that is urgent: the need for an energy strategy that meets economic, environmental, and national security needs.

CHAPTER SEVENTEEN

Energy Strategies for National Security, the Environment, and the Economy

THE UNITED STATES VERY BADLY needs a strategy for energy. Energy is at the heart of modern economies, but we have accepted an energy policy that makes us dependent on foreign dictators, does unnecessary damage to the environment, and creates a danger for our economy. America needs an energy strategy that will pass this three-part test: create jobs and an even more productive economy for the future; marginalize the oil dictators; and protect the environment.

Those on the left who would rely on pain to force change will create a weaker economy with a lower standard of living. For example, in the middle of a recession the Obama administration is already talking about imposing a new energy tax in the form of a cap-and-trade system for carbon. A strategy relying on energy taxes, government regulations, control by bureaucracies, and litigation by trial lawyers will inherently fail to meet the three-part test.

Furthermore, a pain-based energy strategy will inevitably fail on a worldwide basis because neither China nor India nor any other developing country will place the environment ahead of economic development. Their own populations are demanding such dramatic improvements in their standard of living that any government that deliberately slowed its rate of development for environmental reasons would risk serious unrest at home. As the largest of our environmental concerns, global climate change and biodiversity are inherently worldwide challenges, and it is vital to develop an energy strategy that can be adopted by China, India, and other countries.

Incentives

The American experience proves again and again that a market-oriented approach that encourages entrepreneurs to use new science and new technology creates more progress than any other system. It is no accident that the Declaration of Independence and the *Wealth of Nations* were both written in 1776. Adam Smith's understanding of freedom and the moral basis of freedom (his earlier work, *The Theory of Moral Sentiments*, discusses the moral framework within which markets are supposed to operate) is remarkably compatible with that of the American Founding Fathers.

Alexander Hamilton—aide to General Washington during the Revolutionary War, coauthor of the *Federalist Papers*, and first secretary of the treasury—understood that with incentives a market could achieve remarkable things. His "Report on Manufactures" and "First Report on Public Credit" are models of the principles of market-based economic development. In many ways we live in the inventive, productive economy he envisioned more than two hundred years ago.

In the American tradition of progress through technology, Robert Fulton invented the steamboat in 1807, but we did not have laws punishing the sailing ship. The federal government offered huge incentives to get the transcontinental railroad built, but we did not punish stagecoach companies. Henry Ford invented the mass-produced automobile, but we did not tax buggy makers out of existence. The Wright brothers invented the airplane, and the government subsidized the rise of modern airlines through the air mail postal contracts, but we did not tax the long-distance passenger railroad out of existence.

Scientific Breakthroughs

The America that works focuses on inventing a better future and knows that customers will rapidly switch to a better solution. The same will be true for a new energy strategy. We need very large prizes for fundamental breakthroughs. There ought to be a billion-dollar tax-free prize for the first hydrogen car that can be mass-produced for a reasonable price. Hydrogen has to be the ultimate basis for a truly bold energy program because it has no environmental impact and it is universally available as a natural resource. Therefore it would have huge appeal to China and India if it were commercially competitive in price. American technologies for hydrogen vehicles might be one of the biggest economic winners of the next generation.

There should be a substantial tax break for investing in both ethanol and hydrogen supply stations and hydrogen pipelines so the fuel can be delivered when the automobiles are available at a reasonable cost.

There ought to be a tax credit for the auto companies to retool in favor of composite materials manufacturing, which will radically lower the weight of cars and improve gas mileage. UPS has ordered experimental composite delivery vans that reduce weight by 2,000 pounds and increase mileage by 30 percent. Some have estimated that composite materials combined with a hybrid E-85 engine could produce a vehicle that could run for 500 to 1,000 miles on a gallon of petroleum.

There ought to be a tax break for trading in old cars that use a lot of petroleum and emit a lot of pollution. This would help the poor, help the environment, and help the auto industry.

A significant part of the future will be in renewable fuels both in the biofuel world and in solar, wind, and geothermal power. Some of this is a function of new science, such as cellulosic ethanol, which turns all organic material into a potential source of fuel. We must also demand continuous improvement in engineering, such as cheaper, more efficient solar cells, making them more competitive as an electricity source. The future also depends on regulatory decisions, such as getting wind power from South Dakota to Chicago through currently nonexistent power lines.

Nuclear Power

If we are serious about reducing the amount of carbon we are putting in the atmosphere, another part of the solution has to be nuclear power. If America produced as big a share of electricity from nuclear power as France does (78 percent), we would be keeping more than two billion tons of carbon a year out of the atmosphere. That is 15 percent better than the Kyoto Treaty goal in one decision, and would be a 37 percent reduction below current emissions. One of our greenest states, Vermont, actually gets 72.5 percent of its electricity from nuclear power.

With a handful of key steps toward a simple, stable regulatory regime for a new generation of ultra-safe nuclear reactors, it should be possible to build a dramatically better future for the environment and for domestic energy production through nuclear power. Nuclear power has an additional bonus in that nuclear power plants can produce hydrogen for a hydrogen-powered automobile system at night when the electricity grid does not need the power. Thus a significant increase in nuclear technology is also a helpful step toward a hydrogen economy.

Drill Here, Drill Now, Pay Less

In 2008, a spike in world oil prices raised gasoline prices to more than four dollars a gallon for many Americans. Once again, Americans were suffering due to our government's counter-productive anti-energy policies.

In response, American Solutions launched an online petition drive to demand Congress lift the twenty-five-year-old moratorium on new offshore drilling. In just a few short weeks, we collected 1.5 million signatures and presented them to Congress. Our effort sparked a nationwide grassroots rebellion that resulted in the Democratic Congress allowing the offshore drilling moratorium to expire.

Since then oil prices have fallen due to declining demand for oil amidst the global recession. But prices will certainly rise again once the economy recovers, and that may accompany a real energy crunch sparked by numerous factors: there are now efforts to reinstate the offshore drilling ban and to stop any new drilling through frivolous lawsuits; drilling is still banned in key parts of Alaska; and new drilling projects are still being stymied in Colorado, where we have more oil than exists in Saudi Arabia.

I wrote a book in fall 2008 called *Drill Here, Drill Now, Pay Less* and hosted, along with my wife Callista, a DVD documentary called *We Have the Power.* Both projects describe America's vast energy potential and explain how misguided government policies have prevented us from becoming an energy powerhouse.

It is possible to have a dramatically better energy system for the environment, the economy, and national security, and we should insist that the federal government adopt an aggressive strategy to get there.

CHAPTER EIGHTEEN

The Next Generation of Air and Rail Transportation

IF YOU WONDER WHY YOUR GOVERNMENT doesn't work for you the way the private sector does, why bureaucracies take care of themselves rather than you—the customer, the taxpayer—one very big reason is the government employee unions and their union rules. The problem of the Democrats supporting these unions and their unreasonable demands goes beyond the waste of your tax dollars and the debt we're piling on our children and grandchildren. It brings waste, inefficiency, and abuse to everything government touches.

Consider the case of transportation. As the leading economy in the world, America should have the best air and rail transportation in the world, but we don't.

Flying the Not-So-Friendly Skies

Think about how unreformed unions make real change impossible next time you're at the airport and find your plane is delayed by hours.

The current air traffic control system uses analog radar technology from the 1950s. Radar takes anywhere from three to twelve seconds accurately to read the position of an airplane. This necessitates the FAA to require at least a 1,000-foot vertical separation between planes and three to five miles horizontally. In addition, it has been known to mistake puddles on runways for airplanes.

The result of languishing in such an obsolete system while the demand for air travel continues to increase is dramatic:

* In the first nine months of 2007, the average on-time arrival rate at the nation's thirty-two busiest airports dropped from 76.1 percent in 2006 to 73.2 percent. This was before the Thanksgiving and Christmas holiday rush.
* The chances of being bumped from a flight also increased dramatically. The nation's largest carriers bumped scheduled passengers at a rate of .99 per every 10,000 fliers in the first nine months of 2007, up from .7 in 2006.

A new system, called NextGen, that uses global positioning satellites has been proposed and has received initial funding. It determines the position of aircraft once per second, relaying that information to all other airplanes and traffic control. This would allow planes to fly closer together while increasing safety and would boost the capacity of our airways by about 40 percent. It would eliminate nearly all delays, except for those caused by the weather. It would mean more efficient airlines, using less fuel, having higher profits and higher wages, and offering better service at lower costs.

We can see the potential of more accurate positioning systems in several airports that have begun to implement only modest improvements. Hartsfield-Jackson Atlanta International Airport is the world's busiest airport, yet has managed to buck the national trends of decreased on-time arrivals. In 2007, 74.7 percent of flights arrived on time in Hartsfield, compared with 72.4 percent in 2006, and 69.9 percent in 2005. Hartsfield achieved this by maximizing the use of new runway capacity with area navigation technology, which enables planes to navigate along more precise, predictable routes. This has allowed air traffic controllers to introduce another arrival path into the busy airport.

Houston's Bush Intercontinental is another example of how improved positioning technology opens up room for greater capacity. The number of passengers at Bush is steadily increasing, with an additional ten million a year expected by 2015. Still, the arrival time is above the national average at 78 percent, and it actually improved in 2007 even as traffic increased. Rick Vacar, aviation director for the Houston airport system, is optimistic that Bush Intercontinental can keep up its comparatively high level of service despite increased demand. He has said that thanks to new technology that allows for more precise flight paths, the airport can build a new runway between two existing ones.

In addition, portions of Alaska have been using a global positioning system for years due to spotty radar coverage. The FAA reports that since the system was implemented, the fatal accident rate for general aviation has fallen by approximately 40 percent.

Unfortunately, the air traffic controller union understands that a twenty-first-century space-based air traffic control system would reduce the importance and number of air traffic controllers, with initial estimates that the FAA would eliminate about half of its 398 costly radar installations during the switchover to NextGen.

Despite the existing evidence that improved positioning technology increases capacity while improving safety, Patrick Forrey, president of the

National Air Traffic Controllers Association, has said, "It won't do a thing for delays," blaming lack of landing space (which a new system would increase through better use of the existing space) and over-scheduling by the airlines. However, over-scheduling is simply a result of the dramatically increasing demand, and unless a new system is implemented to increase capacity, customers will be met by equally increasing prices. Much like the firemen on trains demanding jobs long after the move to diesel engines had eliminated all work for them, the air traffic controller union opposes improving your travel so that they can continue in an antiquated system. That prices would increase severely without the new system is a secondary concern next to their job security.

And guess who is blocking legislation to modernize the nation's air traffic control system? That's right, the Democrats in Congress, at the behest of the controllers' union. A government program that would work would buy out the surplus air traffic controllers, offer them technical retraining, and encourage them to find new jobs. What we can't do is what the union-controlled Democrats would have us do: remain in an obsolete system to keep government bureaucrats working unnecessarily at great cost to everyone else in America.

At American Solutions we have launched a project to transition our air traffic control system rapidly to NextGen within four years. You can get more details about this project at www.americansolu-tions.com/travelasap.

Amtrak and the Restraints on High-Speed Rail

We should have an amazing rail network in the United States, but we don't. By contrast, in France, high-speed rail captures half the market share on journeys of four and a half hours or less. On routes with two hours or less of train travel time, it wins 90 percent of the market share. Of course, the French have made substantial investments in creating high-speed rail corridors. The Japanese have made similar investments in what they call bullet trains. The Chinese are now following their lead and will presently have more high-speed rail than any other country in the world.

The United States has three corridors that are very conducive to this kind of high-speed train investment. We could build a system between Boston and Washington; from Miami to Tampa, Orlando, and Jacksonville; and from San Diego to San Francisco.

There are three problems with trying to build high-speed systems in the United States and, not surprisingly, all three relate to government. First, union work rules make it impossible, at least if Amtrak has anything to do with it. Second, pork barrel politicians waste money subsidizing absurdly uneconomic routes. (In some cases, we could give away free airline tickets to every rail passenger and we would save money because the subsidy is so massive.) Third, the regulations and litigation involved in large-scale construction in the United States have become time-consuming and expensive. (It took twenty-three years to add a fifth runway to the Atlanta airport, for example.)

Some of the facts about Amtrak are beyond discouraging. It is a case study of how bureaucracy, political pork, and unions fail the public. Consider these facts:

* Amtrak's debt is more than $3.5 billion, and its operating loss for 2005 topped $550 million. For the 2006 fiscal year, Congress approved $1.3 billion in Amtrak subsidies.
* Amtrak has never made money in its thirty-five-year history.
* Amtrak officials estimate union restrictions cost the railroad about $100 million a year.

* Every ticket on Amtrak receives an average federal subsidy of $53, and some routes are subsidized at more than $500 per ticket.

* The Amtrak inspector general recently found that for every $1 in food and beverage sales, Amtrak incurred more than $2 in expenses. According to the inspector general, Amtrak also pays its food service workers 3.5 times the average restaurant industry wage.

I support—and I'm confident that most Americans support—a twenty-first-century rail system that is privately built, run efficiently, and capable of earning its own way. Clearly such a system would require a government grant of authority for construction and might even require an initial program of tax incentives or other help (just as the transcontinental railroad did). But it just makes sense that we the people of the United States should have a railroad system that works for us, and not for the Amtrak bureaucracy and their unions. At a minimum—or for non-high-speed corridors—we should turn railroad lines over to the states, and thereby cut at least one level out of the bureaucracy. But don't expect a solution like that to originate from a Democratic party dominated by unreformed unions.

CHAPTER NINETEEN

The Need for Fundamental Prison Reform

IT IS IMPOSSIBLE TO DISCUSS THE CHALLENGES of the inner city without recognizing the devastating effect crime, violence, drugs, and prison have on a large number of young Americans. In some parts of the country we now see third- and fourth-generation prisoners. In some neighborhoods, going to jail is a sign of status. Prison has become a part of life for many poor Americans, especially poor American males and most especially poor African American males.

Prisons have become nightmares of illegality and brutality, with gang domination, gang rapes, drug trafficking, degrading conditions, and an astounding lack of control. If we can't control people under lock and key, why do we think we can control them after their release?

As a result of the "warehouse" prison model, we have created generations of hardened criminals who are comfortable in prison culture and aliens in law-abiding society. Clearly something fundamental must be changed.

Amazingly, there are glimmers of real hope for a breakthrough in dealing with criminals and preparing them to reenter society as honest citizens with chances for decent futures. Two of the greatest breakthroughs have been Prison Fellowship's InnerChange Freedom Initiative and the America Works program. While they are significantly different in design, each of these approaches has had a positive effect on prisoners.

Prison Fellowship's Inner-Change Freedom Initiative

The Prison Fellowship program creates a faith-based center of commitment and activity aimed at changing the prisoner's outlook on life. Its results have been impressive. Recently conducted research on the graduates of Prison Fellowship's InnerChange Freedom Initiative (IFI) in Texas found that they were two times less likely to be rearrested compared to inmates with similar backgrounds and offenses who had not participated in IFI (17.3 percent to 35 percent). IFI graduates were two and a half times less likely to be reincarcerated. The two-year post-release reincarceration rate among IFI program graduates in Texas is 8 percent, compared with 20.3 percent of the comparison group.

These findings present significant implications for our communities. Fred Becker, the first warden at IFI in Texas, noted, "All but 1,000 of Texas's 143,000 prisoners have an eventual release date. It's up to us to determine what kind of shape they come back to the world in. If we can stop only 10 percent of those inmates from reoffending, it will mean thousands of citizens who never become victims of crime. InnerChange is a step in that direction."

IFI promotes five goals for successful rehabilitation:

* willingness to condemn previous behavior
* recognition that life is a "work in progress" and that spiritual growth is a lifelong process
* replacement of the values of prison society with something more worthwhile
* development of a sense of hope and purpose
* recognition of the need to give back to society

You don't have to believe in the power of faith to appreciate the benefits IFI provides to the community: fewer victims, safer neighborhoods, reduced court cases, and fewer prisoners. In an editorial titled "Jesus Saves," the *Wall Street Journal* wrote, "Critics of the faith-based approach may claim that their only issue is with religion. But if these results are any clue, increasingly the argument against such programs requires turning a blind eye to science."

The American Psychological Association recently reported that "among people recovering from substance abuse, a new study finds that higher levels of religious faith and spirituality were associated with several positive mental health outcomes, including more optimism about life and higher resilience to stress, which may help contribute to the recovery process."

One study of religion's effect on rehabilitation found that religious programs combat the negative effects of prison culture and that religious volunteers are a largely untapped resource available and willing to administer educational, vocational, and treatment services at little or no cost.

The National Center on Addiction and Substance Abuse at Columbia University released a two-year study finding that "tapping the power of religion and spirituality has enormous potential for lowering the risk of substance abuse among teens and adults and, when combined with professional treatment, for promoting recovery."

In another study, the Templeton Foundation funded a four-year recidivism research project by the National Institute of Healthcare Research. After studying inmates in four New York prisons, the Institute concluded that prisoners who attended ten or more Prison Fellowship programs each year were 64 percent less likely to return to prison than other inmates.

It is remarkable that even though these results reflect the potential saving of countless lives over the next generation, many government officials find a faith-based solution unacceptable. They would rather have people commit more crimes and do more prison time than risk changing their lives with a faith-based approach.

America Works

America Works is a unique social services institution based on the profit motive. It helps move people from welfare to work. It was first made possible under New York governor Mario Cuomo. He wanted to apply the profit motive to the social sector to see if it could produce better results than the bureaucratic civil servant model that has dominated government since the 1880s.

America Works works. It is that simple. The program had an amazing track record of moving the hard-core unemployed from welfare to work. They worked closely with hard-to-serve populations and recognized that helping them solve problems was the key to their own success. The result was a remarkably high percentage of successful long-term transition from welfare to work.

In many ways America Works was the single most important model for the 1996 welfare reform bill, which moved 65 percent of welfare recipients into education or a job. Now America Works has begun to focus on helping prisoners reenter the job market with new attitudes and new reliability.

As the America Works president Dr. Lee Bowes explains:

> We currently are doing prison to work programs in New York, Oakland, California, [and] Baltimore, Maryland. We have placed 10,000 [released] prisoners with a 70 percent [job] retention rate at ninety days. We are having a controlled study done on six hundred of the prisoners returning to New York City to establish the extent to which jobs decrease recidivism back to prison. This is a two-year study... and we believe it will arm us with the data to create a revolution similar to welfare reform, where all returning prisoners will be mandated to work immediately upon release. With 675,000 prisoners being released yearly and 67 percent being reincarcerated, committing crimes, and violating parole, the system change is needed. Prison costs in California alone are 9.3 billion dollars and only 3.3 billion is spent on higher education.

Anyone who truly cares for the poorest communities in America has to examine these two models of helping prisoners. We have the power to save hundreds of thousands from reincarceration and to unite families and communities with a bold new approach. No prison should be allowed to operate without one or both of these systems at work. This would be real change, and it would be the right change.

CHAPTER TWENTY

Why the Current Bureaucratic Health System Can't Work and How to Transform It

with Nancy Desmond, president of the Center for Health Transformation

THE CURRENT THIRD-PARTY PAYMENT system for health care is inefficient, ineffective, and fraudulent. It is a classic example of why the buyer-seller model is so much more desirable than the buyer-seller-receiver bureaucratic model, whether public or private.

In the buyer-seller market, the buyer checks out the good or service and decides whether it is worth purchasing at the given price. The seller looks at the offered price, compares it with other offers, and either sells or rejects the offer. In a direct buyer-seller transaction, there is minimum opportunity for fraud and maximum opportunity for satisfaction.

In a buyer-seller-receiver model, the buyer gets nothing of direct value, so he seeks to pay less and to micromanage the seller. The seller knows that the buyer suspects him of fraud or greed or incompetence. And the receiver of the seemingly free good or service has no gratitude because he isn't paying for it. He is never satisfied because he believes the good or service is his right. He always wants more of it, with more convenience and with less accountability and responsibility.

This chapter focuses on the three great side effects of a bureaucratic, government-run health system:

* fraud, leading to financial waste
* lack of choice and control, leading to frustration
* lack of personal responsibility, leading to bad health

Fraud

The more I have studied fraud in government-run health care, the more amazed I have become. Equally amazing has been Congress's unwillingness to fix the fraud and the waste in health care. This is a major opportunity to save money and help balance the budget, yet nothing is done.

Remember that more of your tax dollars are spent on health than on national security. In Washington alone we spent more than $647.2 billion on health in 2006, compared to $521.8 billion for national security. The gap is projected to get bigger and bigger. By 2009 we are expected to spend $737.9 billion on health and $520.7 billion on national security. Not only is the federal government spending more of your tax money on health, but remember that for every state, city, county, and school board, health is a major cost center.

Below are a few examples of the scandals the bureaucratic, government-run health system has produced.

HIV/AIDS Fraud in South Florida

The average beneficiary with HIV/AIDS in South Florida had nine times the average Medicaid claims of beneficiaries in the rest of the county in the second half of 2006, as reported by the Office of the Inspector General for the Department of Health and Human Services. Billing fraud was blamed for the inflated charges.

Miami-Dade, Broward, and Palm Beach counties contain only 10 percent of the nation's Medicaid beneficiaries with HIV/AIDS, but they billed Medicaid for $487 million in the second half of 2006, compared to $489 million in Medicaid billings for patients in the rest of the country. South Florida beneficiaries also took up 79 percent of the billings for infusion drug treatments.

In most geographic areas, the drug claims represented 16 percent of total HIV/AIDS beneficiary charges, but drug claims took up 61 percent of the charges in South Florida. The problem was actually worse in 2005, when the $2.5 billion in HIV/AIDS claims submitted by South Florida providers accounted for 72 percent of the national total.

The discovery of massive fraud in South Florida began when a multi-agency partnership investigated targeted health centers. They hit seventeen centers, finding clinics that had billed that same day, but when the task force arrived, no one was at the clinic, there were no used supplies in the trash, and the space was virtually unused. They immediately filed to revoke most of the licenses. Funny thing is, very few of the clinics challenged the revocations. They just disappeared, likely to open another clinic under another name.

The anti-fraud efforts discovered that schemers in Florida employed amazing ingenuity at getting money from the bureaucracy without doing honest work. One pharmacist compounded his own drugs and then billed Medicaid as if they were name-brand. Dentists drove around in vans or set up shop in warehouses, did not perform any services, and then billed Medicaid.

The key to understanding fraud in third-party payment systems is simple. The bureaucrat enforcing the law is paid a set salary and goes home at five o'clock. The crook who wants your money is willing to work hard and stay after five to perfect schemes to get rich off the taxpayer. In a third-party payment system, the bureaucrat always ends up behind the crook in trying to stop fraud. No place illustrates this better than New York Medicaid.

Medicaid Fraud in New York:
$4.4 Billion a Year of Your Tax Money

The *New York Times*, hardly a critic of big bureaucratic government, ran an amazing series in July 2005 titled "New York Medicaid Fraud May Reach into Billions." Written by Clifford J. Levy and Michael Luo, it told an astonishing story of fraud and corruption. Levy and Luo reported that New York State's Medicaid program had become a "$44.5 billion target for the unscrupulous and the opportunistic." They described dentists like Dr. Dolly Rosen, who "within twelve months somehow built the state's biggest Medicaid dental practice... where she claimed to have performed as many as 991 procedures a day in 2003. Between 2002 and 2005, Dr. Rosen billed taxpayers more than $7 million." They described a Buffalo school official who sent "4,434 students into speech therapy in a single day without talking to them or reviewing their records."

Fraud is not merely a New York problem. Levy and Luo cite the Government Accountability Office's estimation that 10 percent of all health care spending nationally is lost to fraud and abuse. That number, if accurate, would suggest that more than $60 billion a year, nearly a trillion dollars over the next decade, is wasted on fraud and abuse in a bureaucratic system that can never catch up with the crooks.

The *Times* applied this to New York. James Mehmet, who retired in 2001 as chief state investigator of Medicaid fraud and abuse in New

York City, said he and his colleagues believed that at least 10 percent of state Medicaid dollars were spent on fraudulent claims, while 20 or 30 percent more were siphoned off by what they termed abuse, meaning unnecessary spending that might not be criminal. "So we're talking about 40 percent of all claims are questionable," Mehmet said, "an amount that would approach $18 billion a year."

If that figure were true, the amount wasted in government health spending would be in the $250 billion a year range and climbing. With current projections it would suggest we will spend at least $3 trillion of tax money on fraud and abuse in bureaucratic health care over the next decade.

Part of what made the New York experience so interesting was the power of the special interests to protect themselves and the unwillingness of the bureaucracy to follow up on leads. As the *Times* reported: "The investigation found audits on Medicaid spending that were brushed aside, and reports on waste that appear to have been shelved. There have been multiple warnings from watchdog agencies in New York and in Washington that indicate that the program is becoming increasingly porous. Prosecutors said state regulators had all but lost interest in bringing Medicaid thieves to justice, preferring instead to focus on recouping money through a few civil cases that have little deterrent value."

While I often complain about the *New York Times* editorial page, I have to commend them on this extraordinary series on a scale of fraud that is stunning and continues to this day.

It is inherent in a third-party payment system that those receiving the money will conclude the system can be gamed for their personal profit. These problems do not exist only in Florida and New York, but those are certainly classic case studies.

The far greater problem with third-party payment bureaucracies is the degree to which they fail to provide personal choice, and by their rules and regulations slow down innovation and creativity.

Personal Choice: The Power of Markets and the Creativity of Entrepreneurs

The great strength of markets over bureaucracies is that they empower two people who are controlled and limited by bureaucrats: the consumer and the creative entrepreneur. In a bureaucracy, a third party—the bureaucrat—decides on a set of abstract rules that are supposed to control both the buyer and the seller. But no bureaucracy can ever know all the values the purchaser considers at the time of purchase. Those values change constantly: One day you value convenience and saving time. Another day you value efficiency and saving money. On a third day you want to slow down and enjoy a luxury because it is a day to celebrate. No bureaucracy can know all the possible values for every individual.

Markets create environments in which buyers can register their values and the prices they are prepared to pay for them. Equally important, markets create environments in which a new creative entrepreneur can show up and offer a better solution. In contrast, bureaucracies control the buyer and limit the seller. Bureaucracies are inherently anti-innovation and anti-change. No bureaucracy could have invented the fax machine or the iPod. Yet individual preferences for those breakthroughs led to their rapid absorption in the free market.

We know that markets work. We use them in sports, in higher education, in housing, in shopping, in entertainment. (Ironically, left-wing

Hollywood is one of the most commercially competitive and ruthless markets in the world.) We have this strange cultural schizophrenia: we love being customers with incentives, bargains, and choices in the world that works, yet we drop all those values to become passive clients in the world that fails.

How Third-Party Bureaucracies Undermine Personal Responsibility

The deepest and most destructive impact of the third-party bureaucratic system on health is that it shifts responsibility and authority away from the individual and onto other people. In a third-party bureaucratic system, the buyer (the insurance company) pays for the receiver (the patient) and someone else (a doctor) provides a good or service. The patient is essentially passive, and becomes dependent on the insurance bureaucracy to define how he can get care. Then he becomes dependent on the doctor to provide the service the bureaucracy has agreed to pay for. He gets into the habit of waiting for someone besides himself to do something to make him healthy. To make this problem even worse, the doctor who is being paid to take care of the patient grows to expect him to be hopelessly passive.

If America is going to have a healthy future, we need to stress prevention, wellness, early detection, and self-management. Such a future is possible, but it requires recentering the system on the individual responsibility of the patient. That requires a shift away from bureaucratic third-party payment models toward individual accountability and empowerment. This shift could save lives and save money.

A Twenty-First-Century, Personalized, Intelligent Health System

Compare your experiences with the world that works to your experience in health care. It is nearly impossible to find information about cost and quality of treatments, procedures, or providers before you select them. The system remains largely paper-based when nearly every other area of life is electronic. In most cases, it is impossible to access your own medical record or transport it when you change providers. The system also prevents you and your physician from being able to use a database of information to determine the best treatments and avoid many preventable errors.

The result of our health care system's failure to change with the times has had costly and tragic consequences:

* According to the Institute of Medicine, as many as 98,000 people die in hospitals due to medical errors every year.
* In 2003, the Agency for Healthcare Research and Quality estimated that our failure to adopt health information technology is costing America $100 billion and tens of thousands of lives annually.
* Hurricane Katrina was a disastrous reminder of what our failure to create a twenty-first-century, personalized, intelligent health system can cost, as more than a million paper health records were lost at the very time they were most needed.
* The FDA recently reported that approximately 90,000 Americans each year acquire potentially deadly infections, more than half of them the result of treatment in hospitals or other parts of our health care system.

Rather than reforming the current system of health care, we need a transformation to a new twenty-first-century system. We need a new system based on the values of the world that works rather than the world that fails. Many of these values are captured in our Health Values posted at the Center for Health Transformation's Solutions Lab (See Appendix 5).

In a twenty-first-century, personalized, intelligent health system, individuals have accurate, timely, personalized knowledge about their health and treatment options, including information about cost and quality. They have the assurance that their treatment is based on the most up-to-date evidence-based medicine, and there is a focus on preventive care and early intervention. The system encourages and rewards wise health care purchasing decisions and offers more choices of higher quality at lower cost.

A key test for any new system is its ability to provide affordable access to quality care for the poorest and sickest among us. The elimination of health disparities must be a critical goal: no American can be left out. The new system has many characteristics, which can be distilled into three major components.

Component One: Centered on the Individual

Putting individuals at the center of the system requires that they be given the incentives, the information, and the power to make wise choices. However, in the twentieth-century system we inherited, individuals seldom have information about cost or quality, have no financial incentives for wise consumption, and generally have decisions made for them.

Starting with the decision in 1943 to go to a third-party system, we've turned health care into a rental car. The problem is, almost no one washes a rental car. And almost no one feels personally responsible for their own health in the current system.

The Right to Know

The current health care system is absurdly secretive. Americans typically have little opportunity to compare the cost and quality of the various health services, products, or providers they are considering. This situation is tantamount to asking someone to shop for a car when the dealer hides the prices, rolls back the odometers, and does not disclose that his lot is filled with a fleet of rental cars.

Some opponents of making health care quality and cost information transparent argue that the infrastructure and variants to create and maintain this system are unrealistic. Some insist that people cannot be trusted to make these kinds of decisions themselves, yet Americans have grown to rely on electronic systems for many marketplace transactions: ATMs, online shopping, and online travel services are a few examples.

With recent research indicating that 93 percent of the American people believe they have the right to know cost and quality information, we are beginning to see some progress in the sharing of information, even in government. Medicare recently began posting the prices it pays for common medical procedures. Our hope is that in the near future, Medicare beneficiaries—and all other health care consumers—will have the right to know not only the cost but also the quality of the physicians and hospitals they use.

While the vast majority of states hide the cost and quality data they collect, there are some exceptions. Former Florida governor Jeb Bush and his head of the Agency for Health Care Administration, Alan Levine, made Florida the first state in the country openly to report a wide range of cost and quality measures for hospitals and outpatient facilities. FloridaCompareCare.gov has a wealth of information on everything from hospital infection and mortality rates to the cost and frequency of surgical procedures. Knowing which hospitals have the highest and lowest death rates—and the highest and lowest prices— allows the consumer to choose the best-performing, highest-value hospital. What surprises many is that high quality and low price often go hand in hand. By shining a light on the poorest-performing hospitals and outpatient facilities, Governor Bush and his team created a way to save lives and save money for all Floridians.

A second Web site, MyFloridaRx.com, further promotes the consumer's right to know by providing retail pricing information for the fifty most commonly used prescription drugs in Florida. This site helps consumers get the most for their money. A quick search of one ZIP code in Miami shows that, in the case of one drug, the cost of thirty pills ranges from $91 in one location to $220 in another.

Personal Responsibility

In a twenty-first-century, personalized, intelligent health system, patients have certain rights, including the right to be assured that their providers practice the best standards of care. Patients also have responsibilities.

First, individuals are expected to inform themselves and use that knowledge to make wise decisions. It would be futile for us to provide information about cost and quality if people don't use it. Former Health and Human Services secretary Mike Leavitt has a great personal story about shopping around for a colonoscopy. After calling two doctors in the Washington, D.C., area to ask how much the total bill would be, he was astounded to learn that one wanted $6,750 and the other $5,750 for the exact same procedure. He then called Inter-mountain Healthcare in his home state of Utah and found that he would be charged $3,300. Secretary Leavitt, assuming that there must be something wrong with the Utah procedure, researched it and found that it was at least as good as the other two. By shopping around he was able to save $3,450 for the exact same procedure of at least equal quality. After checking best airline prices, he found that he and his wife could fly to Utah for the procedure for a price still under the D.C. estimates. Not only were they able to save thousands of dollars, they were also able to take a trip to visit their family. Incidentally, if he had wanted to undergo the treatment as an outpatient, the procedure in Salt Lake City would have cost him only $950.

Second, individuals have a personal responsibility to engage in (and encourage their children or family to engage in) healthy behaviors, related to both nutrition and exercise, that are proven to prevent ill-nesses and complications. If they develop a chronic illness, they are expected to learn and follow best standards of care to avoid costly complications.

One fascinating wellness program is provided by Healthways, whose myhealthIQ health risk management program gives financial rewards based on quantifiable, improved biometrics. Employees par-ticipate in a wellness assessment and receive a myhealthIQ score. They then receive ongoing online and telephonic coaching, followed by retesting and financial rewards at the end of twelve months if they have raised their score or maintained a healthy score. One large employer reported 83 percent employee participation, resulting in a 52 percent reduction in the number of employees considered to be at extreme risk and a 47 percent reduction in those at high risk.

In addition to preventing disease through programs like myhealthIQ, health management companies can also have an amazing impact on improving the health of people with chronic diseases. Consider asthma, which costs the nation an estimated $14 billion per year and is the leading diagnosis for hospital admissions. Matria Healthcare uses a team of respiratory nurses to provide telephonic education, constant monitoring, and other educational intervention to ensure compliance with physician orders. The result has been a 27 percent decrease in emergency room visits, a 38 percent reduction in hospitalizations, and a reduction of overall costs per month per member of 15 percent.

Prevention, early detection, and good self-management are part of the twenty-first-century focus on health as opposed to health care. While others can develop the tools and provide the lessons, individuals must apply them to their own lives.

Third, individuals are expected to help pay for their care. Everyone should be required to have coverage. Those with very low incomes should receive vouchers or tax credits to help them buy insurance. Those who oppose the concept of insurance should be required to post a bond to cover costs. Allowing individuals to pass their health costs onto others reinforces the attitude that their health is not their problem and adds to the irresponsible, unhealthy behaviors that bankrupt the current system.

Personalized Health and Health Care

A twenty-first-century, individual-centered system will be a personalized system of health, resulting in dramatically better health for everyone. Imagine a future where genetic tests will tell you which specific diseases or conditions to which you are most susceptible can be prevented with lifestyle modifications and medicines. Consider a world where you know that health and treatment regimens are designed specifically for your individual make-up.

We are already seeing glimpses of how the future of medicine is likely to change as we move toward a more personalized system. Not long ago, there was a story about a drug that scientists learned, in reviewing years of data, had a stunning impact on preventing heart attacks in African American males. This was not the original purpose of the drug, and the drug had no such impact on white males. In a twenty-first-century intelligent system, we will be able to recognize these patterns much more quickly and share them more widely. By preventing illnesses, we will save lives and money.

We now know that genetic variations, lifestyle, and the environment play important roles in illnesses like type 2 diabetes. As a result, it is important to understand what carrying a genetic risk variant for a disease means, and how that information can help keep a predisposition from developing into a disease.

Today you can send a saliva or blood sample through the mail and have it analyzed to determine your likelihood of developing specific diseases like type 2 diabetes or of having a stroke or heart attack. Physicians are already using such information to deliver more effective, personalized treatment regimens to their patients. Drug companies are already planning for an era of personalized medicine, in which genetic information is used to determine which individuals will respond better or worse to a drug and is also used in developing new drugs. All this is just a preview of a twenty-first-century system of personalized health that will dramatically change the future.

Component Two:
Information Technology and Quality

A personalized system of health is impossible without an IT-based system. The system must allow easy but secure sharing, analysis, and use of information about health and health history and about the cost, quality, and outcomes of treatments.

We not only have to transform for the future, but we also have to transform to catch up with the last thirty years. Consider gas stations with credit card–enabled pumps, e-tickets, and cell phones—and compare those to the paper-based nature of our health care system.

The difference between health care and other sectors of society when it comes to information technology is dramatic. And it has had a dramatic impact on the lives—and deaths—of many Americans.

Paper Kills

Paper kills. It is that simple. Instead of saving lives, our current paper system is often taking them. With as many as 98,000 Americans dying as a result of medical errors in hospitals every year, ridding the system of paper-based records and quickly adopting health information technology will save lives and money.

But getting physicians and other clinicians to adopt IT has proven to be a Herculean task. A 2005 study by the Centers for Disease Control and Prevention concluded that only 31 percent of hospital emergency departments and 17 percent of doctors' offices have electronic health records to support patient care.

Each day we refuse to move from a paper-based to an electronic system, people are dying needlessly. This is not just conjecture—health information technology's tremendous potential to save lives and money is real and is happening in some of the most forward-looking practices and transformational institutions in our country. Here are two examples:

* Indiana Heart Hospital in Indianapolis reduced medication errors by 85 percent with the completion of a new paperless facility. At the same time, implementation of health IT helped reduce physician administrative time by 30 percent, allowing doctors to spend more time with patients.
* The Central Utah Multi-Specialty Clinic, the largest multi-specialty group in the state, implemented an electronic medical record system provided by Allscripts Healthcare Solutions. During a one-year study, the clinic experienced spending reductions/revenue increases amounting to more than $952,000 over the previous year, and it anticipates savings of about $14 million over the next five years.

E-Prescribing

Doctors write billions of handwritten prescriptions every year. More than 150 million require a call from the pharmacist to the doctor, usually for one of three reasons: the pharmacist cannot read the writing, the drug is not compatible with another drug the patient is taking, or the pharmacist wants to substitute a drug so the patient's insurance will cover it. It is an enormous waste of time and resources on a correctable problem. But more important, written prescriptions kill people. The evidence is overwhelming. Medication errors contribute to more than 7,000 deaths annually, exceeding those resulting from workplace accidents. According to a report by the Institute for

Safe Medication Practices, medication errors could be cut by 55 percent if physicians switched to electronic prescriptions.

Electronic prescriptions are also proven to increase efficiency. A study by Tufts Health Plan found that electronic prescribing saved two hours a day per physician. In addition, the technology helped doctors improve patient safety in several ways: it made prescriptions more legible, it revealed potential drug interactions, and it let doctors know whether patients had been refilling their prescriptions on time.

E-prescribing and electronic health records are only two areas in which we have been slow to adopt health IT, despite the existence of proof that it saves both lives and money. Even bar coding, which has been used in grocery stores for decades, is relatively simple, and has been proven to be dramatically successful in preventing drug errors in hospitals, has been adopted only by about 50 percent of American hospitals. While some providers resist new technologies and cling to paper records, many claim they would like to switch but that the financial costs often put this out of reach. Furthermore, the lack of interoperability, referring to the inability of various technologies to "talk to each other" or integrate with other technologies, increases buyer hesitancy.

Component Three: Health, Not Health Care

The need to transform the current system from an acute care-focused system to one of prevention and early detection is evident. Heart disease, the leading cause of death for both men and women in the United States, accounted for nearly 700,000 deaths in 2002. In 2005, heart disease was projected to cost $393 billion. It is the leading cause of death for American Indians, Alaska Natives, blacks, Hispanics, and whites. More than 300,000 people have bypass surgery in the United States each year.

Heart disease and its complications can be prevented. Among people with heart disease, studies have shown that lowering cholesterol and blood pressure can reduce the risk of dying of heart disease, having a non-fatal heart attack, and needing heart bypass surgery or angioplasty. For people without heart disease, studies have shown that lowering high blood cholesterol and high blood pressure can reduce the risk of developing heart disease in the first place. A system focused on prevention rather than on acute care would provide the incentives and policies to support lifestyle changes needed to control cholesterol and blood pressure. A culture of physical activity and healthy diet choices would replace the current epidemic of inactivity and fattening food.

The increased incidence of diabetes is another example of the impact of a health care system focused on acute care and not prevention. Type 2 diabetes can be prevented. According to Frank Vinicor of the Centers for Disease Control, "Recent studies have shown that people with pre-diabetes can successfully prevent or delay the onset of diabetes by losing 5 to 7 percent of their body weight. This can be accomplished through thirty minutes or more of physical activity most days of the week and by following a low-calorie, low-fat plan, including a diet rich in whole grains and fruits and vegetables."

Diabetes complications can be prevented through control of blood glucose, blood pressure, and blood lipids and by receiving other preventive care practices like eye exams and foot checks. In fact, every percentage point drop in the results of the A1C blood test (used to measure a person's average blood sugar level over two to three months) reduces the risk of microvascular complications (eye, kidney, and nerve diseases) by 40 percent.

However, our current system, by providing reimbursement for volume of care rather than outcomes, discourages the type of care that prevents diabetes complications and acute episodes. One diabetes clinic managed the health of its patients so well that it was forced to close because it did not receive enough reimbursement. In other words, by keeping its patients healthier, the clinic forced itself out of business. This is further evidence that the twentieth-century system we have inherited is measuring and rewarding the wrong things.

The same mindset is evident when it comes to the willingness of the system to pay for technologies and discoveries to keep us healthy. Using diabetes again as an example, our tendency is to pay for dialysis or amputations but to refuse to pay for the education, the tools, or often the medications that can prevent these costly and tragic consequences.

A system that takes advantage of twenty-first-century opportunities will be able to provide a whole new range of technologies, tools, and screening mechanisms. People will stay healthier, avoid or delay many illnesses, and manage illnesses they do develop. Yet the system must also have the mechanisms to pay for, disseminate, and deliver information.

Drivers and Strategies

Moving from where we are today to the twenty-first-century, personalized, intelligent health system will depend on five major drivers:

1. Science: There will be four to seven times as much new scientific knowledge in the next twenty-five years as in the last twenty-five years. This level of change will create both opportunities and challenges. There will be no way for physicians to keep

up with the constantly churning breakthroughs, treatments, and practices without transforming everything from physician training, to physician delivery of care, to the reimbursement systems we put in place. It will become increasingly unacceptable for new best practices to take years to permeate the system.

2. Information technology: Entrepreneurial, science- and technology-based, market-oriented systems have provided dramatic breakthroughs in quality, choice, and declining cost in other areas. Health IT will be at the forefront of driving health transformation.

3. Systems that work: In other fields, there are working systems of productivity that are very powerful. These systems have proven to increase quality and lower cost in other sectors and absolutely must be applied to our system of health.

4. Individual empowerment: An individual-centered system must empower the individual rather than the bureaucracy and must also stress individual accountability.

5. American values: America is strengthened by our work ethic, courage, individual initiative, responsibility, teamwork, energetic effort, savings and investing, recognizing and rewarding achievement, and having high expectations. These American values must be integrated into our health system and will be key to creating a future of better health and lower cost.

In addition to these drivers, there are at least nine key strategies to achieving a twenty-first-century, personalized, intelligent health system:

1. Create information-rich health savings accounts to encourage and empower the individual.

2. Create secure electronic health records with expert systems to maximize accuracy, minimize errors, reduce inefficiencies, and improve care.

3. Develop a new system of health justice to replace the trial lawyer–driven malpractice litigation, with patient safety as a central component of the new approach.

4. Create a buyers' market for pharmaceuticals by building a transparent system for individuals, doctors, and pharmacists of price and efficacy information about prescription and over-the-counter drugs. The system would have an open formulary with an "after-pay" rather than a co-pay.

5. Create a system and culture of rapid adoption of solutions that result in better outcomes at lower cost for both the public and private sector.

6. Establish an intellectually credible, accurate system for capturing the cost and benefits of better solutions, better technologies, and better outcomes. This will create a technically correct model of return on investment for solutions with better outcomes at lower cost.

7. Develop a real-time continuous research database.

8. Combine these electronic systems into an online public health network for health protection against natural outbreaks and a bioshield against deliberate biological attack.

9. By implementing the first eight strategies, turn health and health care from a problem into an opportunity, making it the leading creator of high-value jobs and foreign exchange earnings in American society.

The government must be engaged in health transformation at three levels: as policymaker, as employer, and as provider of health care for the poor, the elderly, and the disabled. In each role government must lead by creating and implementing policies that accelerate the adoption of an individual-centered, IT-rich system focused on prevention, early detection, self-management, and best practices.

Because government controls 45 percent of health care spending and because government policies greatly affect the system, the involvement of government in transforming the system is critical. This means the way government currently works with regard to health and health care must be transformed. Morally, the government cannot turn its back. As President Franklin Delano Roosevelt once said, "The success or failure of any government in the final analysis must be measured by the well-being of its citizens. Nothing can be more important to a state than its public health; the state's paramount concern should be the health of its people."

The challenges and the opportunities inherent in the world today make health transformation not a choice but a necessity. If we are to create for our children and grandchildren a healthy and prosperous future, we must create a twenty-first-century, personalized, intelligent health system that saves lives and saves money. This IT-rich, quality-focused system will be centered on the individual and emphasize prevention, wellness, and best practices.

With momentum building for health care consumerism, chronic care management tools, and the adoption of health information technology, we know what the future will look like: there will be 100 percent coverage, consumers will be empowered, quality and price information will be readily available, early detection and prevention will create a culture of health, reimbursement will be driven by outcomes, and the use of interoperable technology will be ubiquitous. For a more detailed description of the transformations required in these areas, see Appendix 6.

Twenty-first-century challenges require twenty-first-century solutions marked by new levels of patient safety, quality care, and cost effectiveness. We must demand nothing less than an electronic, consumer-centered, personalized health system that will improve individual health, reduce costs, and build a brighter future for all Americans. And we must demand as consumers, parents, voters, and leaders a commitment to embrace, promote, and demand the rights and responsibilities that come with this new system of health.

Our twentieth-century health care system, weighed down by the chains of over-regulation and antiquated bureaucracy, is costing us countless lives, untold suffering, and millions of dollars. We are left with no choice but transformation or decay. Morally, as well as economically, we must choose transformation. And while change of such magnitude is never easy, America has a long history of taking on great challenges and emerging triumphant.

I believe health transformation will become yet another example of American ingenuity turning a monumental challenge into a shining future of greater health, safety, freedom, and opportunity for every American.

CHAPTER TWENTY-ONE

Rethinking National Security and Homeland Security: Where Do We Go from Here?

Before I close, I want to go back to the issue of national security and national survival. It is a simple fact that all our hopes and dreams ultimately depend on our ability to defend and protect ourselves. The insight that convinced me to enter public life back in 1958 is still true. Countries can die. Civilizations can collapse.

Every day we are reminded with child soldiers in West Africa, guerrillas in Colombia, terrorism in Sri Lanka, starvation and killing in Darfur, and a host of other examples that the fabric of the rule of law and the shelter of safety in civilization is much thinner than we would like. Everything we could do here at home will disappear if we fail to defend ourselves and fail to win the war against radical Islamists. Yet the first six years after September 11 have not been very encouraging. Our leaders and other leaders around the world have been remarkably timid and short-sighted in their approach to this large conflict. They have overemphasized the military and underemphasized the intellectual, political, diplomatic, and economic components of winning. They have focused too much on the killers and not enough on the recruiters, the mobilizers, the teachers, and the preachers who make the killers possible and give their murders meaning.

This conflict requires a focus on defeating malignant ideologies as much as on defeating terrorists. It requires a mobilization of national will and national understanding, as did the Civil War and World War II. Our enemies are not as wealthy and organized as Nazi Germany or Imperial Japan, but the rise of nuclear and biological weapons means that they might actually do far more damage to America than any of the dictatorships did in the past. The threat to our civilization, our freedom, our safety, and our way of life may be even greater than the threat in World War II.

One of my frustrations with the bipartisan failure of imagination and leadership is the fact that all this knowledge has been around for a long time. I first wrote extensively about the threats we currently face twenty-four years ago in my book *Window of Opportunity*. In Appendix 7, you can read an excerpt that warned in 1984 about terrorists with nuclear and biological weapons.

One way to measure the gap between where we are and where we should be is to imagine an alternative history of the six years after the September 11 attacks. Imagine that we had been as responsive and as determined as we were after Pearl Harbor. I outlined this alternative history in a speech at the American Enterprise Institute on September 10, 2007, on the eve of General David Petraeus's testimony before the U.S. Congress about the status of U.S. combat operations in Iraq. The speech speaks for itself, and you can read excerpts from it in Appendix 8.

Remember, if we hide from reality and kid ourselves about the dangers that threaten us, the enemies that exist, and the failures in our policies and systems, we will pay the cost in American lives. National security is not an optional concern. It is the bedrock of our safety, freedom, and prosperity.

Conclusion

THE STORY OF THIS BOOK is in many ways the story of a video. Two years ago, I posted a portion of one of my speeches on the popular Web site YouTube. It was a short, three-minute video in which I explained the difference between the world that works and the world that fails, using the example of FedEx and UPS versus the bureaucracy.

The UPS and FedEx systems are so capable and so efficient that they can track, in real time, millions of packages as they move across the country. UPS locates fifteen million packages a day; FedEx eight million—while they are moving. In contrast, the federal bureaucracy can't locate between ten and twenty million people in this country illegally. Perhaps, I said in the video, the federal government should send each of these people a package by FedEx or UPS.

It's a tongue-in-cheek example, but it makes a serious point. Efficient, well-organized, functioning systems like FedEx and UPS are not a theory—they're a reality of the world that works. And they stand in glaring contrast to the world of bureaucracies and special interests—the world that fails.

The response to the speech was immediate and overwhelming. Tens of thousands of Americans viewed it and the word quickly spread. By August half a million people had viewed it. In November, the total passed a million. The success of what eventually became known as the "FedEx versus the Bureaucracy" speech convinced me that there is a great hunger in America for something much better than we're used to from our government and public officials. There's a hunger for someone to tell the truth about what fails in our public policy; to tell the truth about the inefficiency of the bureaucracy and the corruption of the special interests. And even more importantly, there is a hunger for the truth about what works in the world around us, and how we can have more of what works in our government—more competence, efficiency, and excellence and less incompetence, inefficiency, and failure.

That is the essence of what I've called throughout this book "real change." Real change means more than just tinkering around the edges of our political system. Marginal change is not going to produce the results we want. Real change means transforming our system.

The Detroit public school system is designed to pay bureaucrats well and pay them on time, and it fulfills that design. Never mind that it fails to educate the children who pass through it.

So much of America's current political system is designed to reward special interests, protect entrenched bureaucracies, and feed off partisan conflict. And it lives up to its design. For the lobbyists, bureaucrats, journalists, and politicians who have invested in the system, their investment has paid off.

One hundred and forty-five years ago, Abraham Lincoln stood on the battlefield at Gettysburg and resolved that "government of the people, by the people, for the people shall not perish from the earth."

But we no longer have government "of the people, by the people, and for the people." We have government of the bureaucrats, by the consultants, and for the special interests. We have a system that is designed to bypass us, the American people. And so it is up to us, the American people, to change it. That's why I wrote this book. That's why I'm asking for your help.

America today is at an extraordinary crossroads. One path leads to even greater prosperity, safety, and freedom. The other leads to a steady decline from world leader into a country surpassed by China and India and with a declining ability to pay for its health, pension, Social Security, and other programs.

I wrote this book to launch America on the path to a better future for all Americans. But I need your help and your involvement to make sure America takes the right road in the years to come.

The road to a successful American future begins with our ability to take advantage of the coming explosion in scientific knowledge. It continues on the familiar terrain of a proven system of markets, entrepreneurs, and sound economic policy. And it gains speed and direction through the strength of the American civilization, which has worked so brilliantly to increase freedom, prosperity, and safety since the first English-speaking people arrived in North America believing that their rights came from God.

This combination of science, economics, and American civilization will enable us to have a better environment, a better energy system, greater economic growth, a better health system, and the right to pursue happiness for even the poorest and least fortunate Americans.

In the America that works, entrepreneurs, creativity, scientific knowledge, and measurable, real achievement matter. In this successful America, you matter as a customer and as a citizen. In this successful America, we the people have real power over our lives, and we the people get to make real choices.

That's real change.

This book is designed to start a new discussion among citizens, to lead to new demands on our politicians, bureaucrats, and news media, and ultimately to lead to action that will help create real change in America.

This book is designed to give you the arguments to make the case for real change and to give you the hope that together we can make a difference in America.

Real change must begin at the individual level, with each person deciding that the special interests, the bureaucracies, and the forces of the past will not determine the course of the future. Real change has to start with families who don't want to see their quality of life decline even as they work harder to maintain it. Real change has to start with citizens who say to their families, friends, and neighbors that the time has come to insist that their politicians change or they will change their politicians. And once enough Americans decide they've had enough of the world that fails, the movement for real change will have begun. It will roll through the state houses, over the entrenched special interests, the hardened bureaucracies, and the cynical politicians, and it won't stop until it reaches Washington, D.C. Join us and be a part of real change.

Acknowledgments

DEVELOPING THE IDEAS AND CONCEPTS in *Real Change* has been the work of a lifetime; I have been studying and thinking about some of these topics for more than fifty years. The list of everyone who helped shape this book would include hundreds of people. However, there are key people who have made this book possible, and they need to be acknowledged for their help with thinking, writing, and editing.

Vince Haley, research director at the American Enterprise Institute, bore the burden of critiquing, fact-checking, and at times strengthening the entire draft. He made this book vastly better than the version that first left my laptop. He is simply one of the brightest and most dedicated people I have ever worked with. His achievements have been solidly supported and encouraged by Chris DeMuth, the extraordinary president of AEI, and the entire AEI team.

Rick Tyler, my extraordinary press secretary and spokesperson, thoroughly critiqued and improved the text between interviews and scheduling calls. Having worked with me for longer than he cares to imagine, Rick collaborated closely with Vince and me to ensure I captured the best ideas for the book while keeping the language user-friendly for the reader. Additionally, he has worked tirelessly on the Solutions Lab, which we hope will be a very useful tool in the movement for change.

Vince, Rick, and I were able to rely, as always, on my dear friend and mentor Steve Hanser, who kept pushing us to think carefully and write clearly.

At AEI, I owe a debt of gratitude to the generosity of Ken and Yvonne Hannan. AEI also sustains other experts who are very helpful, including David Gerson, Michael Novak, Steve Hayward, Mark McClellan, Kevin Hassett, Danielle Pletka, John Bolton, Sally Satel, Alex Pollock, Charles Murray, James Q. Wilson, and Michael Barone. We have been very fortunate to work with two Navy fellows at AEI, Captain Ron Weisbrook and Commander Donald Cuddington. In addition, Emily Renwick has become an invaluable assistant for us at AEI. Furthermore, Will Coggin, Jay Schweikert, Paul Philippino, Madison Jones, and Scott Baird have been extraordinarily mature interns, providing rapid, detailed research as needed.

Beyond AEI, we relied heavily on a number of wonderful scholars, including Herman Pirchner, Walter Isaacson, John Goodman, Cliff May, Grover Norquist, Ed Feulner (whose leadership of Heritage for more than thirty years is an enormous accomplishment), David Barton, Attorney General Ed Meese, and Andrew McCarthy.

Joe Gaylord, my co-designer of the Contract with America and the 1994 campaign, contributed his vast political knowledge to critiquing and clarifying what worked and what failed over the last two decades. All our initial work rested on the research and analysis of Daniel Ballon, a remarkable young molecular biologist who has a great future in public policy development. Terry Balderson is our general adviser on research. Each day he sends us between eighty and two hundred e-mails with nuggets of knowledge from around the world. He is simply invaluable.

Kathy Lubbers, my daughter and the president of Gingrich Communications, did a great job of representing us in the book negotiation and production. Marji Ross, president of Regnery Publishing, has been extraordinary in her dedication to getting *Real Change* right and in supporting the extra months it took to develop the solutions. Miriam Moore at Regnery did a great job of editing under a very tough deadline. Jeff Carneal, the president of Eagle Publishing, continued to exhort and encourage both the growth of my weekly e-newsletter, the "Newt Gingrich Letter," and *Real Change*.

Once again, Randy Evans, Stefan Passantino, and Anthony Morris brought their legal talents to bear. In addition, Randy is the general adviser and strategist for all my activities and he reviewed everything we were doing for effectiveness. My daughter Jackie Cushman provided innumerable suggestions for improvement and invention. Joe DeSantis, who runs the Newt.org Web site and coordinates our radio and news media outreach, and Jessica Gavora, our newsletter editor, contributed significantly to *Real Change*.

Individual chapters were enhanced by experts with specialized knowledge. In particular, Peter Ferrara, director of entitlement and budget policy at the Institute for Policy Innovation, helped on the tax and Social Security chapters. Nancy Desmond, the president and CEO of the Center for Health Transformation, co-authored the chapter on health. Congressman Bob Walker has helped immensely with his thinking on science, hydrogen, and space. In developing specific issues, Terry Maple, my coauthor on *Contract with the Earth*, helped on the environment. Chuck Colson and Pat Nolan at Prison Fellowship helped on prison reform. Don Eberly helped in thinking through what we need to do build a stronger civil society. Our development of the concept of religious liberty was greatly enhanced by the work of David Bossie and the talented team at Citizens United.

This book is based in considerable part on the extraordinary efforts of American Solutions. Dave Ryan has proven to be a strong leader in launching this new national movement. Pat Saks runs American Solutions as internal vice president. Amy Pass does great work on finances, Dan Kotman, media, David Kralik, developing Internet technology (including our workshop in Second Life), Christine Hall, Paul Kilgore in developing direct mail, Michael Krull as the director of education, and Fred Asbell as the coalition coordinator have all been very helpful.

Polling played a major role in making sure we really understood the values and concerns of the American people. Matt Dabrowski at American Solutions did a great job of coordinating six different national polls of unique design in a very short time. We worked with Kellyanne Conway, David Winston, Gene Ulm, Linda Divall, Randy Gutermuth, Whit Ayres, Jon McHenry, Hans Kaiser, Bob Moore, Bill McInturff, and Frank Luntz. On all polling matters my friendship with Jim Clifton, the head of Gallup (the largest and most prestigious polling institution in the world) has been invaluable. On American opinion Karlyn Bowman at AEI is a stunningly knowledgeable and thoughtful analyst and scholar.

The many projects I am engaged in would all collapse if not for the strong support from the Office of Speaker Newt Gingrich. Sonya

Harrison does an amazing job keeping track of all our activities and schedules, and she is ably assisted by Bess Kelly. In addition, Callista and I have been able to rely on Lindsey Harvey as our superb special assistant.

Finally, my wife, Callista, has made this journey a real joy. As a pianist, French horn player, and professional singer at the Basilica of the National Shrine of the Immaculate Conception, she has an acute sense of the importance of focus, practice, and dedication. In that tradition she has supported my many long hours of thinking, writing, and editing. Our work together at Gingrich Productions (beginning with our DVD, *Rediscovering God in America*) has made this journey even more enjoyable.

The Platform of the American People

A Red-White-and-Blue Platform to Replace the Red-versus-Blue Partisan Split

T HE TWO POLITICAL PARTIES can find many issues about which to disagree. It would be a healthy change if they could begin by recognizing the values and concerns of the vast majority of Americans and jointly agree to a core platform that could bring us together before turning to divisive issues.

Everything in this platform has the support of a majority of Republicans, a majority of Democrats, and a majority of independents. We call these unifying issues the Platform of the American People. Our hope is that beginning with local conventions and up through district, state, and the national conventions, both political parties will consider adopting this platform as a foundation.

Imagine how much healthier America would be if both parties were committed to adopting a series of issues the American people favor by large majorities. If you would like to work to get your party to adopt the Platform of the American People, please go to www.americansolutions.com/platform and sign up. You can also discover others in your community who have agreed to work on common goals for America.

The Platform of the American People: American Values and American Solutions

There are values that unite a large majority of Americans. We want to strengthen and revitalize these core American values. Our goal should be to provide long-term solutions instead of short-term fixes. Government clearly has to change the way it operates by bringing in ideas and systems that currently increase productivity and effectiveness in the private sector. The changes we need in government have to occur in all 513,000 elected offices throughout the country; they cannot be achieved by focusing only on Washington.

English and American Civilization

English should be the official language of government. All election ballots and other government documents should be printed in English. New immigrants should be required to learn English. Government should offer intensive English-language instruction to all who need it, including stipends to help immigrants attend the programs. Businesses should be able to require employees to speak the English language while on the job.

The United States should grant citizenship only to those who want to embrace American values and culture. It is important to have references to God in the Pledge of Allegiance and the Declaration of Independence—that we are endowed by our Creator with the rights to life, liberty, and the pursuit of happiness—because they make clear that certain rights can't be taken away by government.

Statements regarding religion and morality made by the Founding Fathers are just as important today as they were two hundred years ago. We reject the idea that the language in the Pledge of Allegiance and the Declaration of Independence must change with the times. The language in the Pledge and the Declaration is very important and must be protected.

Immigration, the Border, and Assimilation

The American people favor legal immigration, control of the border, ending illegal immigration with an emphasis on employer responsibility, immediate deportation of felons who are here illegally, a requirement to return home to become legal temporary workers, assimilation of those who sincerely want to become American, and a sophisticated, technologically advanced, temporary worker system.

* The American people want to increase the number of visas for highly educated immigrants or those with special skills, the H-1B and H-2B visas.
* There should be a worker visa program making it easier for people to work legally in the United States.
* Allowing illegal immigrants to remain in this country undermines respect for the law. Therefore, to join a worker visa program, workers should have to apply from their own countries.
* When applying for a temporary worker visa each worker should take an oath to obey American law and agree to be deported if they commit a crime while in the United States.
* In a worker visa program workers will receive a tamper-proof identification card that will allow the government to track them.

* Workers interested in coming to the U.S. should have to go to immigration centers in their home countries that will help them find jobs in the United States so they can apply for a visa with a job in hand.

* A real-time verification system should be established to verify immigration status, and it should be outsourced to companies like American Express, Visa, or MasterCard so businesses can immediately identify someone with forged papers.

* No company should market services like credit cards or bank accounts specifically to people who are in the United States illegally.

* There should be heavy monetary fines against employers and businesses who knowingly hire illegal immigrants.

* The Internal Revenue Service should conduct audits of companies who hire illegal immigrants to determine if those companies have paid the taxes they owe.

Science and Technology

There will be incredible possibilities to meet our country's challenges in a variety of fields, because in the next twenty-five years there will be four to seven times the amount of new science and technology in the world as in the past twenty-five years. Therefore we should dramatically increase our investment in math and science education. We must rely on innovation and new technology to compete successfully with India and China.

Prizes

Prizes should be given to companies and individuals that invent creative ways to solve problems. We support giving large financial prizes to companies and individuals who invent an affordable car that gets one hundred miles to the gallon. We support giving a large financial prize to the first company or individual who invents new ways to successfully cut pollution. We support giving a large financial prize to the first company or individual who invents a new, safer way to dispose of nuclear waste products.

Energy and the Environment

We have an obligation to be good stewards of God's creation for future generations. We can have a healthy economy and a healthy environment. We can solve our environmental problems faster and cheaper with innovation and new technology than with more litigation and more government regulation. If we use technology, innovation, and incentives, we do not need to raise taxes to clean up our environment.

Entrepreneurs are more likely to solve America's energy and environmental problems than bureaucrats. We support giving tax credits to companies that cut carbon emissions as an incentive to cut pollution. We want to encourage businesses to voluntarily cut pollution by giving them financial incentives, but if necessary we will require them to do so.

We should give tax credits to homeowners and builders who incorporate alternative energy systems in their homes, like solar, wind, and geothermal energy. We support offering tax credits for people who turn in older, high-polluting cars.

Climate change and global warming are probably happening. We support building more nuclear power plants to cut carbon emissions and reduce our dependence on foreign oil. We should hold city governments to the same standards for cleaning waste water as those applied to private industry. We are prepared to use public funds, and especially public and private partnerships, to preserve green space and parks to protect natural areas from development. We favor property tax credits to private landowners who agree not to develop their land and agree not to sell it to developers.

Our current dependence on foreign oil threatens our economic prosperity and national security by making us vulnerable to dangerous dictatorships. With appropriate safeguards to protect the environment, we should build more oil refineries and drill for oil off America's coasts to lower the cost of gas and reduce our dependence on foreign oil.

Taxes and Jobs

The federal income tax system is unfair. The death tax should be abolished. We favor tax incentives for companies who keep their headquarters in the United States. Taxpayers should be given the option of a single income tax rate of 17 percent, and retain the option of filing their taxes in the current system if they choose to do so. The option of a single rate system should give taxpayers the convenience of filing their taxes on just a single sheet of paper. We support a single corporate tax rate of 17 percent, which would lower taxes for some businesses while also closing loopholes used by some corporations to pay less in taxes.

The United States has one of the highest corporate tax rates in the industrialized world, making it difficult for U.S. corporations to compete internationally. This creates incentives for companies to move overseas. A new tax plan should make America a more attractive place for businesses that provide well-paying jobs.

Social Security and Retirement

It is important for the president and Congress to address the issue of Social Security in the next few years. The current Social Security system is broken, and if it isn't reformed future generations will no longer have it as a safety net for retirement. We favor a Social Security proposal in which personal Social Security savings accounts would be optional; workers could choose to continue to depend on the current system with current benefits.

We favor a Social Security proposal in which workers would use the money in their personal account to buy annuities, a type of financial benefit that will give monthly payments for the rest of their lives. Purchased upon retirement, the annuity will pay at least the same amount that traditional Social Security would.

We favor this Social Security proposal because in the current system, workers cannot pass the money they paid into Social Security on to their family members. We favor a Social Security proposal in which any money in the account left after the purchase of an annuity would be the property of the worker, and the extra money can be left to family members.

Freedom of Religion

References to the Creator in the Declaration of Independence— that we are endowed by our Creator with the rights to life, liberty, and the pursuit of happiness—are very important. Keeping the reference to "one nation under God" in the Pledge of Allegiance is very important. We reject the Ninth Federal Circuit Court's ruling that the Pledge is unconstitutional. The phrase "under God" is perfectly in line with the Constitution, and we reject the claim that it violates the separation of church and state. Separation between church and state does not mean the omission of all references to God in government-sanctioned activities or public buildings. The best way to ensure religious freedom is to protect all religious references and symbols, including those on public buildings, lands, or documents.

We reject banning all prayer in public schools. Children should be allowed a moment of silence to pray to themselves in public school if they desire. We support the display of a Christmas tree or menorah on public property during the holiday season. We favor a law to protect city, county, and state lands that have crosses or other religious symbols.

Many of the problems our country faces originated because America is no longer as religious and moral as it once was. They did not result from changes in the economy, war, public education, or other issues. The Founding Fathers understood that religion and morality were important to creating and building this country, and the statements they made are just as important today as they were two hundred years ago. Throughout most of America's history, this was understood, and it is central to America's success today.

Defending America

We must help defend America and its allies and defeat our enemies. We must be prepared to survive an attack by a nuclear, biological, or chemical weapon. America should take the threat of terror by fanatical religious groups more seriously. Al Qaeda poses a very serious threat to the United States, and it is not possible to negotiate with terrorist groups like it. Furthermore, Iran, Hezbollah, and Hamas pose very serious threats to the United States.

There should be a death penalty for someone convicted of carrying out a terrorist attack in the United States. Congress should make it a crime to advocate acts of terrorism, violent conduct, or the killing of innocent people in the United States. The Department of Homeland Security and other government agencies should develop programs to teach Americans what they can do as individuals to help in the fight against terror. Terrorist Web sites at home and abroad should be closed down using computer warfare.

(Polling data for each platform plank demonstrating why we believe this is the Platform of the American People can be found at www.americansolutions.com/platform.)

The Solutions Lab

AMERICAN SOLUTIONS FOR WINNING THE FUTURE has created a very exciting Web site called the Solutions Lab. The Solutions Lab allows citizen activists and policymakers (both professional and amateur) to collaborate on developing policy solutions to the many challenges facing America. Moreover, this powerful tool is designed to provide elected officials a rich resource for either creating policy solutions or formulating legislative solutions that draw on ideas from both experts and citizen activists.

These solutions, created and posted by community members on their own "My Solutions" pages, can be rated by other members. Members can argue the merits of their solutions, adjust them, or collaborate with other members online. In this way, solutions are challenged and tested over time against the ideas and critiques of the American Solutions community.

Solutions Lab members are encouraged to create communications strategies for their solutions so they can be explained and accepted in the marketplace of competing ideas. Members are also encouraged to create projects to raise awareness of their solutions and to provide definable achievements that can be adopted and implemented by local, state, or federal officials.

Beyond creating solutions for a better America, the Solutions Lab offers tremendous opportunities to learn. For example, members have access to leadership essays on understanding the historic values and principles of the American people. They can also learn more about each issue area from American Solutions experts and other Solutions Lab members.

In this way, the Solutions Lab is designed to allow a great many Americans to participate in policy creation and implementation, vastly expanding the number of citizens working for a better America. To see the Solutions Lab for yourself, please visit www.americansolutions.com/SolutionsLab.

Welfare Reform as a Case Study in Successful Real Change

CONSIDER THE PARADIGM SHIFT from Lyndon Johnson's Great Society in 1965, with its belief in the taxpayers' obligation to subsidize the poor, to the welfare reform of 1996, with its requirements of work, study, and effort as part of citizenship in a healthy society. That was real change.

Beginning when Johnson was still president, Ronald Reagan insisted—with a great nationally televised speech in October 1964 called "A Time for Choosing"—on talking about controversial things. He insisted on returning to America's core values and principles even when such change made people uncomfortable. He insisted on returning to themes that the elites ridiculed and condemned.

In 1966, as a candidate for governor, Reagan first proposed welfare reform. In 1967, in his first inaugural address as governor, he repeated this call. His administration in California convinced President Richard Nixon to approve an initial experiment in "workfare" (as it was then called). As a candidate for president, Reagan proposed welfare reform in both the 1976 and 1980 campaigns. As president he pushed for welfare reform and got the first hesitating steps toward work requirements out of a Democratic House of Representatives.

During Reagan's presidency, Charles Murray at the American Enterprise Institute published *Losing Ground*. This seminal work proved conclusively that welfare increased dependency, drove down education and life skills, and trapped generations of children in poverty. The right to pursue happiness had been replaced by the right to decay on the taxpayer's dime. After Murray's book, the Left never regained the moral advantage it had once exploited to argue for money for the poor. Government money was crippling poor people instead of helping them.

Reagan so popularized welfare reform that Democratic presidential candidate Bill Clinton campaigned in 1992 on "ending welfare as we know it." It was a very clever slogan, allowing liberals to think he would end welfare by improving its benefits and expanding its reach, while conservatives thought he would insist on a work provision.

By 1994, House Republicans included a conservative work- and study-related welfare reform as part of the Contract with America. If President Clinton would not choose between liberal and conservative reforms, we would choose for him.

One of the first phone calls I received after becoming Speaker-elect was from former secretary of education and former drug czar Bill Bennett, who said I had to read Marvin Olasky's *The Tragedy of American Compassion*. He was right. In his book, Olasky outlined the values and principles of the great nineteenth-century social reformers, who all believed that helping people out of poverty required tough love and work requirements. He cited reformer after reformer who condemned the "compassionate wealthy" who wanted to give people something for nothing. These people were convinced that giving away money subsidized bad behavior and encouraged people to remain dependent, and in many cases to remain addicted to drugs and alcohol.

The modern redistributionist model of bureaucratic welfare was an outgrowth of a leftist social critique of society, according to Olasky. He documented the leftists' desire to create a right to money without effort. He cited advocate after advocate on the twentieth-century left who insisted that a large underclass of permanently poor people was acceptable, and that it was cultural imperialism to insist that they acquire habits of discipline and self-management in order to lead full lives as independently productive citizens.

The Tragedy of American Compassion made clear that the fight over welfare reform was at its heart a cultural and moral fight over the nature of being American and the requirements of a full and healthy citizenship. Understood on those terms, the existing welfare system was indefensible.

In 1996, House Republicans passed welfare reform three times. The first two times President Clinton vetoed it. By the third time a national poll indicated that 92 percent of the American people favored welfare reform, including 88 percent of the people on welfare. Exactly half of the House Democrats (101–101) voted with us on fundamental reform of the welfare system.

Ten Lessons from Successfully Transforming Welfare

There are ten big lessons I have drawn from the successful efforts to design and implement welfare reform. I suggest that we apply these lessons to developing solutions that will elevate the condition of our fellow citizens.

1. *Successful reform always starts with a big idea.* Often a powerful idea can languish for many years before it is accepted and adopted, but it has been said that nothing is more powerful than an idea whose time has come. In the case of welfare reform, the powerful idea of replacing welfare and dependence with work and personal responsibility took thirty years to become the law of the land.

2. *Decide whether to repair or replace.* The first and absolutely unavoidable step to real change is to decide whether to marginally improve the current system or replace the laws, the regulations, the bureaucratic culture, and the governmental structures. Successful reformers will have to replace bureaucratic public administration with entrepreneurial public management.

3. *Great change never starts with government.* Great changes come from all over America and are imposed by the American people on the governing system. Governing systems begin to decline when they start shifting their focus to the power structures and away from the people. As one Reagan official said in 1972, "When people in Sacramento start saying 'we' and mean California state government, we know they have been here too long. 'We' means the people of California." And in fact it was the American voter who insisted on real change in 1994. Nine million more Americans turned out in 1994 than had in 1990 to support a positive agenda of reform, including the crowning achievement of welfare reform.

4. *Cheerful persistence is necessary to successfully deliver large-scale reform in a free society.* It is necessary to have a positive vision of a

better future. Americans have always been optimistic, and optimistic positive leadership has almost always beaten negative pessimistic leadership.

5. *Collaboration is critical.* Developing workable, politically popular, and morally grounded reform is very complex. It takes a more decentralized process of parallel effort, and a more collaborative system. The involvement of key governors and their staffs in drafting the welfare reform bill is a classic example of a collaborative approach that reached across formal boundaries to build a team for a specific purpose. This approach was absolutely necessary because the governors themselves would be implementing the policy reforms. Several key governors, like Tommy Thompson in Wisconsin, John Engler in Michigan, and Mike Leavitt in Utah, had already started to lead the way in figuring out the type of welfare reforms that would work. It was important to get ideas from each state in order to diffuse the best approaches across the country. It would have been impossible to craft a system that helped 60 percent of the people on welfare move into jobs or classes without the active help of the governors and those who knew how to get the job done at the local level.

6. *Real change always requires winning the argument.* Successful reformers understand the Margaret Thatcher rule that "first you win the argument, then you win the vote." They understand that defining the argument and organizing the effort to educate and rally the country wins victories in elections or in Congress that would not otherwise be possible. Conversely, successful reformers know when they are starting to lose arguments, because they know that their votes will then be put at risk. Reagan first

proposed welfare reform in 1966; when we passed it in 1996, we knew we had won the argument.

7. *Words matter.* Successful reformers know that words really matter. Successful reformers must acquire the skills to communicate good policy. Any large-scale reform initiative involves learning a new glossary. The new approach has to be outlined in words the public either understands or has to learn. Our vision for welfare reform was one where independence replaced dependency, where opportunity replaced poverty, where responsibility replaced irresponsibility, where self-sufficiency replaced helplessness, where caring replaced caretaking. Over time more and more Americans heard and believed in that vision.

8. *Real change must be consistent with broad American values.* Successful reform can be achieved only if the goals advanced are consistent with American values. The potential for an incentive-led program of reform is increased dramatically by the core nature of American society. It is the nature of America's entrepreneurial free market system to create more choices of higher quality at lower cost.

9. *Opponents of reform must be forced to carry the burden of their positions.* It is necessary to put opponents of popular reform on the defense and force them to explain the logic of their position. In the case of welfare reform, it meant that opponents had to defend a system that kept recipients in a hopeless web of poverty in which they were told not to help themselves, not to look for work, but to sit there and be quiet and wait for the next check. At some point, the opponents could no longer bear the burden of their own position. By then, it was virtually impossible for

Congress to avoid passing it or the president to avoid signing it, which he did after vetoing it twice.

10. *Real change must be citizen-centered.* Successful reform on the scale of the 1996 welfare reform has to be citizen-centered and movement-driven. People have to realize it as their plan for improving their future. Social Security in 1935 was not about FDR. It was about the American people. Welfare reform was not about the Republican Party. It was about giving the poor a much better future. People in power have to constantly remind themselves that they are advocating the interests of the American people.

D–Day Radio Prayer of President Franklin Delano Roosevelt

June 6, 1944

M Y FELLOW AMERICANS: Last night, when I spoke with you about the fall of Rome, I knew at that moment that troops of the United States and our allies were crossing the Channel in another and greater operation. It has come to pass with success thus far. And so, in this poignant hour, I ask you to join with me in prayer:

Almighty God: Our sons, pride of our nation, this day have set upon a mighty endeavor, a struggle to preserve our republic, our religion, and our civilization, and to set free a suffering humanity. Lead them straight and true; give strength to their arms, stoutness to their hearts, steadfastness in their faith.

They will need Thy blessings. Their road will be long and hard. For the enemy is strong. He may hurl back our forces. Success may not come with rushing speed, but we shall return again and again; and we know that by Thy grace, and by the righteousness of our cause, our sons will triumph.

They will be sore tried, by night and by day, without rest—until the victory is won. The darkness will be rent by noise and flame. Men's souls will be shaken with the violences of war.

For these men are lately drawn from the ways of peace. They fight not for the lust of conquest. They fight to end conquest. They fight to liberate. They fight to let justice arise, and tolerance and good will among all Thy people. They yearn but for the end of battle, for their return to the haven of home.

Some will never return. Embrace these, Father, and receive them, Thy heroic servants, into Thy kingdom.

And for us at home—fathers, mothers, children, wives, sisters, and brothers of brave men overseas—whose thoughts and prayers are ever with them—help us, Almighty God, to rededicate ourselves in renewed faith in Thee in this hour of great sacrifice.

Many people have urged that I call the nation into a single day of special prayer. But because the road is long and the desire is great, I ask that our people devote themselves in a continuance of prayer. As we rise to each new day, and again when each day is spent, let words of prayer be on our lips, invoking Thy help to our efforts.

Give us strength, too: strength in our daily tasks, to redouble the contributions we make in the physical and the material support of our armed forces. And let our hearts be stout, to wait out the long travail, to bear sorrows that may come, to impart our courage unto our sons wheresoever they may be.

And, O Lord, give us faith. Give us faith in Thee; faith in our sons; faith in each other; faith in our united crusade. Let not the keenness of our spirit ever be dulled. Let not the impacts of temporary events, of temporal matters, of but fleeting moment—let not these deter us in our unconquerable purpose.

With Thy blessing, we shall prevail over the unholy forces of our enemy. Help us to conquer the apostles of greed and racial arrogancies. Lead us to the saving of our country, and with our sister nations into a world unity that will spell a sure peace—a peace invulnerable to the schemings of unworthy men. And a peace that will let all men live in freedom, reaping the just rewards of their honest toil.

Thy will be done, Almighty God. Amen.

You can listen to FDR's original recording of this speech at www.newt.org/FDRprayer.

Health Values

*Developed by the Center for Health Transformation
(www.healthtransformation.net), these health values define the
transformation that will be required to create a twenty-first-century intelligent
health system that saves lives and saves money for all Americans.*

WE BELIEVE THAT EVERY AMERICAN should be as healthy as possible for as long as possible at the lowest possible cost, within a system of quality, innovation, and evidence-based practices.

We believe that health involves not only physical health but also mental, social, and spiritual health.

We believe in the twenty-first-century pattern of more choices of higher quality at lower cost, which requires a market-based system where innovation and entrepreneurialism are protected and incentivized.

We believe in a solutions-oriented system, where solutions that work are constantly identified and driven through the system as rapidly as possible.

We further believe that a collaboration of leaders is necessary to constantly create new solutions and policies that result in more choices of higher quality at lower cost. The collaboration should include all stakeholders, to maximize the ability to learn, create, and accelerate the adoption of new solutions and policies.

We believe in the importance of having a critical mass of leaders at all levels and across all stakeholder groups. This will also involve every individual playing a leadership role with regard to his own health and his family's health, as well as within his work force, his organization, his community, and America at large.

We believe that creating a movement of citizen leaders, including organizational, government, and industry leaders, is key to transforming the system and accelerating the adoption of twenty-first-century solutions and policies.

We believe that health should be individual-centered, with the individual having the incentives, information, and access to care that will improve health and save lives, which we believe will also save money.

We believe that every individual has the right to own his own health record, to know he is receiving best evidence-based care, to live as independently and with as much freedom and as many choices as possible, and to know that he is safe from preventable medical errors.

In addition to these rights, we believe the individual has the responsibility to make healthy choices, to access available information in order to determine best possible solutions, and to partner with his physician or health care provider to make decisions that lead to better health for himself and his family.

We believe in a personalized health system, built around each person's individual health needs and status, which allows every individual to have access to the treatments and solutions that are best for his personal profile and make-up.

We believe the system should be based on health, not just health care. This means a focus on prevention, early testing, and evidence-based best (or better, since they will constantly evolve) standards of care to manage health.

We believe in an intelligent system, meaning that the system is electronic versus paper-based, is IT-rich, and functions as an inter-connected, interoperable system.

We believe in a systems approach, rather than a siloed approach, meaning that all parts of the system need to work together toward a common vision and common goal. That goal is first and foremost dedicated to saving lives and improving quality of life and secondly focused on saving money, the two of which we believe, in a twenty-first-century system, are inter-related. Better quality of care leads to better health and lower cost.

We also believe that, since changes to one part of the system impact other parts of the system, we must therefore consider the long-term impact on the system rather than focusing on short-term solutions. This approach should govern both clinical and financial decisions that are made, which will require a change in the way government evaluates the way it spends money on projects and programs.

We believe the system should be focused on outcomes and specific metrics, and that we should not only measure metrics but we should also manage according to those metrics.

We believe in transformation, in constant innovation, and in training and empowering every organization and individual to continually improve and strive for a better future.

We also believe that our government should be a collaborative partner, setting standards but not engaging in micromanaging processes or the free enterprise system.

Finally, we believe in a system that creates better health and more choices at lower cost for every American, regardless of age, sex, ethnic or geographic background, or level of disability.

Four Areas Requiring Transformation to Achieve Health Insurance Coverage for All Americans

T O GET TO A SYSTEM OF BETTER HEALTH at lower cost, we have to get beyond fighting over how much it would cost to expand the current system and talk instead about investment and about real change in the four distinct but inter-related boxes of health and health care.

A Twenty-First-Century Intelligent Health System with 100 Percent Insurance in a 300 Million-Payor System Requires Transforming Four Boxes

1. Individual Rights, Responsibilities, and Expectation of Behavior	**2.** Maximize Cultural and Societal Patterns for a Healthy Community
3. Effective, Efficient, and Productive Health Delivery System	**4.** Financing to Enable 300 Milion-Payor Insurance System

Source: www.healthtransformation.net

The Individual

A personalized system of health will work only if the individual is empowered and engaged. This requires each person to be equipped with the knowledge and access that he needs and also to understand, accept, and be encouraged to make responsible choices. As an individual, you will have more rights but also more responsibilities. You will have access to more information and choices but will be expected to become a partner in your own health and health care. Assuming that your health or that of your family is your doctor's problem and not your own will be a thing of the past.

As the wealth of information, knowledge, and scientific break-throughs rapidly expand, you will have to become your own best advocate, as no doctor will be able to keep up with the constant changes and advances related to every condition and relevant to the personal profile of each patient. In addition, you can help drive the transformation—and improve your own health and health care—by selecting providers who embrace the principles and practices of a twenty-first century, individualized, intelligent health system and by voting for policymakers who will advance such a system.

The Culture and Society

We need to maximize cultural and societal patterns for a healthy community. This includes changing the policies, institutions, and environments that affect the choices made by individual citizens. For example, given the current epidemic of childhood obesity, we should absolutely insist that schools serve healthy lunches, offer healthy snacks, and include physical education as part of the daily curriculum. Likewise, if we are encouraging healthy diets but high-risk neighborhoods have no access in their local stores to fresh fruit and vegetables—or it is prohibitively expensive to eat healthy versus unhealthy foods—it is doubtful that we will have much impact.

The Delivery System

We have to create an effective, efficient, and productive health delivery system. This means we must embrace and adopt new technologies, new interoperable systems, and a new culture. A future where the individual is at the center, where learning is constant and real-time, and where innovations are much more rapidly driven through the system will require a different type of delivery system. There will be more partnering, increased reliance on IT-assisted knowledge and expert systems, and a system in which (like at the Mayo Clinic) health professionals are consultants to one another.

One of the central tenets of doing this is moving from a paper-based system to electronic systems. We must bring health care into the twenty-first century through the rapid adoption of health information technology. Many components of the health system are still stuck in a 1950s paper-based model, even though there exist today proven solutions, including electronic health records, remote monitoring, decision support systems, and other technologies proven to save lives and save money.

The mandate is both a moral and a financial one. A recent study by the Institute of Medicine titled Preventing Medication Errors concluded that patients average one medication error for every day they are hospitalized, amounting to more than 1.5 million errors every year, more than 7,000 of which are fatal. Health information technology's ability to dramatically improve the quality of care and to save thousands of lives cannot be ignored.

The System of Financing

Finally, we need to look at the issue of financing to enable a 300 million-payor insurance system. We need a new model of paying for health care. Our current payment system pays doctors and providers for simply delivering care, regardless of the outcome. Doctors, hospitals, and other providers that deliver better care are for the most part paid at the exact same rate as those who provide poorer care. That's like paying the same amount for a Mercedes as you would for a Yugo. Like any other rational market, we need a reimbursement model that takes into account the quality of the care that is delivered, not simply that it was delivered.

As the world's largest purchaser of health care services, the federal government must take the lead. If the federal government were to pay more for risk-adjusted quality outcomes and less for poorer outcomes, particularly through Medicare and the Federal Employee Health Benefits Program, the private market would follow.

Finally, we should insist that everyone above a certain level buy coverage (or, if they are opposed to insurance, post a bond). Meanwhile, we should provide tax credits or subsidize private insurance for the poor. In addition, a national pool for those who suffer catastrophic illnesses or diseases needs to be established in order to ensure that people undergoing the most traumatic and costly health situations be able to access the care they need.

Excerpt from
Window of Opportunity:
A Blueprint for the Future
Newt Gingrich, Tor Books
(September 1984)

T HE FACT IS THAT WE STAND on the brink of a world of violence almost beyond our imagination. The picture is sobering indeed. Imagine the more extreme elements in any terrorist movement with weapons of mass destruction. It is a prospect likely to gray the hair of any reasonable person.

Just as the comfortable Russian landowner before Stalin could not imagine the horrors of collectivization and the comfortable bourgeois German Jew really could not believe Hitler was serious in his speeches, so it is hard for us to believe that these kinds of nightmares are possible. We keep rejecting information about the world around us because it is too far outside our personal experiences, our historical experience, and our shared general view of the world.

It is the refusal to think seriously about the violence we see each night on television and to develop a new explanation for the world we live in which keeps us at a level of shock and surprise. Watch your own reactions the next three or four times you see really violent news reports about a terrorist or a war or the latest atrocity somewhere.

We are going to have to develop an intellectual split-vision which allows us to accept both the reality of our peaceful neighborhood and the reality of a horribly dangerous outside world. If we don't develop a new sophistication to analyze and deal with the dangers from abroad, we will find those dangers creeping closer and closer to our neighborhood. If we don't learn to take serious precautions and to be honest with ourselves about all levels of violence—from individual terrorist-criminal all the way up to a Soviet-American nuclear war—then we increase the danger that these events will occur.

Yet our problem will not come only from terrorist, illegal organizations. There are bandit nations willing to operate outside the tradition of modern international behavior. The three most obvious current bandit governments are North Korea, Libya, and Iran. The leaders of all three countries are inner-directed and likely to do what they personally decide is appropriate. All three leaders have proven themselves risk-takers willing to subsidize terrorist organizations and willing to kill innocent people in the pursuit of their goals. The thought of them having nuclear weapons is daunting indeed.

Furthermore, we must remember that it is only in the West that we focus military power on military engagements. There is every reason to believe that Middle Eastern ideologies will strike at the American heartland rather than at our military power if we threaten them directly.

We have been surprised again and again by other nations because we refuse to study their habits, their culture, and their history. Five hundred years before Christ, Sun T'zu stated, "Know the enemy and you have won half the battle. Know yourself and the battle is yours."

We have a passion for knowing about technology, hardware, and management, but we disdain knowing much about either the capacity of others or ourselves to endure (e.g., Vietnam) or our opponents' techniques and approaches.

Only this willful ignorance can explain our underestimation of the Japanese before Pearl Harbor. Bernard Fall warned us again and again in the early 1960s who Ho Chi Minh was and how long he would fight, but we continued to underestimate the North Vietnamese until they defeated us just as Fall had predicted. We underestimated the Lebanese-Syrian-Iranian-Soviet terrorist connections which had already used vehicle bombs and produced numerous young fanatic volunteers willing to die for their cause, and 241 U.S. Marines died as a result.

Because we reject history as a serious preparation for understanding and operating in the world at large, we find ourselves consistently underestimating how difficult, how intractable, how brutal and violent that world can be. History is powerful precisely because it carries us outside our peaceful neighborhoods and our calm communities. At its best, history can open our minds to possibilities which we would never encounter in our own family or surroundings. The world that has been can be again.

Americans in general tend to underestimate the savagery of the world, but liberals in particular carry the tendency to extremes. Liberals seem to have an ideological block against accepting the notion that there really are dangerous people out there who will do evil things unless they are stopped.

If we do not become practical and candid about the nature of the dilemma we face, we will lose many more men, women, and children to bombings, and we will begin to experience an erosion of civilization here at home. We must develop a doctrine which states clearly American policy toward violence aimed at the destruction of our society. We must take the steps necessary to prove that no terrorist organization can kill Americans with impunity.

The long-term struggle against terrorism will be a dark and bloody one, involving years of vigilant counter-terrorism—a level of surveillance and spying that liberals will call intolerable—and a willingness to strike back with substantial force at the originators of the action rather than the foot soldiers of the terrorist movement.

A free, open society cannot survive by trading violence for violence. If we kill an Iranian extremist every time Iranians kill an American soldier, we will lose the struggle. In the end, no free society can keep pace in enduring pain with a fanatical terrorist organization. We must develop a doctrine which severely and directly threatens the leaders of terrorist movements so that they refrain from attacking the United States because they fear personal consequences. Any other policy is an invitation to a bloodbath in which we will certainly be losers.

The need to develop doctrines and tactics of aggressive counter-terrorism goes against the grain of the American historical memory as taught in modern schools. By blotting out the wars against the Indians, the Barbary Pirates, the pacification of the West, and the campaigns against guerrillas in the Philippines and Central America, it has been possible for the Wilsonian intellectual tradition to dominate—a tradition that argues for a sharp and vivid distinction between war and peace. Liberals dominated by this tradition declare war on a country or are impotent to challenge it; they have no capacity for a long and difficult struggle in the twilight zone of low-intensity conflict.

Only when our professionals master their professions can we begin to design structures that will work. Then we must decide what sort of executive-branch planning and implementation systems are desirable.

At a minimum, we will need closer relationships between the intelligence agencies, the diplomatic agencies, the economic agencies, the military agencies, the news media, and the political structure. There has to be a synergism in which our assessment of what is happening relates to our policies as they are developed and implemented. Both analyses and implementation must be related to the news media and political system because all basic policies must have public support if they are to succeed.

Finally, once the professionals have mastered their professions and have begun to work in systems that are effective and coordinated, those professionals must teach both the news media and the elected politicians. No free society can for long accept the level of ignorance about war, history, and the nature of power which has become the norm for our news media and our elected politicians. An ignorant society is on its way to becoming an extinct society.

"What If?
An Alternative History
of the War since 9/11"

On September 10, 2007, I gave this speech in which I explained why the current strategy, structures, and resources of the American security apparatus are inadequate to meet the challenges confronting the country. Excerpted here, this speech explored the development of a war-winning strategy. The full text of the speech is available at www.newt.org.

THE ESSENCE OF THIS SPEECH is very simple. Six years after the attack of September 11, 2001, we are having the wrong debate about the wrong report. The heart of our problem is in attitude. Wars require bold efforts and undertaking real risks. We must recognize the requirements for change and we must adopt a spirit that it is better to make mistakes of commission and then fix them than it is to avoid achievement by avoiding failure.

Six years after the attack of September 11, 2001, the difference between the debate we ought to be having and the debate we are having is staggering. The gap between where we are and where we should be is so large that it seems almost impossible to explain why the Petraeus Report, while important, will be a wholly inadequate explanation as to what is required to defeat our enemies and secure America and her allies.

Instead, it seems more effective to describe this dramatic gap today by imagining how things might have turned out differently had we made different decisions for our national security starting the night of September 11, 2001. What if we had begun a great national dialogue about the nature of our enemies, the seriousness of their intent, the scale of their capabilities, and the requirements of victory over them? What might then have happened?

We must think about alternative pasts if we are to create a more successful future. America is currently trapped between those who advocate "staying the course" and those who would legislate surrender and defeat for America. America needs a more realistic and more powerful solution to the challenges of our enemies. This rethinking of the last six years is designed to make it easier to be creative about the next six years. The issuance of the Petraeus Report is the right time to challenge both the stay-the-course policies and the legislate-defeat policies.

The Petraeus Report in Context of Winning the Larger War against the Irreconcilable Wing of Islam

Before we assess an alternative past, it is vital to place the Petraeus Report in its correct context. It is a campaign report about a specific campaign. Iraq is a campaign in a larger war just as Afghanistan is a campaign in a larger war.

The Petraeus Report is an important report. The debate over it will be an important debate. Yet this is not a report on "the war." We are not having a debate about "the war." . . .

Beyond the Petraeus Report: the Report on the Larger War

Beyond the Petraeus Report, we need a report on the larger war with the Irreconcilable Wing of Islam. This enemy is irreconcilable with the modern civilized world because its values would block any woman from being in this room, having a job, voting, being educated. It is irreconcilable because it cannot tolerate other religions or other lifestyles. It represents what some have called an Islamofascist approach to imposing its views on others and as such it is a mortal threat to our way of life, to freedom, and to the rule of law.

The Irreconcilable Wing of Islam has emerged as an extremist movement against not only non-Muslims but also against moderate Muslims who wish both to preserve their faith and to be a part of the modern world. . . .

In describing the threat posed by the Irreconcilable Wing of Islam, we don't need to rely on journalists. We can also quote the public speeches of the CIA director. Here is what CIA director General Michael V. Hayden said just this past Friday, September 7, before the Council on Foreign Relations on his own judgment of the strategic threats facing the United States:

> First, our analysts assess with high confidence that al Qaeda's central leadership is planning high-impact plots against the U.S. homeland.
>
> Second, they assess—also with high confidence—that al Qaeda has protected or regenerated key elements of its homeland attack capability. That means safe haven in the tribal areas of Pakistan, operational lieutenants, and a top leadership engaged in planning. Al Qaeda's success with the remaining element—planting operatives in this country—is less certain.

Third, we assess—again, with high confidence—that al Qaeda is focusing on targets that would produce mass casualties, dramatic destruction, and significant economic aftershocks.

This was General Hayden's assessment of the threats just three days ago. In the same speech, General Hayden summarizes the fight at hand with these words:

We who study and target the enemy see a danger more real than anything our citizens at home have confronted since our Civil War. . . . This war is different. In a very real sense, anybody who lives or works in a major city is just as much a potential target as the victims of September 11, or the London subway bombings, or the strikes in Madrid, or any of the other operations we've seen in Morocco, Jordan, Indonesia, Algeria, Pakistan, Kenya, and elsewhere.

Our very survival as a free people is challenged by a large threat, and defeating it on a worldwide basis is inherently going to involve a large effort. That is why Norman Podhoretz has called it World War IV to compare its scale with World Wars I and II and with the forty-four-year-long Cold War, which he calls World War III. It is why the director of the Central Intelligence Agency, General Hayden, is making public speeches to make clear the very real and dangerous threats we face.

We need a debate about a vision of victory for the larger war in which we are engaged and the strategies needed to achieve that vision. We need a debate about the genuine risks to America of losing cities to nuclear attack or losing millions of Americans to engineered biological attacks. We need a calm, reasoned dialogue about the genuine possibility of a second Holocaust if the Iranians get nuclear weapons and use them against Tel Aviv, Haifa, and Jerusalem. We need a clear analysis of the potential for a second Holocaust if the Syrians were to use all the missiles with chemical and biological warheads they currently have targeted on Israel or if they were to transfer those missiles to Hezbollah and Hamas. . . .

We also need an honest, factual, and realistic examination of the progress or lack of progress we are making in the larger war. . . .

Iraq as One Campaign in the Larger War

Iraq has to be analyzed as only one campaign in this larger war. It is a very important campaign and it deserves thorough consideration, but it should not be confused with the larger war. As to Iraq, General Petraeus is as good an expert on counterinsurgency as America has produced in our lifetime. The American team in Iraq has done an extraordinary job in the last few months in finally establishing the right approach and implementing the right tactics. The results are impressive and worthy of our continued support. Furthermore, on both moral and practical grounds it would be extraordinarily destructive for the American Congress to impose surrender and defeat on the United States by legislation which the enemy has been unable to impose by combat against our armed forces.

No one should be under any illusions about the simple test for America in Iraq. At the end of the day, are free people celebrating because the American people have sustained freedom against evil? Or are violent, evil enemies of freedom celebrating because the Americans have been defeated?

Life would be easier if there was a more modulated answer. There is not. In war there are winners and losers. If the American people will sustain this effort we will ultimately win. If the American politicians decide to legislate defeat, America will be defeated. Given that choice, we must support General Petraeus. Furthermore, the Pentagon, the State Department, the intelligence community, and the Office of Management and Budget should be instructed to help him win the campaign in Iraq by meeting his needs rather than weakening him through slow bureaucracy, the imposition of lesser priorities, and the restriction of resources....

What If? Explaining the Larger War with the Irreconcilable Wing of Islam in a Novel Way

Let us build upon this historic pattern of American success and now ask what a realistic alternative history of the war might look like now, six years after September 11. This alternative history is offered to dramatize what we as a nation need to do in the years ahead. And in so doing, see if we can discover a better path to ensure a safer America. So let us look back six years. Let us engage in an exercise and imagine that we, as a nation, stunned by the bitter blows of the day before, now awake the day after and embark upon a different course of action. Let's begin on September 12, 2001.

First, imagine that on the morning of September 12, 2001, the shocked national political leadership in both parties had understood the necessity to take a deep, long look at the Irreconcilable Wing of Islam.

Second, imagine that the president and congressional leaders on a bipartisan basis had mandated a series of public hearings on the scale of the radical Wahhabist financing from sources in Saudi Arabia, the degree of Iranian and Syrian support for terrorism, the various propagandizing and recruiting efforts that were under way to attract terrorists at a rate faster than we could kill or imprison them.

Third, imagine that on September 12, 2001, the news media had begun a series of informative, in-depth explorations of the Iranian war against America (as Mark Bowden described it in *Guests of the Ayatollah*, his book about the 1979–80 hostage crisis) and then went on to examine the goals of the various irreconcilable groups and the religious fervor with which they are willing to die for their beliefs. The Iranian dictatorship had been at war with America for twenty-two years before September 11. The Iranian revolutionaries knew this and acted on it, but we denied it and hid from it. But after September 11, this explicit Iranian violence against Americans began to be outlined in the media and linked together into a continuous story of Iranian attacks and the deliberate self-deception of the American elites.

Fourth, imagine that the great bureaucracies of national security and homeland security had immediately begun to place defeating the enemy above protecting their normal routine systems.

Fifth, imagine that the Office of Management and Budget had been instructed to set aside its peacetime formulas and attitudes and operate within a war footing to facilitate the mobilization and buildup necessary to both win the war with the Irreconcilable Wing of Islam and preserve America's military and intelligence capabilities on other fronts.

Thinking Anew for Victory:
Key Decisions of an Alternative History
since September 11

With this starting context, an alternative history might well have played out with the following key decisions being taken and systematically implemented.

Decision One: Defining the Enemy and Understanding the Threat

In the days immediately after September 11, senior political leaders decided that since the American people are the center of gravity in any American war, an all-out effort would have to be made to educate them about the dangers (nuclear and biological attacks, large-scale civilian attacks) and the motivating forces behind those dangers.

As a result, the history of terrorism and violence in Lebanon, Algeria, and against Israel became major topics for congressional hearings, for news media specials, and for textbooks for high school and college. There were a series of Hollywood films and made-for-television films explaining the enemy and the scale of hatred and planning for violence against civilians. The Algerian experience of 100,000 killed in the 1990s was especially studied for its lessons about Muslim-versus-Muslim violence, which sharply curtailed the claims of those who typically blamed Israel, as so many American and European elites tended to do in the 1990s. The Syrian and Iranian involvement in terrorism in Lebanon was highlighted to emphasize the duration of attacks on Americans going back to 1979 and the ruthless intervention against efforts to create democracy.

Our enemies' religious-political motivation leading to the repression of women, the killing of homosexuals, the violent repression of religious liberty, the elimination of free speech and a free press, and the replacement of a just civil law with unjust religious law were all emphatically placed before the American public. A special effort was made to reach out to the advocacy groups of the Left, for whom in many ways these threats were the most intense.

In addition, a regular system of public information modeled on the World War II efforts was established and was complemented by a weekly briefing for every member of Congress that kept them informed on the activities of our enemies and the progress, or lack thereof, of our efforts. These reports included ongoing estimates of propaganda and financial support coming from so-called allies and active efforts of dictatorships to sustain terrorism. This system of public information was tied directly to a rebirth of public diplomacy as a major instrument of American effort. Every effort was made to engage the public, the news media, and the Congress in a broad bipartisan coalition for protecting America and winning the war.

Decision Two:
Establishing an Effective Homeland Defense

After September 11, since the defense of America is the top priority, a serious and effective Department of Homeland Security was immediately established. The department was organized to address three major functions: protecting the border, preparing to recover from a nuclear event, and preparing for an engineered biological attack....

Decision Three: Mobilizing Public Opinion
at Home and Abroad

As the president prepared for his historic September 20, 2001, speech to a joint session of Congress, it was decided that since a sound effort to defeat the terrorists would have to begin with the support of allies and world opinion, great effort was going to have to be made to mobilize and sustain world opinion and to work closely with every government willing to fight to sustain civilization and the rule of law. The lessons of World War II and the Cold War in developing both overt and covert public diplomacy were applied to winning this new struggle....

Decision Four: A Military Buildup and Dramatic Replacement of Outdated Institutions and Bureaucratic Processes

Within the revised framework of strategic communications, defense, and diplomacy, a major revolution in the national security capabilities of the United States was undertaken post–September 11. The national security system had been grossly underfunded in the 1990s. The intelligence community had been particularly weakened and was suffering from a generation of abuse going back to the Pike and Church Committees. The military itself was preparing for the wrong wars using the wrong doctrine. The State Department had been left underfunded, understaffed, undertrained, and undersupervised.

The requirements for change to prosecute a global war were recognized as immense. In the tradition of Lincoln and FDR, there was a fundamental change in the mentality of government management. The changes to carry out the new requirements were undertaken ruthlessly and with a spirit that it was better to make mistakes of commission and then fix them than it was to avoid achievement by avoiding failure.

The president established a war cabinet with himself as chair. Following the Churchillian model, the president understood that in a modern system the commander in chief had to actually command and drive the machinery if real change was going to occur. This war cabinet met weekly—and in a crisis daily or more often—under the direct leadership of the president. It was routinely expanded to include any agency or department that was relevant to solving a problem. It established a speed of decision and responsibility for implementation unlike anything seen in modern American government. Like Lincoln and FDR, the commander in chief took personal charge of the fight.

The president established a system of metrics based on the Mayor Giuliani achievement system that dramatically reduced crime in New York. An Office of Metrics was established in the White House, and many of Giuliani's best practitioners of planning and implementation were brought in to help the federal government move to a new system of accountability, focus, and constant change, using an evidence-based model of leadership Giuliani had established, a policing system that reduced crime in New York City by 75 percent between 1994 and 2006. This model enables senior leaders to define what matters, monitor what is happening, and change the system until it meets the goals. This new system allowed the National Security Council to shift from an ineffective, slow, and unreliable interagency process to a new accountable, transparent, and highly responsive integrated system that brought all the departments together into an integrated implementation structure and pattern. The president as commander in chief reviewed metrics in the war cabinet setting every week and made changes accordingly.

Every time commonsense solutions could not be applied because of existing federal regulations, the president issued waivers in a timely manner and clearly communicated to Congress and America the reasoning behind such waivers. The goal was to establish a tempo of real change and real achievement. Anyone who longed for the slow old days was urged to retire or find a new career. Anyone who was incapable of achieving results in the new tempo environment was relieved of duty. There was no confusion. After September 11, the U.S. was at war and the entire federal government moved to a wartime posture and adopted a wartime urgency.

Every time something failed to work for systemic legal reasons, the president sent a report to Congress requesting changes in law based on national security and homeland security requirements. The pressure for change in personnel, procurement, and other laws became unending. An advisory committee on federal transformation chaired by Fred Smith of FedEx and involving highly effective CEOs from major American companies such as UPS, IBM, GE, and other high-tempo, high-productivity companies advised the president and educated Congress about standards of management excellence in meeting the new wartime requirements. The World War II rules for dollar year volunteers was reinstated and first-rate entrepreneurs, executives, and celebrities flooded into government to help defend America.

The president established an informal bipartisan advisory committee from Congress, which he met with every two weeks. This was very effective in beginning to establish a human bond that enabled the president to get far more out of Congress with far less partisanship than he could have gotten otherwise. In addition, the president soon discovered that members of the congressional advisory group would bring him bad news and dissenting information that was very hard to get through official channels. This vital information allowed the president and his team to continuously address problems in wartime management of the federal government.

The national security budget for defense and intelligence was set at 5 percent of gross domestic product. While this level of defense funding was arbitrary, it was lower than at any time during the Cold War and represented a smaller increase in overall defense spending than in any previous major war. By comparison, in 1949 under President Truman the United States had spent 7.1 percent of its GDP on national security even though we were at peace. In 1955, under President

Eisenhower we spent 11.4 percent of our GDP on national security even though we were at peace. In 1963, we spent 9.8 percent of our GDP even though we were at peace. In the historic context, a 5 percent of GDP national security budget was very modest and the minimum that could be sustained without major risk. For 2002, this represented a budget of $525 billion compared with the $343 billion which had been originally projected. . . .

The decision to go to a modest wartime funding of 5 percent (the smallest wartime budget in American history) enabled the military to avoid all supplemental spending and thus saved enormous time and effort in managing Pentagon spending. In addition, over the five years (2002 through 2006) after the September 11 attack, the national security system had $627.8 billion more to spend in a rational investment strategy than it would have had under the OMB cheapness strategy and supplemental budgeting strategy that some had advocated.

This enabled the military to prepare for a variety of contingencies in a robust way with timely equipment purchases and no need to rob one area to cover another. It was the American way of waging and paying for war in its most effective manner.

Special note has to be made of one wrenching change in the national security system that was achieved, which was intellectually obvious but bureaucratically almost impossible to carry out. The American army had come out of Vietnam with a deep emotional, cultural, and organizational bias against counterinsurgency operations. The Army wanted to focus on dominating high-technology battlefields against regular opponents. Yet the lessons of Algeria, Afghanistan, Lebanon, Israel, Somalia, Sri Lanka, the Philippines, and elsewhere were that counter-terrorism in the end was a sophisticated urban form of counterinsurgency. The Israeli failure to create a peaceful solution in thirty-four years in the West Bank and Gaza (1967 to 2001) when they had overwhelming military power was a serious warning that the Americans had better rethink their assumptions about how hard this fight was going to be and how difficult it would be to win.

Despite deep objections from the traditional Army and Marines, who wanted to retain their focus on high-technology regular warfare, and the more muted objections of the Special Operations Command, who thought they could already accomplish the mission, the president insisted that the highest investment strategy for the United States would be developing a system that would give the American forces the same dominance in urban terrorist campaigns that they had achieved at sea, in the air, and in regular land warfare.

The team assigned to begin this program reported back that the scale of American investment required to achieve this same level of superiority would be massive. The president responded that that was precisely the point and that any expectation that we could solve this new counterinsurgency challenge on the cheap was foolish. We had become the dominant military power in other zones because we invested the manpower and the capital to create the systems, doctrines, technology, and organizations that could defeat anyone. The commander in chief insisted that we now had to learn to do the same in urban terrorist warfare. . . .

The State Department budget was increased by 50 percent but off a much smaller base. Prior to September 11, the State Department was an obsolescent system with inadequate information technology, inadequate training, and inadequate staffing for teamwork across the system. If America was going to lead the world it was going to have to have a high-tempo, highly trained, highly capitalized State Department, and the personnel of that department had to be numerous

enough to be available for the integrated system, for fellowships outside the Department, for rapid transfer to hot spots, and to studying
and learning from the constant changes in the global war environment....

Beyond an Alternative History:
The National Dialogue We Need Today

This alternative history of the last six years is offered as a thought
experiment. This is an alternative history that could have indeed happened. And how profoundly different would our world be on this
September 10, 2007. Sadly, it is not our history. But nevertheless, we
can draw upon this scenario, learn from it, and now take steps to envi-
sion a better future.

We still need to focus on the larger war. We still need a debate
about what is really at stake. We still need a clear understanding of how
much our enemies hate us, how hard they are working to defeat us,
how serious and real their strategies are, and how much they rejoice
when they find ways to attack us.

The key debate for the next year should not be the Petraeus
Report and conditions in Iraq. The key debate for the next year ought
to be the larger war, the real enemies, the need for a real strategy, and
solutions to the scale of the challenge we face. There is nothing phony
about the threats we face today. There is no question that the risks
today from weapons of mass destruction are real and immediate if the
wrong series of events transpires. If they could acquire them, our enemies would not hesitate to use nuclear or biological weapons to kill
millions of Americans. We fought for survival in the Civil War and
World War II. Our enemies have not yet made the situation danger-

ous enough so that most people understand that this is a battle of survival. The question then for our generation is whether we can learn the lessons of history and understand that this is a battle for survival before we lose millions of Americans, or whether we reject the lessons of history and only respond after a disaster.

Some will read this speech and ask whether the United States would have invaded Afghanistan and Iraq in this alternative history. The answer is not immediately obvious, but the principles are. Afghanistan would have been dealt with in a regional context that would have included the Waziristan section of Pakistan. The Taliban would have been given no sanctuary. From day one, there would have been a dramatic effort to build highways and modernize Afghanistan and open it up so farmers could make money without relying on the illicit heroin trade for a living.

In the Middle East, the challenges of Iraq, Iran, Syria, and Saudi Arabia would have been dealt with as a regional conflict. There would have been no safe harbors for Iraqi dictators to send their money and their key staffs. There would have been no free passage through Damascus for foreign terrorists to come kill Americans. There would have been no tolerance for Iranian subsidies, training, and weapons to kill Americans. A grand strategy would have built up sufficient economic, political, and military power to confront the four nations with a simple choice: change your behavior or have your regimes changed.

In that world, there might have been less violence as weak dictatorships realized they could not survive against the fury of an American people mobilized to action, or there could have been more violence as they banded together to defy America openly and claim the right to finance and support terrorism against civilization and against innocent civilians.

The details of the alternative Afghan and Middle Eastern campaigns might make for a good seminar and even a useful book.

Where We Are and Where We Must Go

While there is much to learn from the past, we are faced with the decisions of the present and the possibilities of the future. This speech was developed to make the case that we need a much bigger context for thinking about those decisions. We are engaged in a larger war, Podhoretz's World War IV, against a determined set of opponents who have survived six years of fragmented American and allied effort. We will never win this larger war with limited efforts in one or two countries in isolation. We must reject legislating American surrender and defeat in Iraq and Afghanistan, but we must also reject "stay the course" as an answer.

We need a new course. We need an honest national dialogue and a determination to be candid about our opponents, honest about the problems, and passionately committed to the survival of America as a free country in which its citizens can be safe. We need to make changes today to have our twenty-first-century national security structures ready for the challenges of the twenty-first century. We need a blueprint for reform and success. It is not acceptable that we have more impediments to action than enablers for action. We need a strategy—not a campaign—to rationalize ends and means to achieve our objectives in this long war against our way of life.

The American people are fully capable of understanding the scale of the threat, the dangers to our lives, the threats to our very survival. The American people showed enormous patience through the great agony of the Civil War. The American people sustained the Cold War for forty-four years until the Soviet Union disappeared. The problem is not with the American people. The problem is with our politicians, our news media, and our bureaucratic elites. They are afraid to tell the American people the truth. They are afraid to explain the scale of the threat and the inevitable scale of the needed response.

Let them trust in Americans. Let us reason together, face the facts, invent the solutions, and mobilize the resources for victory. With leadership, it will be the terrorists who are defeated and the free people who are triumphant. With leadership, the free people of the world will form an unshakable alliance against evil and an enormous system in defense of the innocent. It is in the best American tradition that we have the courage at home that we expect on the battlefield. There is no shortcut. This is the road to victory over evil. This is the road to safety, freedom, and prosperity for the civilized world.

Index